THE PORT-ROYALISTS
ON EDUCATION

T0382375

THE PORT-ROYALISTS ON EDUCATION

EXTRACTS FROM THE EDUCATIONAL WRITINGS OF THE PORT-ROYALISTS

SELECTED, TRANSLATED AND
FURNISHED WITH AN INTRODUCTION
AND NOTES

BY

H. C. BARNARD, M.A., B.Litt.

SOMETIME SENIOR HULME SCHOLAR OF BRASENOSE
COLLEGE, OXFORD; AUTHOR OF *THE LITTLE SCHOOLS
OF PORT-ROYAL*, ETC.

CAMBRIDGE
AT THE UNIVERSITY PRESS
1918

CAMBRIDGE
UNIVERSITY PRESS

University Printing House, Cambridge CB2 8BS, United Kingdom

Cambridge University Press is part of the University of Cambridge.

It furthers the University's mission by disseminating knowledge in the pursuit of
education, learning and research at the highest international levels of excellence.

www.cambridge.org
Information on this title: www.cambridge.org/9781107475182

© Cambridge University Press 1918

This publication is in copyright. Subject to statutory exception
and to the provisions of relevant collective licensing agreements,
no reproduction of any part may take place without the written
permission of Cambridge University Press.

First published 1918
First paperback edition 2014

A catalogue record for this publication is available from the British Library

ISBN 978-1-107-47518-2 Paperback

Cambridge University Press has no responsibility for the persistence or accuracy of
URLs for external or third-party internet websites referred to in this publication,
and does not guarantee that any content on such websites is, or will remain, accurate
or appropriate.

PREFACE

THE contribution which the Port-Royalists made to the cause of education and the influence which they exerted, not only in France but in other countries also, entitle them to a conspicuous place among the world's greatest educators. As such, they merit the attention of all who are interested in the history of European civilisation ; while those whose mission it is to teach the young will find their theories and methods endlessly suggestive. To facilitate the study of education at Port-Royal, therefore, I have endeavoured in this book to give, from the writings of the Port-Royalists themselves, a fairly complete account of the educational doctrines and teaching methods which are associated with the " Little Schools." I have also appended a translation of those sources from which is derived most of our information as to the organisation of the convent-school for girls at Port-Royal des Champs. For a more critical study of the whole subject and for an attempt to estimate the place of the Port-Royalists in the general history of education the reader may be referred to my *Little Schools of Port-Royal.*

In rendering the original extracts into English I have been guided largely by the rules for translation which the Port-Royalists themselves laid down. I take this opportunity of formally thanking my wife and my colleague Mr E. J. A. Groves, L.-ès-L., to both of whom I am indebted for many helpful suggestions.

H. C. B.

March 1918

ERRATUM

p. 50, l. 23 *for* daughters *read* cousins

CONTENTS

INTRODUCTION

I. A GENERAL SKETCH OF EDUCATION IN FRANCE IN THE XVIITH CENTURY, WITH SPECIAL REFERENCE TO THE SCHOOLS OF PORT-ROYAL

THE seventeenth century is one of the most noteworthy epochs in the history of the French nation. It witnessed the setting-up of a strong centralised administration, typified by the *Grand Monarque*—the symbol of patriotism and unity. It saw the French language finally perfected into its present form as one of the clearest and most flexible methods of human expression; and it included a period which is rightly considered to be the golden age of French literature as regards prose and poetry alike. During this century, too, the Church of France, hampered no longer by the Wars of Religion and inspired by the high ideals of the Counter-Reformation, purged herself of many abuses and laid seriously to heart the precepts of her divine commission. It is but natural that, in such a period of awakening, educational activity should be most marked and most fruitful. The beginning of the century saw a reform of the University of Paris; a little later secondary education was exemplified in some of its most striking forms by the great Teaching Congregations; while towards the end of this period elementary education was transfigured by the labours of S. Jean-Baptiste de la Salle. As regards the education of girls, again, which hitherto had been largely neglected, great improvements were made. In every department of the subject, therefore, there is progress to record and the object of this introduction is to sketch in outline the various types of education—elementary, preparatory, and secondary, as we

French Education in the XVIIth Century.

B.   I might call them nowadays—which were given to French children in the seventeenth century.

It must be confessed that during the greater part of this period elementary education in France—as elsewhere—was but little in evidence. It is true that in the last decade of the century two laws were passed to enforce compulsory elementary education throughout France. They were the outcome of the Revocation of the Edict of Nantes (1685), and their avowed object was to impose a Catholic education upon the children of Protestant parents. Both laws, however, were entirely ineffectual. The chief bar to educational activity then, as always, was lack of funds. No schools were available and no money was provided wherewith to build them or to pay teachers. Throughout the century such elementary education as was given was due to the devotion and generosity of individuals. The parish clergy in Paris and some of the other large towns occasionally set up charity schools, in which reading, writing, and simple arithmetic were taught. The pupils also attended Mass every morning in the parish church. But, as might be expected, this work was unsystematised and sporadic; and it was left for an ecclesiastic who gave up wealth and position in order to devote himself to the teaching of the poorest children, to develop this side of education.

Elementary Education—S. Jean-Baptiste de la Salle.

Jean-Baptiste de la Salle—he was recently canonised and we may therefore give him the title of Saint—had his attention drawn to the necessity of educating the poor by a certain M. Nyel, who, with the aid of several other teachers, had been conducting a charity school at Rouen. De la Salle's sound common-sense inspired by a genuine love of his fellowmen led him to organise this teaching band into a teaching Congregation or Order; to it was given the name of "The Brothers of the Christian Schools" or—more shortly—"The Christian Brothers." In order to facilitate the work De la Salle resigned a canonry which he held and devoted his patrimony (which was no small one) to his educational institution. The work of the Society was first started in a formal way in the year 1684. The schools spread rapidly from Rheims, De la Salle's native city, where they were first founded; and they achieved a particularly notable effect in the parish of S. Sulpice in Paris. The education given by the Christian Brothers was gratuitous and their pupils were taught reading, writing, and arithmetic, together with two novel additional subjects— drawing and a manual trade. Another valuable reform introduced by De la Salle was that children were taught to read first in French[1]—not in Latin as was customary in the preparatory schools of the day.

Passing reference only can here be made to the normal school attached to the Congregation—the first training-college in Europe for primary teachers; to the Sunday school for older lads which in many ways anticipated the work of Robert Raikes and the modern continuation school; to the remarkable development of the Congregation throughout the eighteenth and nineteenth centuries; and to the notable work which it still carries on in almost every part of the world. But enough has been said to indicate the importance of this institution; and if elementary teachers wish to find a patron saint for their craft they can surely choose none more suitable than S. Jean-Baptiste de la Salle.

We have next to consider preparatory education such as was given to children aged seven to nine. Their parents

Preparatory Education— The Little Schools. would belong chiefly to the middle classes— the prosperous tradesmen and men of business, the lawyers, the lower government officials, and the like. For children of noble birth the services of a private tutor were almost always engaged. Throughout the seventeenth century the education of the middle classes was of growing importance. Under the personal rule of Louis XIV

[1] This reform was inspired by the example already set by the Port-Royalists (see pp. 150 and 151).

the machinery of government tended to be carried on more and more by subordinate officials who had risen from the ranks. Saint-Simon scornfully speaks of this reign as "un long règne de vile bourgeoisie." Some even of the great ministers of state were no longer of noble but of middle-class parentage; examples are Le Tellier and Colbert. Many of the highest Church dignitaries, again, were of plebeian origin; Massillon was the son of a provincial notary, Fléchier of a grocer. The education, then, of a class from which such men as these could rise has at this period a special interest.

At the age of seven or eight the boy from an ordinary bourgeois family was sent to what was technically known as a *Little School*. Institutions of this kind were allowed to exist only by virtue of a license granted by the Precentor of the Cathedral in each diocese. He had the title of Scholaster (*Écolâtre*) and this right to license Little Schools was a survival from the days when the Precentor was also the headmaster of the Cathedral school[1]. The Scholaster alone had the right to nominate teachers who might be of either sex.

The curriculum in the Little Schools was naturally limited. It included, of course, reading which was taught at first by means of picture letters in the form of animals or common objects—much in the style of our modern illustrated alphabets for young children. But the pupils were made to read Latin, although normally they would be unable to understand the meaning of the words which they spelt. The reason given for this singular procedure was that Latin is phonetically pronounced and accordingly is easier to read than the

[1] A similar control was exercised during the Middle Ages by the Bishop or Ordinary of each diocese in England and as late even as 1802 this control was tacitly assumed by the legislature to exist. Refer to Leach, *Educational Charters*, p. 91; De Montmorency, *State Intervention in English Education*, pp. 12 and 96; Foster Watson, *The Old Grammar Schools*, pp. 69–70.

vernacular. Thus the method, which at first might seem
excessively perverse, did attempt to solve a problem which
will be appreciated by anyone who has tried to teach a very
young child to read. Improved methods of teaching reading
were already being tried in contemporary French schools[1].
They have partially solved the problem, but serious difficulties must always remain in the case of languages which,
like French and (still more) English, are not pronounced as
they are spelt. It is the existence of these difficulties which
supplies one of the strongest of the arguments that are being
put forward, in France as well as in this country, on behalf
of spelling reform.

Writing in the Little Schools comprised the copper-plate
"penmanship" performances with which our grandfathers
were familiar. Letters were ornamented with elaborate flou-
rishes in the form of serpents' tails, birds' heads, foliage, and
similar devices. The other subjects taught in the Little
Schools were the elements of Arithmetic, the rudiments of
Latin Grammar, the explanation of the Divine Offices, the
Catechism, and Singing.

The Little Schools were forbidden to retain pupils who
had passed the age of nine. If any subjects other than those
prescribed were added to the curriculum attempts were made
by the University authorities to suppress the offending schools.
From time to time, also, teachers who had not been licensed
by the *Écolâtre* attempted to teach secretly; but these inter-
lopers were hunted out and their schools shut down. Such
a system as this would never have tolerated the "daughter
of a clergyman" who presides over an "academy for young
ladies," or the charlatan who writes "London University"
after his name on the strength of having matriculated in his
youth, and who by virtue of that magic title attracts pupils
to his private school where a "sound business training" is
imparted. The licensing of teachers by some reputable

1 See *infra*, pp. 144–148.

authority—be it Church or State—may or may not be desirable; but at any rate it does ensure that certain definite qualifications shall be demanded from those who are responsible for a work of infinite importance to society. In this country we have long favoured a *laissez-faire* policy[1]; but one is perhaps justified in regarding the recent formation of a Teachers' Register as an attempt—modified, doubtless, to suit altered conditions—to answer the problem which a past age had long ago faced and for which it had found its own solution.

We come now to a larger department of our subject— the secondary education of boys. Secondary education in seventeenth-century France was carried on by two entirely different types of institution—by the Universities on the one hand and by the Teaching Congregations on the other.

The French university of this period was still to a large extent unlike the university as we understand it to-day, for

Secondary Education. (a) The Faculty of Arts.

it maintained many of its mediæval characteristics. The faculties of Law, Medicine, and Theology provided a course of advanced work for young men which thus corresponded to the modern university course; but the Faculty of Arts was preparatory to this course and so covered the work of our present secondary schools. There is an interesting survival of this mediæval system at Oxford and Cambridge where the first degree is always one in Arts and the faculties of Law, Medicine, and Theology, and even of Science and Letters, are all postgraduate.

On leaving the Little School at the age of nine the pupil would be entered at one of the colleges of the University. At Paris there were some forty or more of these colleges and the provincial universities were modelled upon that of

1 An eminent French educationalist has said : " It is only in England and America that individual liberty has been pushed to the point of charlatanism so that anybody can teach anything." (Langlois, *La préparation professionnelle à l'enseignement secondaire*, p. 101.)

the metropolis although, of course, they were on a smaller
scale. Let us follow in imagination, then, the career of a
little French boy who has already learnt to read, write, and
cipher in a Little School and who has acquired some small
smattering of Latin Grammar. He is put in charge of a
pédagogue or tutor with whom he boards and who helps him
with his lessons. If his parents live near at hand he may
perhaps reside at home as an *externe libre*. He begins his
school-day early. At 5.0 in the morning he is already in
class. After a lesson lasting an hour the whole school assists
at Mass. Then comes breakfast, followed by three hours
of lessons. At 11.0 dinner is served; during the meal the
Bible or a life of one of the Saints is read aloud. After
dinner questions are asked on the morning's work and this
is followed by an hour of so called "recreation" during which
there is another reading from one of the poets or orators.
Afternoon lessons last from 3.0 to 6.0 and are followed by
supper. Then the school attends Vespers and all the younger
boys at any rate are in bed soon after 9.0. Half holidays
are granted on Tuesday and Thursday afternoons. The
school year starts on October 1st; the holidays consist of
eight days at Easter, two at Whitsun, most of the month of
September, and certain Saints'-days.

On entering the college our friend will be placed in Class
VI and his entire energies are there devoted to learning Latin.
To aid him in this task he is given a work which was origin-
ally written in the fifteenth century by a Fleming named
Van Pauteren or Despauter. In this book the rules of Latin
Grammar had been versified with the object of facilitating the
work of committing them to memory. How far this aim was
achieved may be judged if a few random extracts are given:

Rule for the agreement of an adjective with its noun in
number, gender, and case:

> Mobile cum fixo, genere et casu, numeroque,
> Conveniat. Nomen sic vult cognomini adesse.

Rule for the conjugation of certain verbs:

> Bo bi tumque facit. Scabo, lambo, carento supinis,
> Ut cubo, sic proles. Dant scribo nuboque psi ptum.

Rule for construction with comparative and superlative:

> Res similis generis medius gradus, atque supremus
> Poscunt; ille duas, hic plures usque duabus.
> Sin minus ista aderunt, medio gradui dato sextum.

It would take a classical scholar to disentangle some of these lines, and it is not surprising therefore that the more progressive educationalists[1] in France in the seventeenth century were beginning to look upon Despauter with disfavour. Yet in the first part of the century, at any rate, it was still of importance that Latin should be learnt thoroughly. In the University it was the only vehicle of everyday conversation and the only means of conveying instruction. French, in spite of Rabelais and Montaigne, was only beginning to be a literary language[2]. One must remember, too, that Rabelais and Montaigne alike were anathema in the eyes of the Church which controlled contemporary education; and, as a matter of fact, the works of neither would be suitable as school-books. Latin, indeed, was still the only key to all the arts and all the sciences, and a common medium of conversation and communication for learned men in every part of Europe. It was left for Descartes and the Gentlemen of Port-Royal to show that a learned work could be written in good French.

In spite of the fact, then, that it was fast dying, Latin was still a living language. But it was obviously difficult to adapt a classical tongue, which was already standardised and therefore inflexible, to the uses of everyday conversation in seventeenth-century society. To encourage fluency in speaking Latin, numerous Colloquies or materials for conversation

[1] See page 157.

[2] Lavisse even asserts that as late as 1661 the greater number of Frenchmen were still ignorant of the French language. Refer to *Cambridge Modern History*, vol. V, p. 4.

had been published. Those of Maturin Cordier[1] and Erasmus[2] were much used in the Faculty of Arts of the University. Another colloquy which acquired great popularity in this country as well as in France both in the sixteenth and seventeenth centuries was that of the Spaniard Luis Vives[3]. Works of this type often display that inappropriate discursiveness which one associates with the modern "travellers' phrase-book"; but when we remember that they had to furnish materials for conversation out of school hours as well as during them, we can realise the importance of a thorough study of such books at an early stage in the secondary school curriculum[4].

Five hours a day were devoted to class work in the University, but much home preparation in addition had to be done under the guidance of the *pédagogue*. As our French boy progresses in his study of Latin he reads more and more widely and even acquires a smattering of Greek. Normally he moves up one form each year until, at the age of sixteen, he is promoted to Class I, usually known as the Rhetoric. Here he studies points of style, learns passages by heart, and imitates the prose and verse of the best Latin authors. After passing through the Rhetoric course, if he is to find a career in business or in some similar employment, he will probably leave the University. Otherwise he enters upon a two-years' course in philosophy if the institution with which he is connected is a *collège de plein exercice* which provides such a course. The curriculum included Logic, Moral Philosophy, Metaphysics, Physics, and Mathematics; but the

1 For some details see Foster Watson, *The Old Grammar Schools*, p. 91.

2 See p. 243, note on p. 69, l. 16.

3 See p. 247, note on p. 91, l. 20. It was originally written in 1539, but has recently been translated into English by Prof. Foster Watson under the title of *Tudor Schoolboy Life*.

4 There is a good account of the various Colloquies in Keatinge, *The Great Didactic of Comenius*, introd. pp. 120–3.

whole business was merely a study of the corrupt text of
Aristotle and therefore tended to be extremely barren and
formal.   Logic was taught by disputations and the questions
discussed were often of the least profitable character.   None
the less, these scholastic methods in philosophy persisted in
the University with but little change until the middle of the
eighteenth century.

At the end of the philosophy course, when the pupil had
reached the age of eighteen or nineteen, he submitted himself to two examinations with an interval of rather more than
a month between them.   If he was successful in this test he
was awarded the degree of *Maître-ès-Arts*.   Although it carried
with it a license to teach it corresponded not to the modern
licence, but more nearly to the *baccalauréat*—the crown of
the secondary school course in France at the present day.
In passing it is of interest to note how the arrangement of
the classes from VI (the lowest) to I or Rhetoric (the highest),
followed by a two-years' course in philosophy, still exists in
the French secondary school system.   It is the direct descendant of an organised curriculum which dates from the
Middle Ages.

The education given by the Faculty of Arts may be
criticised from many points of view.   The mother-tongue was
entirely neglected; history and geography were not taught as
specific subjects; mathematics occupied only the smallest
part of the curriculum.   The teaching of philosophy was still
conventional and based on a narrow interpretation of the un-
certain text of Aristotle.   Moreover discipline in the colleges
was proverbially bad and—a very usual corollary—punishments were excessively severe.   The moral tone which prevailed
was far from being above reproach.   For many reasons, then,
parents were often unwilling to send their boys to the schools
of the Faculty of Arts.   For such cases an alternative type of
education on more rational lines was offered by the Teaching
Congregations.   These were bodies of ecclesiastics—helped

often by laymen—who were bound together, sometimes by vows, sometimes merely by mutual agreement, to carry on the work of teaching. The congregations which made the most valuable contribution to the science of education were the Jesuits, the Port-Royalists, and the Oratorians.

The Society of Jesus, founded by Loyola in 1540, entered France in 1561. It had two aims—the propagation of the (b) The Jesuits. Faith by means of missions and the conservation of the Faith by means of schools. Education with the Jesuits therefore tended always to become a means to an end. It was regarded not as something good in itself, but as the most powerful safeguard of the Roman Church. Loyola had been a soldier before he became a priest and, as Viscount St Cyres has suggested[1], there is reflected in his order something of the history of its founder. Spiritual matters were defined with a precision and comprehensiveness which suggest a military handbook; the confessor went to his penitents armed with a code of hard and fast rules for resolving every conceivable *cas de conscience;* and in the same way the organisation of the Jesuit schools and the teaching methods which were employed in them were prescribed in elaborate detail. The document which defines them is called the *Ratio Studiorum.* It was first published in 1599 and has remained in force with but few changes down to the present day. Naturally, the curriculum has been adapted to modern tendencies, but the school organisation and methods of teaching remain largely unchanged.

The Jesuit schools present a contrast to those of the University. In the former there was, in a sense, less freedom, for the pupils of the Society of Jesus were rigorously excluded from any contact with the world outside. Communication even between the boys and their parents was discouraged as far as possible. A seventeenth-century publication entitled *The Picture of the Perfect Scholar* gives us an

1 See *Cambridge Modern History,* vol. v, p. 80.

idea of the Society's ideals in this respect[1]. A certain John
Baptist von Schulthaus, a pupil in the Jesuit college at Trent,
was visited by his mother. He refused to shake hands with
her or even to look at her. When the outraged parent en-
quired the reason of this behaviour her son replied: "I refuse
to look at you not because you are my mother but because
you are a woman."

In spite of this unnatural severing of family ties, the
régime of a Jesuit school had much to render it attractive.
Punishments were relatively light and recourse was rarely
had to the cane. Order in class was kept by a kind of co-
operation between master and pupils. Each form contained
a *decurio* or *prætor* whose business it was to collect the work
and keep the marks of his fellows. He had limited powers
of punishing the others and was instructed to inform the
master of any delinquencies on the part of his companions
which he might observe. *Cafards* are detested and despised
as heartily by French boys as "sneaks" are in the schools
of this country, and we may infer that the post of *prætor*
carried with it little popularity. A school method more worthy
of occasional imitation was the division of each class into
two camps—the Romans and the Carthaginians. Examinations were frequent and rewards were given on the results.
The prizes took the form of books or, more often, of the
crowns and other insignia which are still distributed to successful pupils in the elementary schools and girls' schools
of modern France.

We pass on to consider the content of the education
which was given in the Jesuit schools. As in the Faculty
of Arts, Latin was the language of conversation and the
medium of instruction. The aim of the Jesuit college, therefore, was to perfect the pupil in the power of reading, writing,
and speaking Latin. The best authors were studied—freely

1 See Compayré, *Histoire des Doctrines de l'Éducation en France*,
vol. I, pp. 181–2.

expurgated where necessary—and the tendency was to read excerpts rather than whole books. Greek was learnt—more especially in Class II (boys aged 15); and great stress was laid on the power of writing Greek prose. Throughout there was an inclination to emphasise style rather than subject-matter, words rather than things; and thus subjects like history and geography were almost entirely neglected or introduced only by accident in the reading of authors.

The majority of the pupils in the Jesuit schools left at the age of sixteen; those who stayed on for the two or three years' philosophy course were usually aspirants to the ranks of the Society. This philosophy course much resembled that given in the Faculty of Arts. The staple of instruction was the works of Aristotle studied parrot-fashion with no liberty of criticism and no stimulus to individual thought. It was, in fact, an introduction through scholastic philosophy to scholastic theology. In the one case the somewhat uncertain text of Aristotle is the inspired word; in the other, the infallible voice of Holy Church. Freedom of thought was regarded as dangerous impiety and it is for this reason that we find the Jesuits foremost among the opponents of Descartes and his fellow founders of modern philosophy.

It is pleasant to turn from this subject to other aspects of the educational work of the Society of Jesus in which some of the best features of our modern schools are anticipated. It has been customary among Christian teachers of widely-differing schools of thought to despise the body. Charles Wesley, for example, somewhere exclaims:

> A potsherd of the earth am I,
> A worm, a blast, a shade.

S. Simeon Stylites, unwashed and verminous[1], typifies the extremes to which such an attitude of mind may lead. But the Jesuits were eminently sane in these matters and excessive

[1] See, for example, Lecky, *History of European Morals*, vol. II, pp. 111–112.

mortifications or penances found no place in their schools. On the contrary, pupils were not allowed to study for more than two hours on end for fear lest they should overwork. Their food was good and abundant. Physical exercises formed part of the curriculum—fencing, riding, swimming, and singing were all in vogue. Nor was mental recreation forgotten; theatrical representations, which were looked upon askance by almost all contemporary educators, were frequent in the Jesuit schools. Each form, again, had its *académie*, suggested, no doubt, by the French Academy which had been founded by Richelieu in 1637. These academies would correspond roughly to the literary and debating societies of the modern English secondary school. It should be remarked also, in passing, that the education given by the Jesuits was gratuitous. This afforded the Society a great advantage over the colleges of the Faculty of Arts and it helps to explain the success of the Jesuit schools and the decline of those of the University.

The schools of the Society of Jesus, then, present us with a system which in its essence is not educational because it does not develop the reasoning powers of the individual; but at the same time it enshrines school methods which were far in advance of contemporary practice, while the thoroughness of the system and the devotion of those who carried it out cannot but command our respect and admiration.

We come now to the schools of Port-Royal. As they form the main subject of this volume they will merit a somewhat more detailed treatment than can be given, in a mere general sketch, to the other aspects of French education (c) The "Little in the seventeenth century. The Port-Royal Schools" of schools are the outcome of a great controversy Port-Royal. which distracted the French Church at this time. This controversy can be traced back to one who was himself not a Frenchman at all. Cornelius Jansen, or Jansenius as he is often called, was born of lowly parents in the year 1585 near Leerdam in Holland. He was educated at the Jesuit College of Louvain and there formed a close friendship with Jean du Vergier de Hauranne, a young Frenchman of good family who came from Bayonne.

Louvain had recently been the scene of a heated theological dispute. Michael Baius, Chancellor of the University (died 1589), had put forward views which were based upon doctrines which S. Augustine had elaborated nearly twelve centuries before. It will be necessary for us to turn aside for a moment in order to consider them. According to the teaching of the Church, man is a fallen creature because he is a descendant of Adam and participates in the consequences of Adam's fall. To restore man to a position of innocency, grace is necessary; this may be defined as "a supernatural gift freely bestowed by God on rational or intellectual creatures in order that they may attain eternal life[1]." This gift is vouchsafed to man through the merits of Christ our Saviour. Of our own free-will and by our own strength we may certainly do good actions, but they cannot of themselves compensate for the effects of original sin—"By grace are ye saved through faith; and that not of yourselves: it is the gift of God: not of works, lest any man should boast[2]." This doctrine of grace had been championed by S. Augustine in opposition to the followers of Pelagius who had taken up a different standpoint. Their "vain talk[3]" consisted in asserting that Adam's sin was purely personal and affected nobody but himself. Hence his descendants were born in a state of innocence and became corrupted merely by subsequently succumbing to temptation and falling into sin. This meant that original sin had no meaning and that grace was deprived of its paramount importance. The danger of emphasising the doctrine of grace was that it led to a practical denial of the freedom of the will; and Baius has been accused

1 *Catholic Dictionary*, art. "Grace."   2 *Ephesians*, ii, 8.
3 Refer to Articles 9–13, *Book of Common Prayer*.

of pushing the teachings of S. Augustine perilously near this limit.

None the less, the doctrine of grace and all the teaching which it implies much attracted Jansen and De Hauranne. In 1601 the latter returned to Paris and four years later was joined by Jansen whose health had broken down. The two students set before themselves the aim of reviving the teachings of S. Augustine on the subject of grace and of restoring Church life to its primitive purity. With this end in view they retired to an estate belonging to De Hauranne and situated near Bayonne. There followed six years (1611–17) of meditation and study during which a book called the *Augustinus* was planned. Its aim was to set forth the Augustinian doctrine of grace. In 1617 Jansen returned to Louvain and there became Principal of the College of S. Pulcheria and Professor of Theology. He was twice sent to Madrid[1] in order to uphold the claims of his University against the Jesuits who had opened schools of philosophy and had ventured to confer degrees. He also published a pamphlet entitled *Mars Gallicus* in which he attacked Richelieu for his inconsistency in persecuting heretics at home whilst siding with Protestant princes of Germany against the Roman Catholic House of Austria. He contrasted the consistency of orthodox Spain with the illogical attitude of France. Thus Jansen became a bitter enemy first of the Jesuits and then of Richelieu; but his activities attracted attention and he was made Bishop of Ypres. He kept up a close correspondence with De Hauranne and continued to work at his treatise on S. Augustine. In 1636 the plague broke out in Flanders, and Jansen, like a true father in God, devoted himself to the sufferers in his diocese. He caught the infection and died, but not before his *Augustinus* was completed. One of his last acts was to submit its contents unreservedly to the Pope.

1 Louvain was at this time a city of the Spanish Netherlands.

Meanwhile De Hauranne had obtained preferment; in 1620 he was appointed Abbé of Saint-Cyran, near Poitiers. Henceforward he was usually known by the name of his abbey. He had already made the acquaintance of Richelieu and had won a high place in the minister's estimation. When, in 1621, Saint-Cyran left Poitiers for Paris Richelieu was anxious to favour him; he referred to the Abbé as the most learned man in Europe and is said to have offered him no less than five bishoprics. But Saint-Cyran was unwilling to become a tool of the minister and refused all his offers of preferment[1]. From this time onward, therefore, Richelieu's admiration begins to change into dislike and distrust.

On his arrival in Paris Saint-Cyran soon became intimate with several kindred spirits. For some time devout men in France had been grieved by the ignorance and unworthiness of many priests in the French Church. It was said that the priesthood included men who were incapable even of saying Mass correctly, while one at least was found who had been in the habit of praying to S. Beelzebub. Among those who had at heart the reform of these abuses were De Bérulle, afterwards a Cardinal, De Condren, and the saintly Vincent de Paul. With these three ecclesiastics Saint-Cyran formed a close friendship and in time each supplied his own solution to the problem which interested all alike. De Bérulle, imitating the work which S. Philip Neri had already begun at Rome, founded the Congregation of the Oratory of Jesus, or French Oratorians as they are sometimes called (see pages 27 to 30). De Condren became general of this society after De Bérulle's death in 1629. S. Vincent de Paul devised another answer to

1 Under an engraving of Saint-Cyran, which appeared in the *Almanach de Dieu* for 1738, are inscribed the following lines:
>   Hauranne, insensible aux louanges
>   Et caché dans l'obscurité,
>   Sera pour la postérité
>   Un exemple des plus étranges
>   De prudence et d'humilité.

the question how to reform Church life. He founded the Confraternity of Prêtres de la Mission, whose duty it was to go out into all the corners of France instructing and evangelising the poor and ignorant.

Saint-Cyran also had his solution to offer and it was the direct outcome of his association with Jansen in the study of S. Augustine. Like so many other reformers, he felt that a return was needed to the teachings and practice of the early Church. The truths of primitive theology had been clouded by the scholastics and it was to the inspiration of S. Augustine that Saint-Cyran looked for a revival of the true and undefiled religion. But in order to spread these teachings it would be necessary to educate men up to them, and for education men must be caught young. Saint-Cyran therefore—influenced possibly by De Bérulle—formed the idea of founding a seminary. "I had conceived the design," he says, "of building a house which should be a kind of seminary for the Church, in order there to preserve the innocence of children without which I always recognised that they could with difficulty become good clergy[1]." It is at this point then that the first connection is made between Jansenism and the work of education.

The opportunity for Saint-Cyran to put his theories into practice was not long in presenting itself. In 1620 he had met Arnauld d'Andilly, a member of a famous family which will for ever be associated with the abbey of Port-Royal. This abbey had been founded early in the thirteenth century and was situated in a picturesque valley eighteen miles southwest of Paris. In common with most religious houses in France it had fallen into disorder during the sixteenth century; but it was restored to its original simplicity and purity by the energy, steadfastness, and noble example of the Abbess Jacqueline Arnauld, who assumed in religion the name of Angélique. She was a sister of Arnauld d'Andilly. Under

1 *Supplément au Nécrologe* (1735), p. 46.

her rule a second convent was opened in Paris and the two houses—Port-Royal des Champs and Port-Royal de Paris—flourished exceedingly. The reputation of their piety and primitive austerity soon got abroad and occasioned a widespread revival of monastic life in France. When therefore in 1685 a spiritual director was needed for Port-Royal, it was but natural that Angélique, who had already come into touch with Saint-Cyran through her brother D'Andilly, should turn to the Abbé as the most likely priest to sympathise with her aims and to further her reforms. Saint-Cyran rapidly attained a position of great influence at Port-Royal. From this time forward, in addition to the nuns who formed the community, a number of priests and laymen—usually known as "solitaires" or "the Gentlemen of Port-Royal"—began to make the abbey a place of retirement where they could live in retreat under the spiritual direction of Saint-Cyran. Among them may be mentioned Le Maître, nephew of Angélique; Dr Antoine Arnauld; and De Saci, brother of Le Maître and successor of Saint-Cyran as director of the community. A fuller account of these solitaires will be found on pages 40, 42 to 44, and 48.

At the beginning of 1638 it occurred to Saint-Cyran that he might employ some of these Gentlemen of Port-Royal with educational work. As we have already seen, he had originally conceived the design of founding a seminary for the training of aspirants to holy orders. But the teachings of Jansenism on the doctrine of grace inevitably led to a far wider and more general view of the right kind of education for ecclesiastic and layman alike. It has been pointed out that S. Augustine, and Jansen after him, had laid special stress on the doctrine that man from the moment of his birth is a lost creature owing to the taint of original sin[1]. The sacrament of Baptism restores him miraculously to a state of innocence, but it does not safeguard him from falling

1 See also *infra*, pp. 60 and 61.

back into sin. Owing to his corrupt nature, he is still liable to go astray. Moreover he has no power of himself to help himself; his only hope is in the free gift of grace from God whereby he becomes one of the elect. The place of edu cation in such a system of theology was as a safeguard or preventive whereby the soul of the child, regenerated by Baptism, might be developed and strengthened against the attacks of the evil one until eventually it would be strong enough to resist his assaults spontaneously and unaided. But it will be noticed that the whole process is dependent on the free gift of grace—grace for the teacher that he may be enabled to carry out his work successfully; grace for the pupil that he may profit eternally by the education which he receives[1]. And this free gift must for ever be independent of anything which man of himself can do; it lies with God alone to grant or to withhold.

Such was the theology which Jansen developed and it is obviously not a very encouraging one. If carried to its logical conclusion it would have led to complete inanition and fatalism; for if we can never by our own efforts obtain the gift of grace for ourselves and for those committed to our charge, why need we trouble ourselves any further? But the good sense and intense devotion of the Port-Royalists saved them from the consequences of their position; no further proof of this is needed than that which is furnished by the existence of their schools. If grace is withheld when we might have expected it to be granted we must simply acknowledge with reverence that God's ways are not our ways.

The Jansenist theology, with its strong emphasis on

1 Saint-Cyran in a letter to "une dame de grande condition" says: "If it were not for a miracle of grace itself your children when they grow up would never live according to the education which they had received from their infancy upwards. This fact, Madam, does not exempt you from your obligation to give them the best and most Christian education you can procure." (*Lettres Chrestiennes*, vol. I, p. 689.)

original sin and predestination, has never made a wide appeal. Most of us who love children would be tempted to echo the words of the poet[1] who says:

> And fondly he, the passionate saint who steeped
> His virgin soul in Carthaginian mire,
> Found in the weanling babe that laughed and leaped
> Glad from its mother's arm, hate, spite, and ire.
>   They erred. The child is, was, and still shall be
> The world's deliverer; in his heart the springs
> Of our salvation ever rise, and we
> Mount on his innocency as on wings.

Yet from the earliest days of Jansenism down to the present time there have always been a faithful few who, in spite of persecution and difficulties, have clung tenaciously to it. Jansenism certainly savours of the teachings of Calvin and it was therefore condemned by the Catholic Church. It thus happened that the followers of Jansen fell between two stools; while attempting to remain within the pale of the Church and to subscribe to her authority, they were coquetting with doctrines which characterised a recently-formed Protestant heresy; although the Jansenists themselves would have said that they were merely restoring the apostolic doctrine and primitive discipline of Holy Church. If we can forget for a moment the gloomy doctrine of predestination, the terror and contempt of the actual world, and the puritanical distrust of beauty which characterised Jansenism, we may find the conception of an evangelical catholicism both attractive and pregnant with possibilities. Such a theology may doubtless arouse opposition among evangelicals and catholics alike, and this was the fate of Jansenism; but under more favourable auspices and freed from political complications the experiment might perhaps serve to repair some of the rents in the seamless garment of Christendom.

With these general ideas as to the attitude of Jansenism

[1] E. R. Chapman.

towards education, let us return to consider the tuition work which in 1638 was begun by certain of the solitaries under the direction of Saint-Cyran. The convent of Port-Royal des Champs had probably from very early times received girl-boarders (*pensionnaires*) for the purpose of education; but henceforth boys also are taught by the solitaries and it was thus that the famous Little Schools of Port-Royal came into being. They were called "little schools" in order to disarm opposition on the part of the University and the Jesuits, who might scent competition. But as will be gathered from what was said on page 4, the title was a misnomer for the Port-Royal schools offered a complete education for children from the age of eight or nine upwards. Their work, however, was no sooner begun than it was suddenly interrupted. On May 14th, 1638, Saint-Cyran was arrested and thrown into prison at Vincennes. The precise reasons for this step are a little difficult to determine; but it is clear that Richelieu regarded Saint-Cyran as too powerful a person to remain independent. If he would not consent to become a creature of the minister, he must be relegated to a sphere where his influence would be minimised.

The school, in charge of a solitary named Lancelot, was dispersed. It settled for a time at La Ferté Milon, the birthplace of Racine whose aunt, Agnès de Sainte-Thècle Racine, in 1648 became a nun at Port-Royal; but afterwards the school was allowed to return to its original home. In February 1643, two months after the death of Richelieu, Saint-Cyran was set free. He at once took up arms on behalf of the *Augustinus* of Jansen which had recently been published and had aroused considerable criticism. The Jesuits laboured hard to get the book condemned and Pope Urban VIII was induced to censure it[1]. Dr Arnauld joined with Saint-Cyran in championing the *Augustinus* and the whole quarrel was

1 The *Augustinus* had appeared in 1640; the bull of Urban VIII, although dated March 6th, 1642, was not published till June 19th, 1643.

considerably aggravated by the appearance in August 1643 of Arnauld's treatise *De la Fréquente Communion*. This was aimed at the prevailing laxity allowed by the Jesuits and it advocated the necessity of spiritual worthiness before partaking of the Holy Communion.

In the midst of these controversies, on October 11th, 1643, Saint-Cyran died worn out by the rigours of his five years' imprisonment. He has been called the "last of the mediæval theologians," but he was far more than an arid ecclesiastic busied solely with the minutiæ of formal theology. His intense love for his fellow-men, his sympathetic understanding of children[1], his spiritual earnestness, his deep humility— all these qualities combine to make him one of the most attractive of all the many lovable characters which centre round Port-Royal, in strange contrast to the grim and forbidding doctrines which found a home there. It is to Saint-Cyran that the schools with which we are chiefly concerned in this book owe their origin. It is he, and, owing to his influence, Dr Arnauld who gave to Port-Royal its particular religious colouring and set it on the course which eventually won for it a crown of martyrdom. It is easy to see, therefore, that in any account of Port-Royal or of the religious movement known as Jansenism it would be difficult to overestimate the importance of Saint-Cyran.

Meanwhile the community of nuns continued to increase in numbers and accommodation became limited. Accordingly, towards the end of 1646, the solitaries and their pupils removed to a house in the rue Saint-Dominique, a little to the north of Port-Royal de Paris. The school was now organised on definite lines. Saint-Cyran's original idea of forming

---

[1] This trait is illustrated particularly in the letters which he wrote to his little niece and god-daughter—*ma petite*, as he calls her. In the introduction to the 1744 edition of his letters we read: "He knew how to accommodate himself to those to whom he was writing. With children he made himself a child" (p. vi). See also *infra*, p. 69.

a seminary for the priesthood seems to have been set aside, but the schools were from their beginning inspired with his theological views, based on the teachings of S. Augustine. The first headmaster was a certain Walon de Beaupuis and he was assisted by Lancelot, Coustel, Guyot, and Nicole[1]. The school remained in Paris for four years, but its continued success aroused attention and incurred alike the jealousy of other educational institutions and the suspicion of the ecclesiastical authorities. Accordingly, in 1650 the school was partially, if not entirely, broken up. The pupils were divided into three groups and settled at Les Granges, Les Trous, and Le Chesnai—all places in the neighbourhood of Port-Royal des Champs. Other solitaries continued to join those in retreat; in 1655 they added to their number the famous Pascal whose sister Jacqueline had already entered the convent and had just been made headmistress of the girl-boarders. In the same year also Racine, the future poet, became a pupil at Les Granges.

It can be gathered from what has been said that the Port-Royalists were beginning to make powerful enemies. The Jesuits had already found cause to detest them and now the French Court must be added to the list of their adversaries. Saint-Cyran and Arnauld had not hesitated to champion the liberties of the Gallican Church, but Mazarin and Louis XIV after him looked askance at any institution which ventured to defy absolute authority. The *Augustinus* had been condemned at Rome and in 1656 Arnauld himself was censured by the Sorbonne and deprived of his doctorate. Pascal in his *Provincial Letters* took up the cause of Arnauld and of Port-Royal in opposition to the Jesuits. In modern times politics is chiefly responsible for inflaming our passions and perverting our judgments; but in seventeenth-century France with its strong autocratic government there was little scope for free political discussion. Religious controversy was there-

1 See *infra*, pp. 37–39 and 44–48.

fore called in to furnish the necessary pretext for mutual re-crimination and persecution. With the appearance, then, of the *Provinciales* the question of grace ceased to be merely an academic theological discussion. It now became a party cry and excited as much comment and criticism as—let us say—the Dreyfus affair in more recent times. The effect of the *Provincial Letters* was phenomenal; the Society of Jesus was compromised and its very existence was at stake. Port-Royal now appeared as a most dangerous foe which must at all costs be crushed. One of the first results therefore of the *Provinciales* was that the Little Schools kept by the soli-taries—the literary defenders of the society—were suppressed by a royal order engineered by Jesuit intrigue. This was in 1656, but the final destruction of the schools was delayed until four years later largely owing to the impression created by an alleged miracle. Through the application of a relic—one of the thorns which had composed our Lord's crown—Marguerite Périer, a *pensionnaire* of the convent and niece of Pascal, was cured of a disfiguring lachrymal fistula. This was regarded as an evidence of the "manifest protection of God" towards the community. In 1660, however, the schools were once more dispersed and they never reassembled. The masters who had taught in them were scattered abroad; but they have left us several treatises dealing with their school methods and these enable us to gain some considerable knowledge of their educational theories and practice.

The Port-Royal schools endured for at most twenty-two years, and of these for only fourteen as an organised insti-tution. Again, the number of pupils was at no time large. The total of those educated in the schools during the whole of their existence is at most 250. Why then are we justified in regarding the Little Schools of Port-Royal as of first-rate importance in the history of education? The answer is that the influence of these schools and of those who taught in them was very far-reaching and of an almost unique character. We have seen how the teachings of S. Augustine, as interpreted by Jansen and applied by Saint-Cyran, had affected the Little Schools. The emphasis on moral education drawn from these sources was always present at Port-Royal; but there was another thinker from whom the solitaries drew inspiration for their teaching work. Descartes had laid stress on the value of independent thought as opposed to scholastic tradition. Just as Saint-Cyran combated scholastic interpretations of the doctrine of grace and wished to return to S. Augustine, the fountain head, so Descartes opposed scholastic tradition in philosophy and advocated thinking for oneself. Even if he supplied arguments to prove the existence of God he regarded matters of faith and religious experience as outside the province of philosophy. Thus it was possible—or, at any rate, it seemed possible—to combine the philosophy of Descartes with the orthodox Roman religion. It is very doubtful whether Saint-Cyran would have approved of such a step. His aim was to restore the teachings of Holy Church in all their primitive purity; but many of the masters who taught in the Little Schools, and who wrote the educational works which are associated with them, were strongly inclined towards Cartesianism. In this way it happened that Port-Royal contributed to the great and far-reaching intellectual reformation in which Descartes took a leading part.

The solitaries thus brought forth out of their treasure things both new and old. Let us see how this affected their educational practice. On the one hand we have a somewhat puritanical attitude towards art and the theatre; the pupils are kept under continual surveillance to guard against the contamination of the world; and their general environment is regulated with extreme caution. But at the same time children are treated with studied affection, and punishments, viewed in the light of contemporary practice, are extremely mild. Work must be made as easy as possible, for there are in all school tasks so many real difficulties that there is no necessity for the schoolmaster to invent artificial ones. Hence teaching is carried on in the vernacular—not in Latin, as was the almost universal custom of the day; and innumerable text-books were written by the solitaries so that their pupils might use the easiest and most interesting methods of learning. It is enough to refer briefly to these points at this stage for they are dealt with in detail in the translated extracts which form the bulk of this book. Let it suffice to say that the Port-Royal schools were of importance not only because they initiated the application to education in modern Europe of the principle that one should think for oneself, but also because the professional methods employed in them were far in advance of those of the rest of Europe. In the public schools of England many of the practices advocated by Port-Royal were not generally adopted until the latter half of the nineteenth century.

Something now remains to be said about another Teaching Congregation—that of the Oratorians. It owed its origin (d) The Oratorians. to Cardinal de Bérulle who founded an institute of ecclesiastics bound together by no special vows other than those of their holy orders, but whose common aim was to improve the general efficiency of the priesthood in France. Educational work had formed no part of the founder's original scheme, but it was introduced by Pope Paul V and extended by Louis XIII and his successors. The Oratorian Fathers came quickly into requisition as teachers. In 1614 a college was offered to them at Dieppe and this was the forerunner of many similar institutions all over France. By the end of the seventeenth century the society possessed some thirty-four schools chief of which was the famous Collège de Juilly; in addition it had two training-colleges and numerous other institutions not directly connected with the work of education. At many of the Oratorian schools instruction was given free ; at others a small inclusive fee was charged.

In the schools of the Oratory—as in all contemporary secondary boys' schools—Latin was the chief subject in the curriculum. But the Oratorians agreed with Port-Royal and differed from the University and the Society of Jesus in treating Latin as a dead language to be studied for its literary and humanistic value, but not to be used as the vehicle of all instruction. In the Oratory, as at Port-Royal, we never see little boys made to learn to read by spelling out Latin words the meaning of which is unknown to them. But the Oratorians were not so whole-hearted in this reform as were the Port-Royalists. After Class IV, the average age of which would be about twelve, Latin became obligatory as the medium of instruction except in the case of history teaching which was carried on in the vernacular throughout the whole school course.

Although the Classics occupied the greater part of the pupil's time in the Oratorian schools, particular stress was laid on the teaching of history—not only that of Greece and Rome and sacred history, but also that of France. The earliest instruction in this subject took the form of anecdotes and biographies of prominent persons. To amplify the course lessons were given on geography, heraldry, and antiquities. The learning of mere lists of dates was discouraged; and on the whole Oratorian methods of teaching history compare quite favourably with those in use in many of our schools to-day. In the upper forms lectures were given by the master in charge and were taken down in the shape of notes which were afterwards worked up by the pupils themselves. They thus formed for themselves a text-book which was of particular value at a time when historical works were rare and difficult of access to the average schoolboy. Another striking characteristic of the Oratorian curriculum was the prominent place accorded to mathematics. This was the case from the earliest days of the society; the college of Dieppe possessed a chair of Mathematics as early as 1616. Later, under the inspiration of Descartes, physics and natural sciences were introduced and mathematics was made to include algebra, geometry, plane and spherical trigonometry, and the calculus. If, then, in the teaching of the vernacular and of the Classics the Oratorians had not reached the level of the Port-Royalists, it must be confessed that in the teaching of history and particularly of mathematics they had surpassed them. Indeed in this respect they were far in advance of anything done in English schools for nearly 200 years afterwards.

Some reference to Oratorian school-life will conclude what we have to say on this subject. The school-day was much like that at Port-Royal (see page 240). On weekdays the boys rose at 5.30. On descending to the classroom they recited the morning prayers and then prepared lessons until 7.30. Breakfast was served at 7.45 and was followed by more preparation until 9.0. Then came a lesson, after which the school assisted at Mass and recited the Litany of the Holy Name of Jesus. The boys went to dinner at 11.0, and were afterwards allowed a short recreation. Preparation was resumed at 12.30 and lessons in form at 2.0. At 4.30 a light meal was served and this was followed by more preparation until 6.30. Then the Litany of the Holy Virgin was said before supper and after the meal there was another period of recreation lasting until 8.0. There followed half-an-hour's reading—usually of a history book—and at 9.30, after evening prayers had been read, the whole school retired to bed.

Discipline—as was usual in the Teaching Congregations—was relatively mild. The same master accompanied his form throughout their school course from the lowest form to the highest. This is a method which involves obvious disadvantages both from the point of view of the teacher and that of the taught alike; but it has not been unknown even in more modern times and in this country[1]. At the end of the term a report was sent to each boy's parents. It comprised the following headings: Church; Piety; Proses; Translations; Commentaries; Conduct; Work; Politeness. This curious mixture of things sacred and profane was evaluated according to the following scale: excellent; very good; good; moderate; doubtful; bad. The estimation of moral qualities by means of such a scheme may appear ridiculous to the modern critic; but it does remind us of a fact which is sometimes overlooked now that the value of education is judged so largely by examination results—the fact that mere intellectual knowledge is only a part of what the school must inculcate. The development of character and the awakening of a sense of responsibility and of public spirit are doubtless realised to be of even greater importance. If then we can evaluate and report upon the results of school training in the intellectual sphere, it might be argued that an attempt should be made to do likewise in reference to the moral development of our pupils. As a matter of fact, schemes of this kind have actually been introduced of recent years into certain schools of a progressive type in this country. For example, in a well-known public boarding-school in the north of England and in a large boys' day-school near London masters are asked to report on their pupils under such headings as *honesty, courage, public spirit, power of leadership, religious sense*, and the like. To fill up such reports satisfactorily is extremely difficult—often, perhaps, impossible; and to be required to do so is apt to be resented by overworked schoolmasters at the end of term. But the system, even if at present in its infancy and often wrongly applied, has its possibilities, and it is interesting to see how it was adumbrated in the practice of the Oratorian schools.

Little has been said so far about the education of girls.

[1] See, for example, D'Arcy Thompson, *Day Dreams of a Schoolmaster*, ch. iii, p. 29.

In the case of the parish schools which gave a rudimentary
The Education kind of education[1] there was even less provision
of Girls. for girls than for boys. The chief reason for this
(a) Element-
ary Educa- was that the bishops were strongly opposed to
tion. mixed schools. The question, therefore, which
confronted the founders of parish charity schools was whether
boys or girls should be educated; for, owing to the episcopal
ban, the two sexes were mutually exclusive. In almost all
cases it was the boys who benefited. Another difficulty was
to find suitable women to whom the Precentor's license could
be. granted and who could take charge of "little schools."
Single women of education or who possessed dowries usually
retired into convents; and the teaching of little girls outside
of the convent schools was left to uneducated and incompetent persons who tended to treat their charges with extreme
severity and were unable to teach them anything beyond
reading and the elements of writing.

To remedy this state of things a notable attempt had been
begun in 1606 by a lady named Anne de Xainctonge, aided
by her sister Françoise. They were natives of Dijon and were
impressed at once by the vigour and efficiency of the Jesuit
college of their native town and by the absence of any ade-
quate provision for the education of girls. The enthusiasm
of the two sisters overcame all the obstacles which the pre-
judices of their family, their friends, and the municipal and
ecclesiastical authorities put in their way. They consulted
the Jesuits, who were at this time the only Teaching Congregation in France, and to some extent modelled their
methods on those of the Society of Jesus. Their object was
to set up free schools, not attached to any convent, for the
benefit of girls who came from poor families. The curriculum
included reading, writing, and arithmetic, and "all those
accomplishments which beseem their sex and can help
them one day to become good mothers of families." Similar

1 See *supra*, p. 2.

attempts to provide poor girls with gratuitous instruction in the three R's and domestic accomplishments were made by such societies as the *Filles de la Congrégation de Notre-Dame* (1607), the organisation of which was closely modelled upon that of the Society of Jesus, and the *Institut de l'Enfance* (1662), and by a community established at Troyes by Nicole in 1678, and entrusted to a certain Madame Aubry whose daughters entered the convent of Port-Royal.

Let us turn now to the education of girls of the middle-class. Fénelon, writing in 1683, says, "Nothing is more neglected than the education of girls[1]." It must be confessed that the average bourgeois *père de famille* of the seventeenth century strongly sympathised with Molière's Chrysale in his strictures on female education[2]. There was throughout a tendency to believe that the education of girls should be rigorously confined to instruction in religion and in domestic duties—*Küche, Kinder, und Kirche*, as a modern reactionary has phrased it. Woman always occupied a subordinate position—in religion to her superior or her confessor; in domestic life to her husband. The corollary of this was—"Do not teach her too much," with the únexpressed apprehension "lest she forget her proper position." This attitude of man towards his womankind reminds us of that adopted by "persons of quality" during the seventeenth and eighteenth centuries towards members of the "lower classes." As a rule, therefore, girls were sent to the schools which were attached to convents, where there was little fear of their being overburdened with instruction. They picked up a smattering of reading, writing, and arithmetic, together with a large amount of religious instruction and a great deal of information as to the sinfulness of the world outside.

There were several orders which devoted themselves almost exclusively to the education of girls. As examples we

1 *De l'Éducation des Filles*, p. 1.
2 *Les Femmes Savantes*, Act II, Sc. vii, 61–66.

may take the nuns of the order of S. Elizabeth, the Angeli-
(b) Conventual cals, or the Ursulines, who, although expelled
Education. from France by the recent Congregations Act,
still carry on their noble work elsewhere. Typical of this
conventual type of education were the Port-Royal girls'
schools, details of which are given in Part IV of this book.
Teaching seems to have been regarded less as a benefit
which could be conferred on the pupil than as a penance
which would prove a valuable aid to the spiritual development of the teacher. The *régime* tended to be severe—witness the long silences, the continual surveillance, the emphasis on instruction in religion almost to the exclusion of
other subjects. It may be difficult for us from our modern
standpoint to have much sympathy with a type of education
such as this; yet in the seventeenth century it was the usual
lot of the bulk of French girls who received any education
worth speaking of. Perhaps it did not weigh so heavily upon
them as we might at first be tempted to suppose. At Port-
Royal, at any rate, there was ever a motherly affection and
a shrewd knowledge of child-nature which helped to temper the rigours of the school regulations. We have indeed
evidence that old pupils often looked back with affectionate
recollection to the time which they had spent in these conventual schools[1]; but we shall none the less agree with Fénelon when he criticises this hot-house type of education and
says: "A girl leaves a convent like one who has been reared
in the darkness of a deep cavern and is brought out suddenly
into broad daylight[2]."

Towards the end of the seventeenth century a most
(c) Madame de important experiment in the education of girls
Maintenon— was made. Mme de Maintenon does not
the School at
Saint-Cyr. usually figure in our history books as a great

1 Cf., for example, p. 191, *infra*.
2 *Avis de M. de Fénelon à une Dame de Qualité sur l'Éducation de
Mademoiselle sa Fille.*

educational reformer, yet she has many claims to the title. After several experiments in the education of girls, she was instrumental in founding the celebrated school of Saint-Cyr. It must not be confused with the military school established in the same place at a later date by Napoleon. Mme de Maintenon's institution was designed for the education of girls of noble birth whose fathers had lost their wealth or their lives in the service of their country. Louis XIV, who always distrusted monastic schools—witness his treatment of Port-Royal—laid it down explicitly that at Saint-Cyr "nothing should savour of the monastery, either in the external practices, or in the wearing of a habit, or in the religious services, or in the daily life, which last should be active but unrestrained, easy, and free from austerity[1]." Even though the school had its conventual aspects it was none the less a real advance upon the *régime* which is typified, perhaps at its best, in the girls' schools of Port-Royal.

Mme de Maintenon may, perhaps, be not unfairly described as a "schoolma'am" writ large. She first comes into prominence at the French Court as governess to two of Louis XIV's illegitimate children, and subsequently she seems to have assumed somewhat the same relationship towards the King himself. She was indeed eminently fitted to become the controlling spirit of such an institution as Saint-Cyr, where —as in all well conducted schools for young ladies—due consideration was given to morals and deportment. Mme de Maintenon threw herself whole-heartedly into the life of her school. She busied herself alike with the physical and mental well-being of her pupils. She was in the dormitory when the girls rose and in the class-room while lessons were in progress. She gave the utmost attention to developing on desirable lines the character of each individual pupil and her activities were inspired by a very real love for her charges.

[1] Mme de Maintenon, *Extraits sur l'Éducation*, ed. Oct. Gréard, p. xxviii.

The girls—there were 250 of them—were divided into four groups distinguished by the colour of their sashes. The reds (aged 7–11) studied reading, writing, arithmetic, grammar, the catechism, and sacred history; the greens (11–14) in addition learnt music, geography, and mythology; the yellows (14–17) took French, music, religion, dancing, and drawing; while the blues (17–20), who wore the royal colour, specialised in French, music, and morals. These groups were subdivided into "families" or classes of eight to ten pupils each. The aim of the school was to produce good women who would make good wives and mothers—an aim which was often lost sight of in contemporary conventual schools. Mere instruction, however, was too much sacrificed at Saint-Cyr. Reading, on the whole, was discouraged; at any rate, it was confined to a few religious books; in fact Mme de Maintenon obviously dreaded lest her charges should develop a tendency to *préciosité*. On the other hand, all kinds of domestic work held an important place. The girls did their own housework and gave much time to needlework.

There was one department of intellectual education, however, which for a time was in evidence at Saint-Cyr. The girls were encouraged to give dramatic representations, and Racine's *Esther* and *Athalie* were originally written for the pupils of Mme de Maintenon's school. The Court attended the performances and the brilliance of these functions drew much attention to the young actresses and their school. It then struck Mme de Maintenon that such popularity might not be good for children; the girls were too much petted and were in danger of becoming self-conscious and affected. In 1691, therefore, this department of life at Saint-Cyr came to an end.

We can see in this school one of the earliest realisations in France of the truth—not yet universally appreciated—that girls have, no less than boys, every right to a full and fruitful education such as will best fit them to serve most effectively the society to which they belong. It marks one of the first

avowed attempts to educate girls of the "upper classes" not
for the religious life of the convent, but for the duties of wife
and mother in the home. It would, indeed, have been strange
if a period which saw a few women of extraordinary brilliance
taking a leading part in French intellectual, social, and
political life, had not witnessed also a reaction against the
contemporary conventual education of girls.

In this short *résumé* of French education in the seventeenth century it has been impossible to do more than review
Conclusion. rapidly a number of subjects, treating none with
the detail which it deserves. It is indeed a
chapter in the history of education which merits further study.
Schoolmasters are a notoriously conservative class and the
schoolroom afforded a refuge for some of the least desirable
characteristics of the mediæval scholastic tradition long after
it had lost its power elsewhere. But enough, perhaps, has
been said to show that there were schools in France in the
seventeenth century which were already filled with a new
spirit—the spirit which has since regenerated education
throughout Western Europe. We too, in these latter days,
have something to learn from these striking instances of the
deep earnestness of purpose and wonderful clarity of thought
which have always characterised the French people.

II. Notes on the chief Port-Royalist Writers on Education

Saint Cyran

Some account of the Abbé de Saint-Cyran (1581–1643)
and of his connection with Port-Royal will be found on pages
15 to 23. He was the founder of the Little Schools and
his theological views largely determined the character of the
education which was given in them. We have no evidence
that he ever actually taught in the schools, but he inspired
and controlled those who were responsible for the teaching
and even after his death this work was carried on along the

lines which he had indicated. His *Lettres Chrestiennes* were written chiefly during his imprisonment at the castle of Vincennes (1638–1643). He had already acquired a considerable reputation as a "director of consciences," and many persons of rank and eminence had welcomed him as their spiritual adviser. When therefore he was cast into prison, he continued—though with some difficulty—to exercise his ministry by correspondence. As might be expected, most of his letters deal with purely religious topics; but it has always proved difficult to separate such matters from questions of education; and as we have seen (pages 19 and 20), education and religion in Saint-Cyran's opinion were vitally connected. We therefore read in the preface to his correspondence: "Fathers and mothers will see in these letters the care which they ought to exercise in bringing up their children as Christians—that is to say, as children of God, for such they are by baptism, and not merely as children of men, as if they were heathens[1]." He continually inculcates the solemnity of the responsibility which is laid upon parents; "the smallest flaw in the heart is enough to prevent its movement towards God, just like dust in a clock or dirt in the eye. Children belong to their parents only as regards the body, but to God as regards the soul. Love your children for the sake of God and less than God[2]." The extracts from Saint-Cyran's letters given on pages 57 to 60 form the most detailed exposition of his views upon education that is left to us in his own writings.

Lancelot

Claude Lancelot (1615(?)-1695) was of humble origin. He began his ecclesiastical career at the age of 12 when he entered the community of S. Nicholas du Chardonnet at Paris. There he remained for some ten years, studying the Fathers; but when he contrasted the saints of whom he read with the ecclesiastical dignitaries of his own day, he was filled with doubts and difficulties and knew not where to look for help.

1 *Lettres Chrestiennes* (1645 ed.), vol. I, p. 4. 2 *op. cit.* vol. I, p. 229.

"There are no longer," he says, "men like S. Chrysostom, S. Augustine, and the rest; if there were even one only I would start this moment and go to seek him even to the end of the world, to throw myself at his feet and to receive from him so trustworthy and so salutary a guidance[1]." Stranded thus, "like a man who has been thrown up by the sea on the coast of some island and who is waiting till a vessel happens to pass and take him off," he heard of Saint-Cyran as being the type of director for whom he was looking. He hastened to put himself into the Abbé's hands, nor was he disappointed. He became Saint-Cyran's most faithful disciple and most devoted admirer. He tells us how he used to "pause sometimes and look upon M. de Saint-Cyran as one of the most living images of Christ" that he had ever seen. Lancelot was put in charge of the teaching of Greek and Mathematics in the school which had recently been started. In 1644 he published his *New Method* of learning Latin, in which the rules of Despauter (see pages 7 and 8) were given in French verse. Judged by present-day standards, Lancelot's doggerel rhymes have but little to recommend them, but they marked an important advance in educational practice at a time when children were commonly made to learn the rules of Latin grammar in Latin itself. In 1655 appeared his *Greek Method*, which sought to simplify the learning of Greek grammar, and in 1657 he published his *Garden of Greek Roots*, the aim of which was to facilitate the acquiring of a vocabulary. The latter volume (see page 178) is of little value owing to the faulty etymologies of which it is full; it has none the less proved extraordinarily popular in French schools[2] and has undergone many revisions and improvements; it is

1 *Mémoires de Saint-Cyran*, vol. I, p. 5.
2 It was also imitated. In 1706 Étienne Fourmont published *Les Racines de la langue latine mises en vers françois;* while, at a later date, Masclef wrote a *Racines hébraiques sans points-voyelles*, which was also in verse.

mentioned, for example, in "André Laurie's" popular school-story *Mémoires d'un Collégien*. When the Little Schools were suppressed in 1660 Lancelot was appointed tutor to the young Duc de Chevreuse and afterwards, in 1669, to the two Princes de Conti. He resigned the latter position in 1672 rather than take his pupils to the theatre. The Port-Royalists were unanimous in their condemnation of the stage (see pages 108 and 110–112); but here, as always, they are faithful to the teachings of S. Augustine[1]. In 1672, then, the educational work of Lancelot came to an end and he retired to the abbey of Saint-Cyran, then under the control of Martin de Barcos, nephew of the famous abbot. Upon De Barcos' death in 1678, Lancelot became involved in the general persecution of the Jansenists and was forced to retire to Quimperlé in Brittany where he died in 1695.

Since he was not only one of the chief teachers in the Little Schools but also a writer whose books have played some considerable part in the history of education, we shall have several occasions to quote from his works. His *Mémoires touchans la Vie de M. de Saint-Cyran* serve to amplify the abbot's educational theories as outlined in the *Lettres Chrestiennes*. His Latin and Greek *Methods* indicate the teaching practices which he adopted in the Little Schools. His letter to De Saci, giving an account of how he educated the Princes de Conti, shows us Saint-Cyran's theological view of education applied under special conditions to a particular case. This letter is preserved for us in the *Supplément au Nécrologe*[2] —a collection of records and documents relating to the convent of Port-Royal. In addition to the books already mentioned, Lancelot was the author of an *Italian Method* and a *Spanish Method*, and he contributed to the *General Grammar* (see pages 141–143 and 144–146).

[1] See, for example, *Confessions*, bk III, ch. ii. The theatre had also been condemned by Jansen in his pamphlet *De la Réformation de l'Homme intérieur*.   [2] (1735) pp. 161–7.

De Saci

Louis Isaac Le Maître (1613-1684), usually known as De Saci—an anagram of his Christian name Isaac—belonged to the Arnauld family which played so conspicuous a part in the history of Port-Royal (see page 18). He was brought up with his "little uncle," the afterwards famous Dr Arnauld. Unlike the latter, however, he showed no taste for the studies of the Sorbonne and was therefore put under the care of Saint-Cyran. From his earliest youth he had shown a strong inclination towards holy orders and although, when the time came, he felt some misgivings as to his fitness for so sacred an estate, he was finally persuaded by Saint-Cyran's nephew De Barcos. He was ordained priest in 1650 and became director of Port-Royal. He thus had charge of the community during the period when the Little Schools were most flourishing. As early as 1638 he had been set by Saint-Cyran to teach some boys, and he remained deeply interested in the work of education. His best-known contribution to literature is the famous Mons Bible—a translation of the Scriptures into French, for which he is largely responsible. He also published for school use several French renderings of Latin authors. In Fontaine's *Mémoires sur MM. de Port-Royal* (see page 41) there is also a passage dealing with De Saci's views on education. Parts of this are given below (pages 104-105 and 107); throughout the reader will notice the close resemblance of De Saci's theories to those of Saint-Cyran. De Saci died on January 4th, 1684; during the anxious time of persecution he had continued faithfully to fulfil his sacred duties as director to the perplexed and harassed nuns of the community.

Fontaine

Nicholas Fontaine (1625-1709) entered Port-Royal at the age of nineteen and De Saci, following the example of Saint-Cyran, entrusted to him the instruction of several boys. Throughout his connection with Port-Royal he occupies a somewhat subordinate place; he was attached more particularly to De Saci to whom he acted as secretary, and he followed his master into captivity in the Bastille from 1666 to 1668. When attempts were made to procure his release, he said: "My liberty is to be with M. de Saci." His chief importance from our point of view is that he wrote a *Mémoires sur MM. de Port-Royal* which gives us a charming picture of the community and incidentally sheds considerable light on the educational doctrines of Saint-Cyran and De Saci. The latter part of his life was overshadowed by the persecutions levelled at the Jansenists and he died in 1709, the last survivor from that golden age in the history of Port-Royal with which the Little Schools are inseparably connected.

Varet

So far as the present writer has been able to ascertain, Varet (1632–1676) took no actual part in the teaching work at Port-Royal. He was, however, an historian of the Jansenist movement and is mentioned in the Port-Royal *Nécrologe* —an annotated list of persons connected with the convent, and arranged according to the days on which they died. Varet's death, as a matter of fact, occurred while he was on a visit to Port-Royal des Champs and he was buried in the abbey. In 1666 he had published his treatise *De l'Éducation Chrestienne des Enfans*[1]. This book is of interest because it emphasises and develops the theological conception of education as set forth by Saint-Cyran in his letters; for example, Varet elaborates the doctrines of original sin and baptismal regeneration in all their rigour. And since these doctrines are inherent in the Jansenist view of education it has been thought wise to include in this book some characteristic extracts from Varet.

---

[1] An English translation of this book appeared as early as 1678; it was published by "J. B. Coignard at the Golden Bible in S. James' Street."

De Sainte-Marthe

In the *Supplément au Nécrologe* there is preserved a letter which deals with the aim of the Port-Royal schools and explains some of the methods adopted in them; a translation of this document has therefore been included in this book. It was written to a certain M. Chamillard (see page 73) by Claude de Sainte-Marthe (1619–1690). The author is one of the lesser-known figures at Port-Royal; he chose the path of pious obscurity and followed it in spite of everything. From 1669 to 1679 he acted as confessor to the convent. It is said that when the persecution of the Jansenists was renewed in 1679 and the gradual strangling of the community began he would come by night to Port-Royal des Champs and climb a high tree which grew outside the garden wall; thence he would address words of comfort and hope to the disconsolate nuns, huddled together in the darkness below. De Sainte-Marthe died in 1690 and the nuns testified to their gratitude for the services which he had rendered them during those dark days by inscribing upon his tomb the words of the Psalmist: *Pavit eas in innocentia cordis sui*—"he fed them according to the integrity of his heart."

Dr Arnauld

Antoine Arnauld (1612–1694)—"le grand Arnauld," as he is often called—was the youngest brother of Mère Angélique. He had an unusually successful academic career and was already making a name for himself at the bar when he came under the influence of Saint-Cyran who was at the time a prisoner at Vincennes. Arnauld retired to Port-Royal and decided to relinquish his prospects of worldly fame. After a brilliant course in the theological faculty of the Sorbonne he was ordained priest and admitted doctor in the year 1641. When the *Augustinus* (see page 16) was attacked, Arnauld took up the cudgels on its behalf and soon showed himself one of the chief literary champions of Jansenism and Port-

Royal. His activities provoked the most strenuous opposition. He was marked down for persecution, deprived of his doctorate, hunted from one hiding-place to another, driven into exile and poverty; but nothing could stifle his voice uplifted, as he believed, in the cause of Truth. He died at Brussels at the age of eighty-three.

Next to Saint-Cyran, Arnauld is the most conspicuous figure of all those who are connected with Port-Royal. As regards the purely educational work of the community, however, he does not merit so important a place. He took very little part in the actual teaching, but he had many fruitful ideas upon the subject of education. He wrote a *Mémoire sur le Règlement des Études dans les Lettres Humaines* which suggested reforms in the Faculty of Arts of the University (see pages 6 to 10); several extracts from it have been included in the present selection. Dr Arnauld was also a collaborator— probably the principal one—in the Port-Royal *Logic* and the *General Grammar*, and he wrote an *Elements of Geometry* which Pascal considered superior to a work of his own on the same subject.

While we are right in regarding Dr Arnauld as the chief champion of Jansenism (with the possible exception of Pascal who wrote the *Provincial Letters*), the fact remains that he does not altogether represent the primitive spirit of the movement as it is typified by Jansen himself or by Saint-Cyran. Arnauld more than any of the solitaries had come under the influence of Descartes[1]. The Cartesian philosophy was anathema to De Saci, as it would certainly have been to Saint-Cyran also, had he known of it. Again, when we reach the polemical activities of Arnauld we have left behind that Port-Royal in which the primitive austerities of the Cistercian Order had been revived by Angélique and which was the scene

[1] Arnauld wrote a long letter in answer to a treatise by Le Moine, dean of Vitré in Brittany, who had attacked certain aspects of the Cartesian philosophy. (See *Œuvres* (1780), vol. XXXVIII.)

of the ministrations of Saint-Cyran. In this earlier Port-Royal there was ever a distrust of the world of affairs, together with a spirit of self-repression, of contemplation,—even of mysticism, which at times suggests the teachings of Mme Guyon, the foundress of Quietism[1]. These characteristics are illustrated, for example, in many of Saint-Cyran's writings, in the Regulations for the Port-Royal girls' schools, and still more in the letters of Mère Agnès, Angélique's sister. But they are very foreign to the lust for battle with which the indomitable Arnauld returns, bruised but not beaten, to the charge, or to the inexhaustible energy for controversy shown in the answer which he gives to his tired and timid follower Nicole: "Have we not all eternity to rest in?" But since it is with the earlier Port-Royal—that of Saint-Cyran—that the scholastic work of the community is chiefly connected, the great Arnauld—heroic figure though he be—is of less interest to an educational historian than many another less famous Port-Royalist.

Nicole

Pierre Nicole (1625–1695) first came into contact with Port-Royal while he was a theological student at the Sorbonne. An aunt of his was already a religious of the community, and when in 1646 a Little School was established in Paris (see page 23), Nicole became a master there. Teaching, however, occupied only part of his time for he continued to study for his bachelor's degree in theology. The troubles which arose at the Sorbonne consequent upon the publication of the *Augustinus* determined Nicole to relinquish his academic career and he now devoted his attention exclusively to teaching in the Port-Royal schools. He became a friend of the celebrated Dr Arnauld and helped him to defend the com-

1 S. Theresa, the Spanish Mystic, from whom Mme Guyon drew much of her inspiration, was held in particular honour at Port-Royal— see page 249, note on p. 109, l. 7.

munity by polemical literature. He assisted at the composition of Pascal's *Provincial Letters* and afterwards translated them into Latin. He also contributed to the *Logic* and the *General Grammar*. His *Hérésies Imaginaires* and *Visionnaires* are an imitation of Pascal's work. It was in one of these letters that Nicole set forth views on the theatre which gave great offence to Racine and caused a temporary breach between the dramatist and the community which had educated him (see pages 49 to 50). In 1671 appeared the first volume of Nicole's *Essais de Morale* which in their day had a great vogue[1]. In the second book of these essays is a *Traité de l'Éducation d'un Prince*. Under so pronounced a monarchical *régime* as that of Louis XIV it was not unnatural for the would-be social reformer to look to the enlightened despot as the most effective and accessible instrument for the fulfilment of his hopes. Hence Nicole, like so many other writers of the period, considers that the proper education of those who are the most influential of mankind is a matter of vital importance. At the same time what he has to say relates not merely to the education of those in high places; it has a far wider application for it reflects his own experience as a teacher in the Little Schools of Port-Royal[2]. None the less Nicole—like Dr Arnauld—is not directly inspired by Saint-Cyran. It is even true, perhaps, to say that he was only half-heartedly a Jansenist and his continued services to the cause were possibly due in large measure to the influence so long exerted over him by Dr Arnauld. We are not surprised therefore to find that when Nicole treats of education he concerns himself less with the fall of man and baptismal regeneration than with the development of the reason and the formation of the judgment.

1 Mme de Sévigné refers to them frequently in terms of high praise—see several letters of 1675–6 and especially that of Jan. 12th, 1676.

2 Nicole himself says in his preface: "Most of the recommendations made in this book can be applied under any conditions."

Nicole died in 1695. After the dispersion of the Little Schools his life had been devoted largely to assisting Dr Arnauld in his spirited defence of Jansenism. But in 1679 Nicole's natural timidity and longing for a quiet life overcame his devotion to his master, and he spent his last years in that peace and retirement which he had so long desired. He was not of the stuff of which martyrs are made and it was of that rare metal that the true disciples of Port-Royal were fashioned. Sainte-Beuve sums him up as "le cousin-germain de Port-Royal[1]."

Walon de Beaupuis

When the educational work of Port-Royal was formally organised and a school opened in the rue S. Dominique (1646), Walon de Beaupuis (1621–1709) was selected to be its first headmaster. He was a native of Beauvais and had had a brilliant career at the University of Paris. He was led by reading Dr Arnauld's *Frequent Communion* (see page 23) to ally himself with Port-Royal and he was identified with the work of the Little Schools throughout their troubled existence. He afterwards acted for a time as tutor to Pascal's nephews and was ordained priest in 1666. When the persecution of the Jansenists was renewed in 1679 Walon de Beaupuis was deprived of his benefice and retired to his sister's house where he lived a life of meditation and rigorous asceticism until his death in 1709. We still possess an account of the manner in which the school groups at Port-Royal des Champs were organised. It was drawn up by De Beaupuis' brother, Georges Walon, a merchant of Beauvais who had himself been a pupil in the Little Schools. This *Règlement* is given, word for word the same, both in the *Supplément au Nécrologe*[2], and in Fontaine's *Mémoires sur MM. de Port-Royal*[3]. A more detailed set of rules for the school group of Le Chesnai, of

1 *Port-Royal*, vol. IV, p. 502.
2 pp. 58–61.   3 pp. cxviii–cxxiii.

which De Beaupuis for a time had particular charge, is also given in the *Supplément au Nécrologe*[1]. Although these two regulations cover much the same ground it has been thought advisable to include both in the present volume so as to give as complete a picture as possible of the organisation of the Little Schools.

Coustel

Pierre Coustel (1621–1704) was a native of Beauvais and was attracted towards Port-Royal through the influence of his friend and fellow-townsman Walon de Beaupuis. He had already been a schoolmaster in his native city and when the Little Schools were established in Paris (1646), Coustel was appointed to teach in them, his special subject being Latin. After the dispersion of the schools in 1660 he became tutor to the nephews of the Cardinal de Furstenberg, Prince-Bishop of Strasbourg, who was a creature of the French king and whose elevation to the Archbishopric of Cologne in 1688 was the immediate cause of a European war. To this prelate Coustel dedicated his *Règles de l'Éducation des Enfans* which appeared in 1687. We have evidence that this book is based directly upon the educational practice of the Little Schools (see page 140 and note on p. 253). It is permeated with the spirit of Saint-Cyran, tempered somewhat by experience gained in the class-room. This work, therefore, in spite of its somewhat prolix style, is one of our most valuable sources of information as to the methods employed by the Port-Royalist teachers, and frequent quotations from it will be found below. Unfortunately the book is very rare (see page 52); the copy which is perhaps most easily accessible is that in the *Musée Pédagogique* at Paris. Coustel also translated for school use some Latin authors and wrote a tract condemning "comedies." The gist of the latter work is contained in the extract from Varet which is given on pages 110–112.

[1] pp. 54–58.

Guyot

Of Guyot we know very little. He was one of the masters in the school of the rue S. Dominique and afterwards at Le Chesnai. But in later life he deserted the Jansenists and went over to their bitterest enemies, the Jesuits; consequently the records of Port-Royal pass over his name in silence. Yet he made a valuable contribution to the educational work of the community. He translated several Latin authors into French and furnished them with introductions which have a permanent interest for the educational historian, because they adumbrate school methods which were far in advance of those in contemporary use.

Du Fossé

Pierre-Thomas Du Fossé (1634–1698) has a peculiar interest for us because he was a pupil at Port-Royal and has left us an account of his school-life in his *Mémoires pour servir à l'histoire de Port-Royal*. A record from this particular point of view is of unique value for supplementing the treatises of those who were responsible for the organisation of the schools or for the teaching methods employed in them. Du Fossé derived much help and encouragement in his work from Le Maître, brother of De Saci, who had renounced a legal career of exceptional promise to become a solitary at Port-Royal. "He gave me," says Du Fossé, "several rules for good translation in order to enable me to make progress in it[1]." These *Règles de la traduction française* are given in Fontaine's *Mémoires sur MM. de Port-Royal*[2]; they form a *résumé* of the suggestions on this subject which are put forward in greater detail by Coustel and other Port-Royalist writers.

Du Fossé remained at Port-Royal des Champs until 1656, when he went to Paris. There he continued his studies in company with his old school-fellow Le Nain de Tillemont

[1] *Mém.* vol. I, p. 156.   [2] Vol. II, pp. 176–8.

who afterwards won fame as a church historian. Like all those who remained faithful to Port-Royal, Du Fossé did not escape persecution. He was even imprisoned in the Bastille at the same time as De Saci and Fontaine (see page 41), but was released at the end of a month. Du Fossé and De Tillemont died within ten months of each other in the same year—1698.

Racine

The poet Jean Racine (1639-1699) was for three years a pupil at Port-Royal. He entered one of the school groups in 1655 and there continued his education which he had already begun at the Collège de Beauvais in Paris. But if he is the most famous pupil of the Little Schools he is in some ways one of the least representative. Anyone who reads the original documents and memoirs relating to Port-Royal cannot but be struck by the small part which Racine plays in them. For example, he is never mentioned by Du Fossé who was intimately connected with Port-Royal during the whole time that Racine was a pupil there and who published his *Mémoires* in 1697 by which time Racine's fame was well-established. In the *Nécrologe* (p. 166) a few lines are devoted to him; he is described as a poet, and the works attributed to him are *Cantiques Spirituels*, an *Abrégé de l'Histoire de Port-Royal*, and the tragedies of *Esther* and *Athalie* which he composed for Mme de Maintenon's school (see page 35). The reason for Racine's break with the community has already been indicated. Port-Royal distrusted his poetic genius and his worldly tendencies, and the breach was widened in 1666 by Nicole's attack on the theatre which Racine assumed to be directed at him (see page 108). He replied in a bitter letter, the agile sarcasm of which reminds one of the *Provinciales*. He was doubtless justified in defending his art, and the sympathy of the modern critic, at any rate, is entirely on his side. But Racine forgets what he owes to those who

B. 4

watched over his education with such loving care and who gave him that knowledge of Greek and that appreciation of good literature which were destined to bear such wonderful fruit. Happily the story does not end here. In later life Racine made full and honourable amends. After the appearance of *Phèdre* in 1677 he was reconciled to Port-Royal and spent the latter part of his life as a respectable *père de famille* and a close friend of the community. In spite of his youthful lapse, he had been at bottom a deeply religious man and more nearly akin to the spirit of Port-Royal than is, perhaps, sometimes realised. But it remains true to say that the earlier Port-Royal—that of Saint-Cyran and the Little Schools—either distrusted or did not appreciate his genius; and for this reason, as Sainte-Beuve[1] points out, it was not until the eighteenth century that Jansenism became proud of him.

Two quotations from Racine's prose writings are included in this volume. His appreciation of the girls' schools (see page 191) is taken from his *Abrégé de l'Histoire de Port-Royal*. Racine was connected with the convent of Port-Royal by many family ties; his aunt, for example, Agnès de Sainte-Thècle Racine, was for a time abbess of the community, and one—if not more—of his daughters was educated in the girls' school. It has also been thought of interest to quote a short essay on "How to write History," which was composed by Racine probably while he was a pupil at Port-Royal.

Domat

Jean Domat (1625–1696), like Blaise Pascal, was a native of Clermont in Auvergne. He won renown as a lawyer and about 1681 was invited by Louis XIV to come to Paris. There he became intimately associated with Port-Royal although he was never a solitary or formally connected with the community. He was a particular friend of Dr Arnauld

1 *Port-Royal*, vol. 1, p. 6 n.

and of Pascal. He is best known as the author of a legal work entitled *Les Lois civiles dans leur ordre naturel.* In book 1, chap. vii of this work he treats "des Universités, Collèges, et Académies, et de l'usage des Sciences et des Arts libéraux par rapport au public." His attitude throughout is essentially that of the Jansenist theological writers on education and it has therefore seemed advisable to cite a few short extracts from his book, illustrative of special points, although he himself was not directly connected with the Little Schools.

Jacqueline Pascal

The nuns of Port-Royal, like those of many other convents, devoted some of their attention to the work of education. But the girls' school attached to the community must be clearly distinguished from the Little Schools for boys which were carried on by the solitaries. The only connection between the two institutions is furnished by their common dependence upon Port-Royal and a certain Jansenist bias in the organisation of each which that dependence implied. An account of the girls' school is given in the *Règlement pour les Enfans* which was written by Jacqueline Pascal (1625–1661). She was the younger sister of the famous Pascal. Like her brother she had abandoned a worldly career of unusual promise and had chosen to hide her extraordinary gifts in the seclusion of the religious life. She took the veil at Port-Royal in 1653, assuming the name of Sister Euphémie. In 1655 she was given charge of the educational work of the convent. The letter to her brother (see page 144) is dated Oct. 26th of this year. In 1657 she drew up her *Règlement pour les Enfans* in response to a request made by Antoine Singlin who had assisted Saint-Cyran to begin the community's educational work for boys and who now held the office of director of Port-Royal. These regulations have been quoted at length because they illustrate seventeenth-century conventual education in general, and the spirit of Port-Royal in particular.

III. BIBLIOGRAPHICAL NOTES

FOR those who desire to obtain their information at first hand there are in this country two valuable collections of original Port-Royal authorities. One of them is in Sion College, London, and the other at Keble College, Oxford. Unfortunately neither of them contains Coustel's *Règles de l'Éducation des Enfans* nor any of Guyot's translations with their valuable prefaces. These works are also unrepresented in the British Museum Library and in the Bodleian Library at Oxford. It is upon these sources that we rely largely for our knowledge of the teaching methods employed in the Little Schools; and it would be interesting, therefore, to know whether copies of these books exist anywhere in this country.

Of modern works dealing with the community, Sainte-Beuve's *Port-Royal*, in seven volumes, is and will long remain the standard book on the subject although his account of the schools is somewhat sketchy and is, of course, not treated from a professional standpoint. The first book which introduced the Port-Royalists to English readers was published in 1829 by a Quaker lady, Mrs Schimmelpenninck. In 1861 Charles Beard brought out his *Port-Royal*, in two volumes In the writer's opinion this is the best account of the subject in the English language, and since the book is now not very easy to obtain it might repay reprinting. Of recent years there have appeared several more books on the subject and reference can here be made only to a few of them. Mrs Romanes' *Story of Port-Royal* is sympathetic and well written. *Angélique of Port-Royal* by "A. H. K." is a most interesting psychological study of the character of Port-Royal's greatest abbess. It gives the reader an insight into the moral and spiritual value of conventual life at its best; the book should be supplemented by Dr Lowndes' *Nuns of Port-Royal,* which consists largely of translations from original sources bearing on the history of the convent and of certain of its members. The present writer's *Little Schools of Port-Royal* deals in some detail with the educational work of the community, while the Rev. H. T. Morgan's *Port-Royal and other studies* contains some excellent essays on the more theological aspects of the subject. For shorter articles dealing with Port-Royal, the following may with profit be consulted: Sir James Stephen's *Essays in Ecclesiastical Biography*; Monroe's *Cyclopædia of Education* (vol. IV, art. *Port-Royal*); and the *Cambridge Modern History* (vol. V, art. *Gallican Church*). There is also a well-written modern novel—*La Maison du Péché,* by Marcelle Tinayre—which throws an interesting sidelight on the subject. The hero is a young Frenchman of the present day whose family has strong Jansenist traditions, and whose education has been conducted along the lines which were prescribed by the solitaries of the Little Schools. The conflict between his Jansenist upbringing and his passion for a woman of the world is described with all the intimate detail which one associates with the modern French psychological novel. But the book none the less affords food for thought and one wonders whether it deals with an experience not unknown to certain past pupils of the Little Schools themselves, but to which allusion is never made in the grave writings which the solitaries have left to us.

In conclusion, it is interesting to note the wideness of the appeal which Port-Royal has made. The French philosopher and statesman Royer-Collard (1763–1845), himself an inheritor of the Port-Royalist tradition, has said: "Who knows not Port-Royal, knows not human nature"; and truly it would seem that one touch of Port-Royal makes the whole world kin. There is indeed something in its spirit which awakens a response wherever it breathes. It is surely not without significance that writers so diverse as an eminent literary critic like Sainte-Beuve, a unitarian minister like Charles Beard, a lady of marked protestant and evangelical views like Mary Anne Schimmelpenninck, a "High-Church" clergyman like Henry Morgan, an impartial historian like Dr Mary E. Lowndes, and—one may perhaps be pardoned for adding—an ordinary schoolmaster like the present author, should all have found in the writings of the Port-Royalists something to attract and to inspire. If this little book can succeed to any extent in directing the reader to those writings and in helping him to share in that inspiration, it will not have failed of its object.

IV. A LIST OF DATES ILLUSTRATING THE SUBJECT-MATTER OF THIS INTRODUCTION

(Events directly concerned with Port-Royal are shown in **bold type**)

1597. Filles de la Congrégation de Notre-Dame founded.
1599. Jesuit *Ratio Studiorum*.
1600. Henri IV reforms the University of Paris.
1606. Anne de Xainctonge begins her educational work at Dijon.
1611. Oratorian Order founded.
1614. Oratorian College at Dieppe opened.
1617. **Jansen becomes Professor of Theology at Louvain.**
1629. Death of Cardinal de Bérulle.
1635. **Saint-Cyran becomes director of Port-Royal.**
1637. **Beginning of education of boys at Port-Royal.**
French Academy founded.
1638. **Arrest of Saint-Cyran. Port-Royal Schools dispersed.**
Oratorian Collège de Juilly founded.
1639. **Schools return to Port-Royal des Champs.**
1640. **Publication of Jansen's *Augustinus*.**

1643. Saint-Cyran released (Feb. 6th); died (Oct. 11th).
Arnauld's treatise *De la Fréquente Communion.*
1644. Lancelot's *Nouvelle Méthode Latine.*
1646. Schools removed to rue S. Dominique, Paris, and reorganised.
1650. Schools again dispersed and organised in three groups.
1651. Jean-Baptiste de la Salle born.
1653. Jacqueline Pascal takes the veil at Port-Royal.
1655. Blaise Pascal becomes a solitary. Racine enters Port-Royal as a pupil. Lancelot's *Méthode Grecque.* Beginning of the *Provincial Letters.*
1656. Dispersion of boys' schools.
1657. Lancelot's *Jardin des Racines Grecques.*
1660. Final dispersion of boys' schools.
1661. Dispersion of girls' schools. Death of Jacqueline Pascal.
1662. Port-Royal *Logic.*
1666. Varet's *De l'Éducation chrestienne des Enfans.*
1669. Peace of the Church. Port-Royal girls' schools restored.· Temporary respite in persecution of community.
1671. Beginning of Nicole's *Essais de Morale.*
1679. Renewed persecution of Port-Royal. Girls' schools finally dispersed.
1684. Brothers of the Christian Schools start their educational work.
Death of De Saci.
1686. Mme de Maintenon founds Saint-Cyr.
1687. Fénelon's *De l'Éducation des Filles.*
Coustel's *Règles de l'Éducation des Enfans.*
1690. Death of De Sainte-Marthe.

1694. Death of Dr Arnauld.
1695. Death of Lancelot and Nicole.
1698. Death of Du Fossé and De Tillemont.
1699. Death of Racine.
1704. Death of Coustel.
1709. Death of Walon de Beaupuis and Fontaine.
       Destruction of Abbey of Port-Royal des
          Champs.

EXTRACTS

I

EDUCATIONAL THEORY

The extracts under this heading may be divided into two groups: (*a*) i–vi, which deal with the *theological* conception of education as put forward by the Jansenists; these extracts are taken from the writings of Saint-Cyran and those who were most directly inspired by him; (*b*) vii–ix, which show the more modern *psychological* treatment of the subject, and which are taken from the works of men who were responsible for the actual teaching work of the Little Schools.

i

(*Lettres Chrestiennes et Spirituelles de Messire Jean du Vergier de Hauranne, Abbé de Saint-Cyran*, 1645, Vol. II, pp. 228–232.)

To a person of quality. He deals with the education of children.

SIR,

Since you wish to have my opinion upon so important a subject as that upon which you have been pleased to consult me, I will give you my views in a few words.

We must show God that what we desire above all things 5 for our children is their salvation. This is the primary duty and the most sacred aspiration of a father or a mother. Just as they hasten to have their children baptised, so also should they hasten to have them educated; and whatever is done for children, if that is left undone, only serves to call down 10 the wrath of God upon the father and the mother; for they are, as it were, visible guardian angels, and it is their duty to lead heavenwards, by the means laid down in the Gospel, those whom they have brought into the world. It is a

mistake to imagine that we can win salvation by other good
works, if we neglect this which ought to be regarded as the
most important of all and by which alone it is possible to be
saved, even though we have no means of doing anything else
5 all our life. We have an example of this in S. Monica who
by her great zeal and ardour for the salvation of her son gave
to the world a leader and to the Church her greatest doctor.

True piety consists in doing what God commands us and
not what we ourselves choose. This is why the apostle says in
10 the fifth chapter of the First Epistle to Timothy, that the first
good work which ought to be taken into account in the case
of a widow, is whether she has brought up her children well.

After having shown God that this is our heartfelt desire,
we must use every effort to prevent the education of our chil-
15 dren from falling into bad hands or into a bad environment.
If we are thwarted in our endeavours, we must still do our
very utmost to help our children in the environment where
they happen to be. Although there is a danger in keeping
them at home, this is always less than if they are sent away
20 elsewhere; because by having them at home we are enabled
to carry out with regard to them the rule *Take ye heed, watch
and pray*, which imposes on us the duty of keeping constantly an eye upon them, even as God watches over us so
long as seems good to Him, keeping us from evil in all our
25 actions. For if He turn His eyes but a little even from the
just, they are straightway troubled. Hence the necessity for
watchfulness, for constant prayer, and the need for us to act
in this same manner with regard to our children. We must
lead them with a similar watchfulness and gentleness, and at
30 times even we should ask rather than command. We must
for a while suit ourselves a little to their whims so as to make
them capable of dispensing with this indulgence in the future,
and of entering upon a better and a safer path....

God dealt thus with the Jewish people. He used to check
35 them in their desires and in their lust for earthly possessions,

in order to lead them afterwards to a love of poverty and penance through the grace of Jesus Christ. This is why the first Church, the mother of all the others, was composed of 3000 Jews who had been converted by S. Peter and who at first gave up everything and embraced voluntary poverty.   5

However, we must be careful to exercise great caution and disinterestedness in showing indulgence, doing this in the same spirit as that which God Himself has shown. We must always remember that it is not for us to remain at that stage; but that if we stoop to their level we do so only in 10 order to be able to raise them with ourselves, to lift them by degrees from their degradation, and not to model our own desires on theirs or to deal indulgently with them owing to the weakness of our nature. For we must always keep before our eyes—both on their behalf and on our own—the words 15 of Jesus Christ when He commands us to be perfect even as our Father in heaven is perfect; in other words, we must aim unceasingly at that perfection which consists in putting into action the feelings of love which flourish in our hearts only when we cease to lavish them upon objects which please our 20 senses. With this end in view we must labour unceasingly during this life, and towards it we must direct all that we do alike for our fellows and for ourselves. Otherwise our charity is unreal, our acts of mercy are not disinterested, and our goodwill towards others is nothing but a weakness and a 25 veritable falling from grace which have not, as their motive, knowledge of God and love for Him, but love of self and of the world.   *Vincennes.* August 1640.

ii

(*Saint-Cyran: op. cit.* Vol. I, p. 685.)

I was once pointing out to a man the various rocks hidden in the sea upon which he was sailing; and I made him 30 admit that well-to-do people, who profess to lead Christian lives, can be the sole cause of their own children's ruin, not so

much for the other reasons which might be brought forward
as for that with which we are now dealing—the lack of care
which they take in having their children educated from the
time when they leave the cradle. For there is a prophecy
5 in Isaiah which says in definite terms that a time will come
when children must be taken from the breast if they are to
be brought up in the truth and knowledge of God—to say
nothing of the knowledge of Jesus Christ which inspires less
awe when it is held up as an example because it was revealed
10 to the eyes of men during His life on earth; whereas God and
the knowledge of Him have always been beyond our reach
and were not made manifest to men before the time of Jesus
Christ, save by the precepts of the holy word of the Old
Testament. *Vincennes.* July 17th, 1641.

iii

(Fontaine: Mémoires sur MM. de Port-Royal, 1738,
pp. 189–192.)

15   M. le Maître asked M. de Saint-Cyran what was his belief as to the state of infants [who die without baptism] and
whether they endure physical sufferings. M. de Saint-Cyran
replied: It is certain that the devil possesses the soul of an
infant in its mother's womb. S. Augustine upholds this view
20 in opposition to the Pelagians and defends it by the Church's
ceremony of breathing upon the infant at baptism in order to
drive away the evil spirit. As to physical sufferings, it is un-
questionable that Divine Providence, foreseeing the difficulty
which the human intelligence would have in comprehending
25 this, has willed that it should be demonstrated clearly by the
fact that infants constantly and before our eyes undergo un-
accountable sufferings and even die. For it is an undeniable
fact that divine justice can no more punish those who are
without sin or make them endure evil, than it can refrain
30 from punishing the guilty. From this S. Augustine concludes

—in opposition to the heretics—that since infants are always suffering, it necessarily follows that they must have some sin, and this is none other than original sin. According to the teachings of this saint and also according to plain and irrefutable reason, the suffering which infants endure in this life 5 is suffering as a punishment for original sin; and since this suffering is physical and sometimes terrible, it is obvious that original sin merits bodily pain as its punishment. Experience itself therefore refutes the argument put forward by those who reject this truth and who say that original sin ought not to be 10 punished by bodily pain. You have so clear a judgment that I am sure that this alone will be enough to convince you of what I have just said. This is one of the points which are most surely established both by Holy Scripture and by the tradition of the primitive Church; and it shows us that we 15 must not be surprised if we find that we have departed from the teaching of our fathers in many less noticeable points, preferring the interpretation of reason to that of faith and Christian doctrine....

But since we are on the subject of children, I must thank 20 you for the kindness you have shown in undertaking the education of young D'Andilly and De Saint-Ange; and I must apologise for having taken the liberty of suggesting this to you. I did so only after being thoroughly assured of your willingness to do this. As to the work itself I will merely 25 say that you could find no better means of winning God's favour than by devoting yourself to educating some children well. If God had not several times charged us with this duty, we might possibly have had doubts on the subject. I am struck by the importance which God gives to things which 30 seem small in themselves. This makes me have a feeling of respect for everything. When matters which seem least important have some reference to God, then—in my opinion— they should be regarded as of great importance. Properly speaking, there is nothing which is important in itself; so also 35

is there nothing which may not be important in God's eyes. And since God has chosen what is weak in order to overthrow what is strong, since the object of Jesus Christ in the redemption of the world was to put down the mighty and to
5 exalt the humble and meek, confounding the wisdom of the world by the foolishness of the cross, we must regard His action with the deepest reverence. We must put our trust not in what has some show of greatness, but rather in the lowliness which Jesus Christ has exalted by taking it upon
10 Himself in order to render it worthy of our esteem.

The pupil named De Saint-Ange, mentioned in the last extract, did not turn out so well as had been hoped. On hearing of this Saint-Cyran speaks to Le Maître as follows:

iv

(*Fontaine: op. cit.* pp. 195–198.)

There is this consolation in work which one undertakes for God, that He demands of us the work and not its success. As He says in the Holy Gospel, we must be content with this, without being concerned whether we are successful or the
15 reverse in the efforts which we make to instruct our neighbours. A conscientious farmer will deserve no less from God if his fields and vines bear no fruit, although he has cultivated them to his utmost, than if they bear corn and grapes in abundance.
20 We must always pray for souls and always watch, keeping guard as though in a beleaguered city. The devil is prowling outside; he very soon assails the baptised; he comes spying out the land; if the Holy Ghost has not taken up His abode there, he will do so. He assails children and they do not
25 resist him; we must therefore resist him on their behalf. A tare sown while we are slumbering is enough for him. He looks merely for tiny rifts in the tender soul…, that is to say, their weakest places which he regards as good openings for

bringing about their downfall. Separation from the world,
good examples, and prayer are the chief means of assistance
which we can render them. We must humble ourselves to
their level. We must learn a lesson from the Incarnation;
Jesus Christ made Himself like us in order to make us like 5
Him. We must make allowances for children's weakness in
order to raise them again; but we must not utterly abase
ourselves. Jesus Christ stoops down to put the lamb on His
shoulders; but He does not do more than this.

Experience shows us that there is hardly any other occu- 10
pation in which wisdom and patience are more necessary. It
takes a long time for anyone to acquire virtue and this is
especially the case with children.... But it is not so with
vice. As the devil became suddenly wicked, so the souls of
the wicked become corrupt at birth; and a knave is sometimes 15
a knave at ten years old as well as at forty. It is good to make
children appreciate the magnitude of original sin by telling
them that Adam before he sinned was like a diamond, but
after sin became as a coal. Children—and in fact most
Christians—almost always completely fail to realise how 20
difficult it is to return to God and to be truly converted after
once having lost baptismal innocence. We can hardly be
surprised. Who would ever have believed under the Old
Dispensation that the law would be of no avail whatever for
the salvation of the true-born Jew, and that on the contrary 25
it would merely serve to increase his guilt, even though the
Jews themselves believed the reverse? There is a similar
ignorance among Christians touching the difficulty of returning to God after having broken the covenant of baptism
by a mortal sin. They believe that any absolution can do this, 30
just as the Jews believed that the law of itself was sufficient
for this purpose. The dew of grace never descends upon the
heathen among whom the preaching of the Gospel has never
been heard; what wonder is it, then, if it does not descend
so often as we think upon Christians who have spurned it 35

and have crucified Jesus Christ? Indeed it descends upon them only at rare intervals and is very difficult to obtain save only on condition of sincere penitence. If we once obtain remission of our sins after baptism and then fall again
5 into mortal sin, the difficulty of returning to God increases more and more, according as our sins are multiplied and our absolutions annulled—and it matters not whether these have been properly or improperly granted. For if the latter is the case, absolution is a mere sacrilege; if the former, the sin
10 which annuls the absolution is by so much the greater and therefore more difficult to be forgiven. Happy are they who like you, Sir, endeavour to defend children from this.

I am sorry for parents. They love their children only out of vainglory or self-interest or because they look forward to
15 leaving an heir for their house. If a father is beginning to think about God and sincerely wishes to serve Him, before putting his house in order and busying himself with its smallest details, he should devote his chief care to his children; so much so that he ought to resolve for the future to train
20 them as a Christian father should, since otherwise salvation is impossible for him. Just as—in the words of S. Augustine —the piety of a king is valueless if it operates merely within the limits of his court and his house, when it should make itself felt throughout his kingdom, so also the piety of one of
25 his subjects is valueless if it is confined to himself and does not stimulate him to train his children properly. When before God he makes up his mind to lead a good life, he should at the same time resolve that he will induce his children and his servants to do likewise. Be thankful to God, Sir, for having
30 spared you these responsibilities and delusions. You are adopting these children; but I am sure that in doing so you will be fulfilling your duty. You are right in not being in a hurry about having them confirmed. You know that each individual has his Pentecost, like the Church herself. The
35 sacrament of Confirmation is the Christian's Pentecost; and

we abuse it if we have it administered indiscriminately to quite young children. We should be extremely careful lest they lose in any measure the grace which they have received; and all the more so, because this sacrament, unlike the Eucharist, can never be again administered. Although the Apostles had 5 been baptised and had heard truths from the lips of Jesus Christ Himself, it was only after they had received the Holy Ghost that their faith overcame all obstacles.

v

(*Varet: Éducation Chrestienne des Enfans*, 1669, pp. 45–46.)

Education alone can banish all the vices which dominate the world, because it alone can instil a horror and a fear of 10 them. It alone can revive among Christians the spirit of poverty by inspiring the hearts of those whom it influences with a contempt for the things of this world. It alone can restore among Christians love of suffering—by restraining from the luxury of the age bodies which are still immature 15 and accustoming them early to suffering; reverence and sub-mission towards superiors, whether secular or spiritual—by making children practise complete obedience; love and con-sideration for one's neighbour—by inculcating regard and kindly feeling for all men. In short, education on these lines 20 is alone able to change the face of Christendom, to effect a much-needed reformation throughout the Church, and to preserve in children the innocence and grace which they have received at baptism.

vi

(*Lancelot: Mémoires touchans la Vie de M. de Saint-Cyran*, 1738, Vol. II, pp. 330–335.)

He thought that the whole course of one's life was deter- 25 mined by one's early years, and that if only the young were well brought up, it might be hoped that public positions would be filled by more worthy officials and the Church by more virtuous souls, and that the State and private families alike would derive therefrom incalculable advantage. We might then almost say that this good work, which at present 5 is so utterly neglected, is in a sense the one thing needful; consequently if this could be successfully carried out, almost every other disorder would be set right; whereas if this groundwork is lacking, it necessarily follows that the results are felt throughout the rest of life.

10 M. de Saint-Cyran therefore used to say that whatever other virtues parents might possess, if they did not do their duty in obtaining a good education for their children, this fact by itself was sufficient to condemn them; and a good education nowadays is more rare and difficult to find than 15 one would think. He never ceased to be amazed at the blindness of most parents who do not see that, even if no question of eternity were involved, their own interests should lead them to perform this duty properly; for it happens only too frequently that the children whom they have brought into the 20 world to be—as they think—a support and an honour to their family, prove its disgrace and ruin, through lack of a good education. He could not understand why, when it is a question of putting children into some position or employment or secular office, parents will exert themselves as if everything 25 were at stake, although often they succeed only in providing the means for their children's downfall; whereas, when it is necessary to have them properly educated, in order to satisfy their own consciences and to secure the true well-being of their children, they cannot find the means and grumble at 30 even the smallest expenditure. And in truth by so doing they show clearly that they are not true Christians, since such conduct is not only like building one's house on the sand, but also like throwing oneself into the onrushing waves in company with all who compose the house and who should 35 be its support. He used to grieve over the misfortune of our

age, in which the devil had found a means of destroying the
children of the Church, more easy than that employed of old
by Pharaoh, king of Egypt—who was, in reality, nothing but
a type of the devil himself. This curse is all the more terrible
inasmuch as the devil often utilises the negligence, greed, or 5
other vices of the parents in order to bring about the ruin
of their children; whereas the Israelites at any rate were
conscious of their unhappy position and did their utmost to
save their children from the tyrant's wrath.

M. de Saint-Cyran was impressed by the fact that the Son 10
of God, while exercising the highest functions of His ministry, was unwilling that little children should be forbidden to
come to Him; and that He embraced them and blessed them
and has bidden us so strongly not to despise or neglect them.
He used therefore to show towards children a kindness which 15
amounted almost to a sort of respect, in order to express his
reverence for their innocence and for the Holy Ghost dwelling
in them. He used to bless them and make the sign of the cross
on their foreheads; and if they were capable of appreciating it,
he would make some pious remark which was, as it were, 20
the seed of some truth sown in passing and in the sight of
God, in the hope that in due course it might take root. On
one occasion when he was visiting us he went into the children's class-room and, with his customary cheerfulness and
kindheartedness, caressed them and said: "Well, and what 25
are you doing? You must not waste time, you know; and
what you do not occupy the devil takes for himself." They
showed him their Virgil which they were studying, and he
said: "You see all these beautiful lines? In composing them
Virgil achieved his own damnation because he made them 30
in a spirit of vanity, for the sake of glory; but as for you,
you must win salvation by learning them in a spirit of obedience, to make yourselves fit for the service of God."...

M. de Saint-Cyran had so high an opinion of the love
shown by those who devote themselves to educating children 35

in a Christian manner that he used to say that there was no
employment more worthy of a Christian in the Church; that
next to the love of which it is said: *greater love hath no man
than this*, and which makes us willing to lay down our lives
5 for our friends, this was the greatest; that it was an easy way
of retracing the false steps of one's youth and so making
amends for one's past short-comings; that at the hour of
death one of the greatest consolations that we could feel was
to have contributed to the good education of some child; and
10 that, in short, this occupation by itself was sufficient to sanctify one's soul, if only it were carried out in a spirit of love
and forbearance. He used to say that we ought to be not
merely the guardian angels but in some sense the Providence
of the children committed to our charge, because our chief
15 care should be to direct them gently and lovingly to what is
good, just as we need that God should direct us to it and
make us act upon it. He usually summed up our duty in
respect to children in these three maxims: *Speak little; endure much; pray still more.*

20 He wished us to bear long with their faults and weaknesses, in order that thereby we might induce God to have
mercy upon our own, and afterwards perhaps to strengthen
these tender plants when they should learn what patience we
had exercised in respect to them. He used to add that we
25 ought to show special love and pity for those who appear
most defective and backward—those, that is to say, whom
original sin has most deeply wounded. He could not bear
us in dealing with them to use too stern a look or too domineering a manner, which savoured somewhat of contempt or
30 was likely to discourage them and render them spiritless; for
we are definitely forbidden to do so by the Prince of the
Apostles. On the contrary, he wished us to treat them with
genial familiarity which would win them over by studied kindness and by a truly paternal affection; and this should lead
35 us to be sympathetic with them. For we can do nothing so

long as they have no confidence in us and do not realise that we have kindly feelings for them. This explains why, during his imprisonment, M. de Saint-Cyran would often condescend to play at ball on a table with children of seven or eight years old. 5

vii

(Coustel: Les Règles de l'Éducation des Enfans, 1687, Vol. I, pp. 5–13.)

By the word education I do not mean the care which parents take of their children's bodies; it is merely a natural instinct which makes them do this, as is indeed the case with all animals. But I mean the care which they should take of their children's souls by cultivating their two chief 10 faculties—*i.e.* the intellect and the will; the intellect by making children study the humanities, and the will by training them in virtue....

But besides virtue and knowledge, which are the greatest benefits which parents can procure for their children by a 15 good education, they should also (as Erasmus says) be careful to have them instructed in good manners. It is then in these three things—virtue, knowledge, and good manners that I sum up all the education of children, upon which subject I am about to give some rules. Let us begin by 20 showing the utility—nay rather the necessity, of education....

If education is of advantage for the parents it must undoubtedly be advantageous also for the children whose intellects and wills it develops. In fact whatever intellectual gifts a child has, he profits greatly by being well taught from 25 his youth upwards, just as soil profits by being well cultivated whatever be its natural properties. For we must acknowledge as an invariable fact that education can no more change the natural properties of the intellect than agriculture can change the natural properties of the soil. 30

If then by good fortune the intellect of a child is of a

high order, we see by experience that with careful training he will make marvellous progress in his studies. If, on the contrary, he is neglected, he either deteriorates gradually or else becomes an adept only in wickedness and vice; just as
5 we often see that the best soils are those which produce most thorns and brambles. But if a child is of only mediocre intelligence, a good education can none the less be of use to him by ridding him of his most uncultured mannerisms; just as even the least fertile soil can still bear a little grain
10 if it is well cultivated.

If education is of such value to the intellect, it is unquestionably of far greater value to the will; for it checks unreasoned impulses and corrects evil tendencies. It was this that made the ancients say that the will is able even to over-
15 come nature. Of all animals man is the most headstrong, for he gives way to his passions and obeys the unruly impulses of ambition, anger, and envy. For this reason it is good for him from his youth upward to be kept within bounds which check him and prevent him from overstepping the limits of
20 reason. It is this which the Holy Ghost would have us note when He says: It is good for a man that he bear the yoke in his youth. "This yoke," says S. Gregory, "should be borne from the earliest years upwards in order that in later life we may have grown accustomed to a rigid discipline; otherwise,
25 if the bearing of the yoke is put off too long, there is a danger that one's soul may be pierced by the sharp stings of conscience, that one may be troubled by an already acquired habit of committing sin, and that thus, being continually engaged in fresh warfare, one may experience in one's soul
30 the disturbance caused by these onslaughts which are sometimes successful and sometimes repulsed. On the other hand, if a man submits in his youth to the yoke of God's word, he will enjoy unbroken peace, having set his soul in perfect order.

He will enjoy, I say, unruffled calm by subjecting the flesh
35 to the spirit; and having taken his place upon the tribunal

of reason, as though in a court of law he will issue whatever edicts and decrees he wills, and his inclinations, like so many citizens, will obey them faithfully."

viii

(*Nicole: Essais de Morale*, 1714, Vol. II, p. 242.)

To educate is to form the judgment—that is, to give the mind a taste for the good and the power to recognise it; 5 to make the mind keen to recognise false reasoning when it is somewhat obscured; to teach it not to be dazzled by a show of vain talk with no sense in it, or satisfied with mere words or vague principles, and never to be content until one has penetrated to the very bottom of a thing. It is to 10 make the mind quick to seize the point at issue in an involved matter and to recognise what is irrelevant. It is to fill the mind with those principles which help it to find the truth of all matters and especially of those where the truth is most needed. 15

ix

(*Nicole: op. cit.* Vol. II, pp. 277–278.)

The aim of instruction is to carry the mind to the highest point that it is capable of reaching. It does not impart memory or imagination or intelligence, but it cultivates all these faculties by strengthening one of them by means of the others. Memory helps judgment, and imagination and judgment to- 20 gether assist memory. When some of these faculties are lacking they must be supplied by the others. Thus a master shows his skill by setting the pupils under his care to those tasks which are most congenial to them. There are some children whose exercises should be practically confined to memory work 25 because their memory is good and their judgment weak; there are others who should at first be set to tasks involving judgment because in them this faculty is stronger than memory.

Strictly speaking, it is not their masters nor the information which they gain from without that enables them to understand; the most these can do is to expose things to the inner light of the mind whereby alone they are understood. Unless, therefore, this light is there, instruction is as futile as showing pictures in the dark. The greatest minds are only partially illumined and they always contain some dark and obscure corners; but children's minds are almost entirely filled with darkness and they can only catch glimpses of tiny rays of light. Thus the whole secret is to make the most of these rays, to increase them and to illuminate by means of them what we wish to be understood. The result is that it is difficult to lay down general rules for the education of all and sundry, because we have to accommodate it to this mingling of light and darkness—and they vary in proportion in each individual case, and particularly so with children. We must find out where the light is and bring to it what we wish to be understood; and for this reason we must often try different methods of getting at their minds, and then confine ourselves to those which prove most successful.

None the less, generally speaking, we may say that the illumination which children possess depends very largely upon the senses and that therefore, as far as possible, instruction should be given through the senses and made to enter not merely by the hearing but also by the sight, since there is no other sense which makes so vivid an impression on the mind and which gives such clear and distinct ideas.

II

GENERAL EDUCATIONAL METHODS

As might have been expected from the theological foundation
upon which much of the educational theory of Port-Royal is based,
the emphasis in the Little Schools tends to be on the inculcation
of morals rather than on the giving of mere instruction. This
point of view is expressed in extracts i–iv which follow.

i

(*Supplément au Nécrologe de l'Abbaye de Notre-Dame de Port-Royal des Champs*, 1735, pp. 48–51.)

The following account of the Little Schools was written in
1664 by M. de Sainte-Marthe (see p. 42). It is addressed to a
certain M. Chamillard, a doctor of the Sorbonne and a bitter
persecutor of Port-Royal. He had been forced upon the community by its enemies as its confessor ; and De Sainte-Marthe's
account is therefore a kind of *apologia* for the schools which had
recently (1660) been suppressed. The account throughout is based
on the *Règlemens qui s'observoient dans l'École du Chesnai*, which
were written by Walon de Beaupuis and which are preserved in
the *Supplément au Nécrologe*, pp. 51–53.

The following were the reasons for founding the Little
Schools in which young people were to be brought up in the
fear of God. There is only too much occasion for sorrow in
that we see children of Christian parentage who give practically no signs of the grace which they received at baptism. 5
As soon as they begin to possess reason, they show nothing
but blindness and weakness ; their minds are closed to things
spiritual and they cannot take them in ; whereas, on the other
hand, they keep their eyes open for evil, their faculties are
alive to every kind of vice, and they have a natural tendency 10
which inclines them forcibly towards it. In this condition it
is well-nigh impossible for them to retain their innocence for

long amid the world. There the very air they breathe is infectious; there every sight they see serves only to destroy them; there they hardly ever hear mentioned those Gospel truths which alone could save them from their ignorance and
5 their evil tendencies. They grow accustomed to hear indecent songs and expressions; they often hear sinful actions commended; they are allowed every kind of frivolity; they are permitted impure pastimes; all kinds of books are left in their hands, and when the devil has once engendered in their
10 hearts a curiosity to find out what is evil, their whole mind is soon filled with it. For since they have as yet neither the power nor the will to resist it, they eagerly proceed to put into practice all that they have learnt.

When their hearts have thus become corrupt, they easily
15 take a dislike to virtue and hate the attempts which are necessary to attain it. Besides, there exists so close a correspondence between their natural corruption and the corruption of the world, that they willingly assent to all its teachings, as soon as they are able to learn them. They love only such things
20 as please their senses; their idea of happiness consists in laziness, effeminacy, intemperance; in short, their only rule of life is to follow every inclination, to go with the multitude, and to let themselves be carried away on the stream of worldliness.

When they go to school they take with them all these
25 vices or else learn them there; the example of a large number of other children who are already well advanced in wickedness helps to make them bold to commit shameful deeds, though they no longer regard them as such because they have become habitual. I do not for a moment accuse the masters of con-
30 niving at these irregularities, but if they wish to bear witness to the truth they will confess that whatever they do is of no avail to prevent them. Even the best-intentioned masters, for the most part, have charge of too many pupils to be able to keep an eye on them all and on all that they do. Yet it
35 is impossible for several children to be together for long, with

nobody looking after them, without their acquiring many evil habits which increase with age.

It is a precept of the Gospel that as we have an enemy who sleeps not, we are compelled to be ever on the watch so as to resist him; as soon as we cease to do this he enters the 5 heart, regarding it as an empty house, and he does therein whatever he pleases; but as children would not know how to keep watch over themselves, nor over their faculties— which are as it were the gates to their hearts—they need someone to keep watch on their behalf; and they cannot 10 remain long without falling into the clutches of their enemy unless they have a faithful guardian who is always beside them and who takes care to remove from before their eyes or their feet all that might cause them to fall. No sooner are the sheep abandoned by their shepherd than they become 15 the prey of wolves; but children act like wolves one to another when they have no master and no guide. If several children are put together, there are always a few whom the devil employs to sow in the hearts of the rest, by some act or word, the deadly seeds of every kind of sin.   20

I might say in the words of S. John Climacus that every- one sees this conflagration by which almost all the young are consumed, but hardly anyone makes an attempt to extinguish it, no one seriously bewails it, no one troubles about it. For there is nothing in this world which arouses so little interest 25 as the ruin of human souls.

M. de Saint-Cyran's love, being as catholic and universal as his faith, was bestowed even upon these little lost souls; and since Jesus Christ shed His blood for their salvation, he esteemed himself happy in devoting his life to helping them. 30 It was this love which gave him the idea of founding the Little Schools at which you are so scandalised and the prin- ciples of which I should like to lay before you.

It had been realised that children often owe their mis- fortunes to negligence or lack of intelligence on the part of 35 their teachers. An attempt was therefore made to choose for this duty none but persons whose piety, ability, discretion, and disinterestedness were beyond doubt. Such men would bring themselves to undertake a duty so arduous and so 5 difficult only through love; and their chief aim would be to preserve in their pupils the spirit of Jesus Christ Who dwells in them after they have been consecrated in the waters of baptism. They would feel constrained to bring up those entrusted to them in a way far different from that which is 10 customary. Children learn in the world everything of which they ought to be ignorant, and they are allowed to be ignorant of everything which they ought to know. On every side they see nothing but lively images of all kinds of coarse vice which arrest their senses and enter their souls, even against their 15 will. No one ever talks to them of those spiritual vices which can be avoided only by those who have sufficient knowledge to recognise them. The result is that such children are exposed to all that infection of which the world is full and of which they know only too much. They are the victims of 20 spiritual vices of which they know nothing; and what finishes their ruin is that they are hardly ever instructed in a single truth which can strengthen them against these horrible temptations.

To remedy such great abuses we were trying in the Little 25 Schools, of which you make a crime, to remove from our pupils everything which might harm them. We took care that they never heard or saw anything which might wound the modesty and purity which are so delicate at that age. We tried to leave them in blissful ignorance of all things the 30 knowledge of which might hurt them, and to keep their eyes always closed lest they should ever see anything, the mere sight of which can deal the soul a mortal wound. But while it is good that children should never leave this happy ignorance which preserves in them Christian innocence, it is 35 desirable that they should grow in knowledge and wisdom, that they should not be blind to the good, nor careless when evil is to be avoided. This is why we tried to teach them whatever might help them to progress in virtue. We used to speak to them about the things of God so far as they could appreciate them. We gradually inculcated in them a salutary 5 hatred of sin. We tried to kindle in their hearts a love of eternal blessings. We used all our industry so as to enlighten their minds that they might be able, by the general teaching of the Gospel, to have sufficient knowledge of evil to flee from it, and to inspire them with such a horror of it that they 10 might never stop to gaze upon anything which, through the medium of the senses, might carry poison to the soul.

This is what the masters of these schools—which you condemn, knowing nothing of them—were trying to do. And it was with the object of fulfilling these duties that they used 15 to watch continually over this little flock of Jesus Christ, so that they might say with Jacob: "In the day the drought consumed me, and the frost by night; and my sleep departed from my eyes." Love gave them enlightenment for instructing their pupils and they endeavoured never to lose an oppor- 20 tunity of so doing. They made themselves children, if I may say so, in order to win them for Jesus Christ. They sympathised with their weaknesses, bore with them patiently and were never tired of serving them. They used to regard them as a precious trust which God had confided to their keeping 25 and of which He would demand from them an account. Their whole aim was to preserve their pupils in the innocence of their baptism. For this reason they kept them always in their hands, that they might make of them a work worthy of heaven. One might almost say that they carried them in 30 their hearts, since—lest they should labour in vain—they offered their pupils every day to God, to draw down His blessing upon them.

Since it is practically impossible that children, who are as yet utterly enslaved to their senses, should not do what 35

they see others do, the masters tried to instruct them more
by their actions than by their words; and they even took
special care to have only the most respectable servants so
that the children, never seeing any but good examples, might
5 be fortunate enough to be induced to do only what they saw
done, and to walk in the path in which they were led. On
the other hand, since they were kept busy, to the full extent
of their capacity, in the study and practice of piety, all leisure
to busy themselves with evil things was taken away from
10 them; but they were none the less fortified against the
teachings of the world. They were shown that in it there are
pitfalls everywhere. They were taught that they must be in
the world but not of it, and that in order to overcome it they
must love neither its wealth, nor its honours, nor its pleasures.
15   Those from whose care the children have been torn away
should humble themselves before God; perhaps they were
not worthy to contribute to so good a work; perhaps, again,
this age was not worthy of seeing the establishment of so
great a good. The judgments of God are always inscrutable;
20 but they are never more terrible than when He allows to be
destroyed at their very beginning works of piety which might
have contributed to the salvation of many souls.

ii

(Lancelot: Mém. de S.-C. Vol. II, pp. 337–339.)

[M. de Saint-Cyran] thought that the most important
factor in the good education of children was the good example
25 which could be set them and the general organisation of the
institution in which they were being brought up. A Father
of the Church, speaking to a mother about the education of
her little girl, once said: "Remember, you who have brought
a virgin into the world, that she should be taught more by
30 example than by words....She should never hear anything
which does not relate to the fear of God. Keep her from that

reprehensible license to which children are addicted; be careful that the girls and servants who are her associates do not mix with worldly companions lest they teach their pupils even more of the world's evil than they themselves would have learnt from it of their own accord." And it is this which 5 M. de Saint-Cyran used to advise should be done for boys as well as for girls; for he wished us to be particularly careful to curtail their opportunities for mixing with the outside world, from which they might receive undesirable influences. He would often say that contact with the world exposed them to 10 an infection which does as much harm to souls as the plague does to bodies. Again, he was unwilling that they should be entrusted with money. One day when he was sending some sweetmeats to a little girl, he gave this warning to a person who had charge of several children : "In no wise accustom 15 them to the pleasures of the world, which make them lose the taste for those of God."

He could not endure that mere knowledge and study should be made the chief end of education, as is commonly done at the present day. He looked upon this as one of the 20 greatest injuries which could be done to the sacredness of this employment; and he used to point out that in addition to disheartening backward pupils and making the others vain, such a course recoiled with even greater force upon the State and the Church; for it burdened the Spouse of Jesus Christ 25 with a number of persons whom she had never called, and Society with innumerable lazy people who fancied themselves superior to everyone else because they knew a little Latin, and who would feel it beneath their dignity to follow a calling which befitted the station of life into which they had been 30 born. For this reason he used to say that even though one were given complete charge of a large number of children, quite a few only should be made to study—that is to say, those alone who were seen to be especially tractable and who had shown some signs of virtue and sincere piety.   35

Having this conception of the education of the young and regarding it as a duty of the utmost importance to both the State and the Church, M. de Saint-Cyran used to say that he would have been delighted to devote his whole life to this
5 task. But in saying so he did not intend to enslave himself to the caprice and inconsiderateness of parents who burden us with their children merely in order to relieve themselves of this responsibility, so long as their children are nothing but a trouble, and then carry them off again from us as soon
10 as it suits them, in order to sacrifice them to their greed and vanity. Such conduct might be described as turning an occupation worthy of angels, a work of pure love, into utter contempt and sheer drudgery. Indeed, if anyone is forced to submit to such conditions it would be far better for him to
15 learn a trade or to till the ground. He would at any rate have the consolation of performing the same penance as that which God imposed upon the first man ; and he would escape a multitude of evil results which often accrue to the teacher or to those who are educated in this utterly heathen manner ;
20 moreover the labour of this occupation, when it is not directed by the will of God, is much greater—if one is fairly conscientious—than that of tilling the ground and it undermines the constitution more and greatly accelerates the approach of death.
25 As for M. de Saint-Cyran, he would never take charge of children unless he had hopes of obtaining complete control of them and unless he was well assured of the intentions of the parents. For this reason, when the late Duchesse de Guise sent him a message with a view to the education of the
30 present M. de Guise, who was intended for the Church, he did not shrink from the proposal which was made, but went so far as to make certain promises ; for he was always even more anxious to see persons of high rank well educated than other people, because he realised that in their case it was
35 more important. At the same time he gave his consent only

on the understanding that the Duchess would refrain from
any interference and that she would completely surrender to
him the care of her son. Mme de Guise did not feel herself
sufficiently inclined to do so and accordingly he withdrew
his promise and did not wish to have the matter mentioned 5
again.

iii
(*Coustel: Règles, etc.* Vol. I, pp. 184–188.)

We can distinguish three kinds of life which every Christian leads—that of the body, that of the mind, and that of
the soul; or, to put it otherwise, animal life, intellectual life,
and spiritual life. Each of these types of life has also its own 10
appropriate nourishment. Bodily life is maintained by the
bread and meat which God has created for this purpose; intellectual life is fostered by the various branches of knowledge and the noble sentiments which are to be found in
good authors; while spiritual life, which is strictly speaking 15
the Christian life, is preserved by truths drawn from the Holy
Scriptures.

Such being the case, I assert that a teacher must impart
to the children under his charge every kind of good instruction—not merely that which may help to form their minds 20
and judgments, but also that which may feed their souls. To
this end he must carefully husband whatever he finds in his
authors—even in profane authors. For instance, in Cicero,
Horace, or Seneca what a wealth there is of excellent maxims
which can serve not merely to instruct a young man in good 25
manners and the duties of civil life, but also to attract him
towards virtue and draw him away from vice, provided that
the master is skilful enough to develop them a little and give
them the requisite turn. I know quite well that it is not here
that we must look for the essential and fundamental truths 30
of our religion. But it is advisable always to utilise the

B.   6

occasions to which these authors give rise, for saying things to our pupils which may be advantageous to them.

To give children good instruction is not enough; we must also try to give them good examples. Nothing makes greater
5 impression on the mind—and particularly on the minds of children, who pay far greater heed to what they see their master do than to what he may tell them, and who can feel nothing but contempt for the good which he sets before them so long as his actions do not bear out what he says. And in
10 fact, how can one listen to a man who does not listen to himself? Is it possible to believe that he is persuaded of the truth which he preaches to others if he does not take the trouble to practise it himself? The teacher then must be for his pupils like a clear looking-glass wherein they can see
15 mirrored their faults and blemishes; or rather, like a gauge which, by its own correctness, sets right whatever is imperfect or faulty. He must speak to them far more by his actions than by his words and show them, by acting rather than by speaking, the path which they should tread. If he himself
20 does everything that he enjoins upon those who are in his charge, not only will he correct their faults, but he will also safeguard himself against the just reproach which the Apostle levels at those who do not act thus—"Thou therefore which teachest another, teachest thou not thyself?"

iv

(Guyot: Billets que Cicéron a escrit (sic) *tant à ses amis communs qu'à Attique son amy particulier,* 1668, Preface—no pagination.)

25 What Cicero lacks is not intellect but heart. It is absolutely essential to distinguish these two things which as a rule are not sufficiently distinguished. There are men who have plenty of intellect, but little heart. Now a man is governed by his heart; it makes him what he is and to a very

large extent determines his actions. If he has a noble heart, his whole character is noble; but if his heart is mean all the rest of him is mean; and this nobility or meanness of the heart must not be measured by the loftiness or baseness of a man's position, but by the loftiness or baseness of his senti- 5 ments. Noble and generous hearts may be found in men of lowly and humble degree, just as there are base-hearted men in lofty and distinguished positions. The distinctive mark is not the gown, nor the sword, nor the train of attendants, nor the splendour and magnificence of apparel. One man has 10 the heart of a king, though he is clad in rags; another, the heart of a menial, though he wears a golden crown....

Since then the heart is the most important part of a man, we must pay far more heed to it than to the intellect; and one of the greatest though commonest faults in the education 15 of children is that the intellect is highly trained, but the heart very little. None the less, it is the heart that makes a man good or bad, just or unjust, grateful or ungrateful, brave or cowardly, modest or boastful, generous or miserly, good-humoured or ill-humoured, unselfish or selfish, kind or un- 20 kind, honest or dishonest, forbearing or passionate, merciful or revengeful, pitiful or cruel. This is why Holy Scripture bids us: "Keep thy heart with all diligence."

Now the lesson of the heart is a lesson of example, while that of the intellect is a book-lesson. Acts teach the heart, 25 words the intellect. The heart learns through the eyes, the intellect through the ears. To instruct the intellect one must work, meditate, and study; but to instruct the heart one must act well and live well And since we are often surrounded by naught but evil actions, evil words, evil thoughts, evil 30 examples—in fact, an evil life, whether it be led by the parents, the servants, the friends, the teachers, or in short by every-body with whom children are connected—we must not be surprised if their hearts are less well educated by what they see, than their intellects by what they hear. We treat the part 35 which is least affected, whilst exposing to attacks of every kind the part which has already received innumerable wounds; for it is indisputable that the corruption of the heart is infinitely greater and more widely spread than that of the mind. 5 This shows us with what caution and discretion we should behave in respect to the young, and how careful we should be to do and say nothing in their presence which might harm them or offend them.

Emphasis on the importance of moral education implied a belief that the schoolmaster's office is one of the utmost importance, and that to fill it worthily he must be a man of irreproachable character, endowed with very special gifts. Passing reference to this topic has already been made in extracts i and iv. Extracts v–viii deal with the subject more definitely, but in general terms; while in extract ix we have a specific instance—the ideal schoolmaster according to Port-Royal.

v

(*Lancelot: Mém. de S.-C.* Vol. II, pp. 339–344.)

We should be the less surprised at M. de Saint-Cyran 10 being so anxious to induce everybody to perform acts of kindness towards children as he did not refrain from doing so himself; or at his belief that neither the worth nor the rank of any individual gave him any right to look down on children, since God considered them worthy of His angels. 15 For, as Jesus Christ has said, "In heaven their angels do always behold the face of My Father which is in heaven." But it is perhaps one of the devil's most crafty devices that he has brought into contempt that method by which he foresaw that very many souls might be snatched from him, by 20 preserving children in their innocence. It is not difficult to induce persons of any condition to devote themselves to works of piety; but merely to suggest the work of education to them would be thought a mistake. There is no hesitation about exposing them to the infection of prisons that they may visit the prisoners, to the vitiated atmosphere of hospitals that they may care for the sick, assist the poor, and dress wounds—disgusting as these sometimes are. Yet it would be thought that they demeaned themselves too much and gave themselves too great labour if they merely undertook the 5 education of a child. I know quite well that it is not everybody who can do this; but if the gift is rare that is no reason for despising it; and if some are already debarred from this work through lack of aptitude, it is to my mind most unreasonable that still more should be debarred by public opinion.   10

I have sometimes wondered why, when the profession of a doctor involves his seeing so many foul and disgusting sights and often exposes him to dangerous infection, many are none the less found to embrace it because men are so attached to life that this profession is considered honourable; and why 15 at the same time these very men have so few qualms about despising a profession which can do most to secure the eternal salvation of their children, and upon which their own very often depends as well. And I have been equally astonished by the fact that although S. Paul the Apostle has so explicitly 20 stated that: "If ye have judgments of things pertaining to this life, set them to judge who are least esteemed in the church," we nevertheless see nobody in such high positions as those who are concerned with such matters; or again by the fact that although one of the great successors of the Apostles has 25 assured us that the direction of the most insignificant soul is a greater thing than the government of a whole world, we see no occupation more despised than that which is concerned with laying the foundations of a good character. But it is still more astounding to see duties and offices, which are in them- 30 selves base, so exalted in princes' households (*e.g.* majordomo, or master of the horse); while what concerns the care and education of rational beings, redeemed by the blood of God, is regarded as the lowest employment in nature. Truly it must be confessed that great is the blindness of men.   35

I am well aware that most worldly people would laugh at me if they heard this. But let them laugh, so long as Thou, O God, dost not laugh at it. For we shall be judged not according to what *they* think, but according to Thy divine
5 word and the precepts of Thy servants, one of whom teaches us that the wisdom of this world is foolishness in Thy sight, and that what is foolishness with God is greater than all the wisdom of men. Let them say as often as they will that this is the way of the world, that custom cannot be changed, that
10 men will never be persuaded to think highly of a profession which they have always treated with disdain. Let them not hope then to persuade us to pity them very much when—as often happens—misfortunes come upon their families through their lack of esteem for education ; or rather, let them not
15 prevent us from pitying them with all our hearts, since the love of Christ constrains us to censure this unhappy custom. "Woe is thee, thou torrent of human custom!" says a Father of the Church. " Who shall stand against thee ? How long shalt thou not be dried up? How long roll the sons of Eve
20 into that huge and hideous ocean, which even they scarcely overpass who climb the cross ?"

Since M. de Saint-Cyran was very enlightened and far removed from these worldly ideas, and since he knew the importance of caring for children and educating them, he
25 looked upon this task in quite a different light. However tedious, however degrading it was in the eyes of men, he none the less did not fail to employ in it persons of repute, though they were not to think that they had a right to complain, for they saw with what zeal and charity he put into practice the
30 advice which he gave to others. For I have often seen him giving lessons to his nephews who lived with him, looking upon them—so he once told me—not as nephews but as children whom he was trying to bring up in a Christian manner.

One day when he went into a shop to buy a pair of
35 stockings he saw a little boy of promising appearance. He

was sorry to hear that the child was to be sent to a *collège* where he ran the risk of being spoiled; and he asked the shop-keeper to send the lad to ĥim and he would teach him along with his own nephew. This he did for a time; but as the child did not turn out so well as he wished, he was obliged to send 5 him home again.

During his imprisonment, as I have already said, there were three young children whom he took the trouble to teach; and when he put me in charge of M. d'Espinoy and M. de Villeneuve he was kind enough to send me word that he 10 would be their "under-master," and that if God restored to him his liberty, he would take them under his care.

It was in this way that M. de Saint-Cyran used to put into practice his theories and his knowledge of what was right; and it was in this spirit that he used to give advice to 15 others. For when first M. Singlin submitted himself to his direction he was delighted with M. de Saint-Cyran's suggestion that he should devote himself to children; and the Abbé intended him to take up this occupation for which—as he said to me on another occasion—God had sent him. Some time 20 before this he had assigned his nephew, M. de Barcos, to M. d'Andilly, to take charge of the latter's children at a time when Cardinal Richelieu would have been glad to secure his services. He entrusted M. de Saci with the education of a little boy who had been taken away from him during his im- 25 prisonment; and for his guidance he wrote two admirable letters, in which it is striking to notice with what care and precision he goes into the minutest details. When later he put this child under my care he wished M. de Saci still to take charge of him in the mornings because I was busy at 30 that time in church. When M. Arnauld submitted himself to M. de Saint-Cyran's direction he suggested that he should take charge of a young marquis who gave signs of a desire to withdraw from the world. In short, we know that he set everyone, whenever there was a chance, to this employment. 35

vi

(Suppl. au Nécr. pp. 162–163.)

De Saci had asked Lancelot for an account of the manner
in which he was educating the Princes de Conti (see Introd.
p. 39). This extract is taken from a letter which was sent in
reply.

In acceding to your request, Sir, I may call your attention
to the following fact: If anyone who has a real call to this
occupation (described by the greatest man of recent years
as an occupation of penance and of love) considers the dic-
5 tum of S. Gregory, who tells us that to control the smallest
soul is a greater and a more difficult task than to rule the
whole world, then he will no longer have any difficulty in
realising the importance of this occupation and the attention
which he should devote to it. He might also be told—what
10 the Fathers themselves recognised—that a schoolmaster's
first duty is to consider himself in the place of a parent with
regard to his pupils ; and this, as one of the wisest of them
points out in another place, implies a reciprocal duty on the
part of the pupils.

15   Such then, Sir, were the views of the ancient world on
this subject, and this is why the greatest conqueror the world
has ever seen is reported to have said that he felt more indebted to his tutor than to the king his father. It was this
again which made the great Theodosius exalt so highly the
20 occupation of Arsenius and desire that his sons should show
so deep a respect towards him. The author whom I have
quoted adds that this dutifulness—*pietas*, he calls it—is of
the greatest assistance to children in their studies; and it is
of still greater value in the training of character, since, as
25 S. Ambrose says, children have no greater stimulus to ad-
vancing in virtue than the regard which they have for their
master.

I will not labour this point, for I might be accused of being prejudiced. Nowadays we are over-particular about what concerns the world and careless about what concerns God and His servants. We even think ourselves wiser than the ancients; we persuade ourselves that they did not know 5 how to live, and their customs have gone quite out of fashion. No one knows better than you do, Sir, how this doctrine has revolutionised the directing of souls. Undoubtedly it has made it incomparably more difficult in the case of children; and it is without question one of the devil's stratagems, since 10 under such conditions there are so few who succeed in saving themselves from shipwreck; whereas they might almost all be preserved—as the late M. de Saint-Cyran used to say— if a good system of education were set up. But it will always be practically impossible to make children feel thus well-dis- 15 posed towards their masters and so increase their own happiness, so long as men hold in contempt an occupation upon which the well-being of both Church and State almost entirely depends and which is so difficult that men can be found for any other good work sooner than for this.   20

None the less, schoolmasters must not be disheartened; on the contrary they must redouble their efforts, they must foster this fatherly affection for their pupils, and they must think themselves happy to devote their labour, their interests, their lives to those little ones whom God has entrusted to 25 them. Children are all the more worthy of our pity in that they cannot as yet realise the benefits which we are conferring upon them; and in this, as M. de Saint-Cyran used to say, they do but typify our own far greater ingratitude towards God. Unless a schoolmaster adopts this frame of mind he 30 will never accomplish anything. If the reverse is the case he will soon find that grace is no less powerful in operation than nature; and his love for his pupils will help him to find more ways of being useful to them than all the advice that could be given to him.   35

vii

(*Coustel: Règles, etc.* Vol. I, pp. 128–136.)

In order that a field may prove productive it is not enough that its soil should be good; in addition it must fall into the hands of a farmer who perfectly understands the art of cultivating and sowing. It is the same with education; in order that
5 it may prove successful it is not enough for a child to have intelligence; he must also have the good fortune to come into the hands of a master who knows how to plant the rudiments of knowledge in his mind and to sow the seeds of piety in his heart. Such a master must possess certain good quali-
10 ties which are as estimable as they are rare. It may be said that these qualities are as a rule either inward or outward. People who are led only by what strikes their eyes (as is the case with most mothers) are attracted chiefly by the latter; and when a man is of fairly good appearance and knows how
15 to make a bow or a well-turned compliment, he has little difficulty in winning their approval. But there are many other qualities to be desired:

(1) In the first place a master must be a man of good morals and virtuous character. " The first care of prudent
20 and well-advised parents, " says Quintilian, "should be to make choice of a man whose life is well-regulated and beyond reproach. " This is also one of the things which is strongly recommended to parents in the statutes of the University. For since it is the master who has to sow the seeds of true
25 piety in the hearts of the children under his charge, and since he is the pattern on which they should model themselves, it is essential that all his actions should be so well regulated, his words so discreet and carefully guarded, and his whole conduct so prudent and so consistent that the copies may be
30 able to reproduce some of the beauty and perfection of their original; and that—as S. Chrysostom says—some of the

master's good and virtuous qualities may be transmitted to
his pupils. Indeed, it would be shameful if one who professes
to teach the art of living well did not himself observe the rules
which he lays down for others.

(2) Knowledge is the second quality which is absolutely 5
indispensable in a schoolmaster. For this reason it is classed
with good character both by Quintilian and in the University
statutes. Pliny the younger, writing to a lady on the subject
of the education of her son, speaks as follows : " Put in charge
of him a person who will teach him first morals and then 10
rhetoric which cannot be learned aright if separated from
morals. " The first Council of Milan, again, combines knowledge with piety in masters who are chosen to instruct the
young. The reason why knowledge is indispensable in a
schoolmaster is that a half-educated person as a rule merely 15
confuses and obscures the authors which he explains ; whereas
a capable man can always so turn them as to reveal all their
beauties and make them absolutely clear and comprehensible.
For this reason the former is as hurtful to children as the
latter is useful. Erasmus, Vives, and Juvenal are not content 20
even with a moderate knowledge ; they claim that a schoolmaster ought to know everything and to have read carefully
every author so as to be able to help his pupils to understand
them easily. Quintilian also desires that if a schoolmaster is
only moderately educated, he should at any rate thoroughly 25
realise the fact ; for nothing is so dangerous as those who
wish to appear what they are not. For this reason he compares them to small men who stand on tip-toe in order to
appear taller than they really are.

(3) It is not enough that a schoolmaster should have his 30
memory well filled with a multitude of beautiful things ;
besides this it is desirable that he should possess accuracy of
judgment—*i.e.* he must always be competent to praise what
is praiseworthy and to blame what deserves blame : and he
must not only set everything in its proper light, but must do 35

this in a pleasant and interesting manner. For we do not give children a schoolmaster merely for him to teach them Latin and Greek, but for him to develop their minds; and everything should contribute to this end—games, conver-
5 sations, reading, visits, walks; in short, all the events of life.

(4) Again, a master must have plenty of method and system. For unless he makes the children under his charge keep to a certain regularity in their studies and everything
10 else, they will become like travellers who go further and further astray the more they try to progress on their journey.

(5) In addition to these inward qualities which are indispensable for a schoolmaster, there are others which are at any rate much to be desired; for example, prudence which enables
15 him to guide the morals and the studies of his pupils and skilfully to keep them within the bounds of discipline without irritating or discouraging them or giving them a dislike for their lessons or prejudicing their health; for any kind of stumbling-block invariably does harm.

20 (6) Experience again is necessary, especially for those who have to educate children of rank upon whom it is difficult to make one's apprenticeship. *À propos* of this subject, it may be remarked that it is somewhat astounding that in this occupation one follows an entirely different course from that
25 which is adopted in all the other arts. For example, a man who has never been on the sea does not venture to lay hold of the tiller of a ship and ply the trade of a pilot. If a man knows nothing of the different constitutions of the various kinds of diseases, and of the doses to be prescribed, we do not ask
30 him to play the *rôle* of physician. Teaching is the only profession in which men sometimes take upon themselves to act as master without having first served an apprenticeship; and they often tamper with the instruction and direction of others at a time when they themselves still stand in need of instruc-
35 tion and direction.

(7) I add here the authority and influence which are given by age and a good appearance.

(8) Lastly good-breeding and knowledge of the world and of etiquette are at any rate much to be desired.

viii

(Nicole: Essais de Morale, Vol. II, pp. 257–260.)

The most necessary qualification for a tutor who has to educate a prince is a certain quality which has no specific name and which is not associated with any particular profession. It is not merely knowledge of history, mathematics, languages, or philosophy. Deficiencies in these can be made up; but deficiencies cannot be made up in this essential characteristic which qualifies a man for this task; it can never be borrowed from anyone else nor is it in any way possible to acquire it by preparation. In origin it is a natural gift; it is developed by long practice and much thought; and thus those who have it not and are of mature years are incapable of ever possessing it.

I cannot explain myself better than by saying that it is the quality which leads a man to blame always what is blameworthy and praise what is praiseworthy, to look down upon what is base and appreciate what is noble, to judge everything wisely and fairly, to express his judgments in an attractive manner suited to those whom he is addressing, and on every subject to turn towards the truth the minds of those whom he instructs. It must not be imagined that he always does this by definite remarks or that he is continually stopping to lay down rules as to what is good or bad, true or false. On the contrary, he does this almost always imperceptibly. It is the clever turn which he gives to things which shows up what is noble and worthy of note, and hides what ought not to be

revealed, which makes vice ridiculous and virtue attractive, which imperceptibly leads the mind to appreciate and discriminate what is good and to feel disgust and aversion for what is bad. Consequently it often happens that the same
5 story or the same dictum which helps to develop the mind when it is handled by a skilful and judicious person, only serves to corrupt it when handled by a person of the opposite character.

Tutors as a rule consider themselves under an obligation
10 to instruct princes only at definite hours, when they are giving what is specifically termed a lesson. But the man of whom we are speaking has no fixed time for his lesson, or rather he is always giving his pupil a lesson; for often he gives him as much instruction during games, visits, conversations and
15 discussions at table with those who are present, as when he makes him read books; for since his chief object is to develop his pupil's judgment the various subjects which chance to turn up are often of greater value for this purpose than prepared discourses, because nothing makes less impression on
20 the mind than that which comes in the somewhat unwelcome guise of a lesson or instruction. But as this method of instruction is not apparent, the benefit resulting therefrom is also in a way not apparent—*i.e.* it does not manifest itself by obvious and outward signs; and it is this fact which leads
25 unthinking people astray, for they imagine that a child educated in this way has made less progress than another because, perhaps, he cannot produce a better translation from Latin into French or because he does not repeat more correctly a lesson of Virgil; and so, judging of the education of their
30 children only by such trifles as these, parents will often make less account of a really able man than of another who has merely a superficial knowledge and an unenlightened mind.

ix

(Du Fossé: Mémoires pour servir à l'Histoire de Port-Royal, Rouen complete edition, 1876, Vol. I, pp. 165–169, 197.)

Du Fossé is speaking of the school which in 1646 was started in the cul-de-sac Saint-Dominique, not far from Port-Royal de Paris (see Introduction, p. 23).

We had for our master one of the most lovable men I have ever known. He came from Chartres and was called Le Fèvre. He had nothing of that which usually characterises members of this profession—I mean that lordly and some-times ridiculous air which nearly always accompanies what 5 they say to those who are in subordination to them and which makes their pupils tremble in their presence and ridicule them behind their backs by even giving them opprobrious names such as "pedant."...For it is indeed extraordinary that this kind of little tyrant thinks that everything is allowed him and 10 that, although in the realms of the law it is possible to appeal even against the judges of the sovereign courts, yet there is no appeal against him, who instead of striking fear into his pupils by his transports of rage sets them every day an ex-ample of rage by his own conduct.   15

Monsieur Le Fèvre, whom we were so happy as to have for our master, was far removed from this character of foolish pride or ignoble brutality. His nature was kind and gentle; his spirit noble and far above the ordinary; his mind, open and adapted to everything great. He knew something of 20 everything, being a good classic, a clever philosopher, a learned theologian, well-read in history, skilled in astronomy and to some extent also in medicine—not the ordinary kind but that which is founded on a knowledge of minerals and vegetables and natural principles. It was this that gave him 25

great advantages, for he had so genial a disposition that he
was able to win the affection of his pupils and attach them
wholly to himself. For since he knew how to be familiar with
us without in any way losing that importance which a master
5 ought to have, he used always to introduce into his conversation something interesting according to the various subjects
which offered. And by the charming way in which he employed this for our benefit—making it his aim to appeal to
our sense of honour and to win us over by this means—he
10 knew so well how to gain our confidence that we loved him
dearly as a friend and none the less respected him as a master.
In short, his attitude to us was such that there was not a
pupil in the school who did not envy us our position, as if
it were a kind of benefice, and who did not consider himself
15 unfortunate in comparison with us. Thus I can say that we
made much progress under such a master and learnt from
him many interesting things which the rest did not know....

Nothing, I think, can give a better idea of what I have
said in praise of M. Le Fèvre than the way in which he won
20 over one of his pupils who was of the most extraordinary
disposition and seemed the least amenable to any correction
or improvement. This was De Bohebert whom his parents
regarded as a suitable object for exercising the patience of
his masters; for there was no trace of docility or obedience
25 or tractableness in his nature. However, although the rest
had never ventured to hope it, M. Le Fèvre carried the work
through by the great assiduity with which he remarked not
only all his faults, but also all the means which he could
discover and which were best suited to engraft into his mind
30 what was said to him, and to make him assimilate it. M.
Le Fèvre won him over, then, in such a way that he used
to do whatever he wished and he made him tractable, so far
as so rough a nature was capable of it....

[In 1649, owing to the disturbances of the Fronde and the
Jesuit attacks on Port-Royal, Du Fossé and several other pupils

were sent in charge of Le Fèvre to Magny, a village near Port-Royal des Champs.]

We spent six months there in a private house which we rented. It is true that this time seemed to all of us a real holiday because of the pleasure which we found in the company of so accomplished a master as ours was. We devoted ourselves to study during all the study hours; but at recrea- 5 tion times we used to be in a way even more attached to him because of the innumerable interesting things which he used to tell us. At evening during the fine summer weather, when we walked in the country with him, he used to take pleasure in pointing out to us the various constellations and 10 in showing us the planets and principal stars, which we used to look at with great interest; and I have never learned anything of these subjects except what he taught us then in lost time—which however was not lost for us, because he knew how to make us reap great benefit from it. Our happiness 15 was too short and we lost far too soon this admirable man by a violent illness which carried him off in a few days.

The Port-Royalist's belief in the supreme value of moral education will explain the attitude taken up in the following extracts towards boarding-schools and day schools (x); the expurgation of texts used in class (xi and xii); foreign travel (xiii and xiv); novels and the theatre (xv–xvii).

X

(Coustel: Règles, etc. Vol. I, pp. 103–120.)

I. *Education at Home.*

There are as a rule three considerations which induce parents to bring up their children at home. The first is that it is more easy to look after their health there, especially if 20 they are still young or of a weak and delicate constitution. The second is that the presence of the parents acts as a

restraint and as a deterrent; and in their desire to please them they are without difficulty induced to study. The third reason (which appeals most to them) is that they can more easily learn the usages of polite society by noticing the
5 behaviour of visitors; and by often being obliged themselves to receive them or entertain them, they become imperceptibly perfected in the duties of social life and in the manners and customs of well-bred people.

But although something can be said in praise of this
10 system of education, it has none the less many disadvantages :

(1) It is difficult to keep to regular hours of study because the times of the meals, upon which those of the lessons depend, cannot be fixed owing to business affairs or visits which
15 intervene unexpectedly and often can neither be foreseen nor avoided.

(2) Children have their attention perpetually distracted by their inborn curiosity to know everything that is going on around them or who it is that is coming or going.

20 (3) The tokens of love and affection, which parents cannot resist showing them, merely serve to render them soft and unmanly.

(4) The indulgence and obsequiousness of the servants, the obscene conversation and behaviour of the footmen —
25 from which at times it is hardly possible to exclude them— make an impression on these tender minds which in many cases can never be effaced.

(5) The life of the parents, again, is often a most powerful hindrance to the well-being of their children. For children
30 are just like apes; they are extremely prone to imitate whatever their parents show them, because they think that they are wise and always right. Thus, when their tutor exhorts them to spend their time well so as to make progress in their studies and keeps them with him in the schoolroom for this
35 purpose, what will be the result of this restraint, if they see

their parents spending the whole day at the gaming-table or
on the promenade, but to give them a dislike not only for
their studies but also for him who keeps them imprisoned, as
if he were their gaoler?

(6) Nothing is more detestable than the conduct of 5
certain parents who, being ignorant of the value of knowledge
and the true worth of virtue, treat like a hireling a tutor who
is trying to improve the minds of their children, and whose
attitude towards him makes their children and servants look
down upon him.   10

(7) There are again some parents who are eccentric
enough to imagine that a tutor ought to be able to perform
miracles—i.e. that he can transfer all his knowledge to the
minds of their children however stupid, idle, and unfitted for
a literary education they may be. They know quite well that 15
a farmer, for all his labour, cannot change the nature of a
barren or sandy soil; that a fountain-maker can never compel
water to rise higher than its source, and that a gardener is
not asked for fruit from a newly-planted tree and at too early
a season. But they are not so reasonable. Their natural 20
affection puts a bandage over their eyes which prevents them
from seeing what justice and good feeling would have them
do. They are so annoyed at the stupidity and ignorance of
their children that they cannot keep silence, and they find
the tutor the most handy person upon whom to vent their 25
spleen. "He's an incapable person," they say. "He has
neglected my son and made him fritter away all his time"—
and other similar remarks, quite as unjustifiable.

(8) Finally, since parents in their desire to show their
children how much they love them cannot refrain from telling 30
them continually of the antiquity of their family, of their
wealth and the plans for getting them a good position in the
world—that is to say, intoxicating them with ambition and
vanity—this again adds to the mortification of the tutor who
has charge of them. For prudence compels him to hold his 35

tongue, not only for fear of losing the respect which he should have for the parents, but also lest his trouble should be wasted In fact, if he took this liberty would it not serve merely to bring down upon him the effects of their unjust 5 indignation?

II. *Education in Boarding-Schools.*

The most usual custom in France with regard to the education of children is to send them to boarding-schools. Parents are induced to do this by four considerations which are noted by Quintilian in the first book of his Institutes:
10   (1) The first is that they make there profitable acquaintances and friendships which are often of lifelong duration.

(2) The second is that they can there easily develop the mind and the judgment by associating with those of their 15 schoolfellows who are cleverest and best behaved.

(3) The third is that they find there more competition which incites children to work with much more diligence and rescues them from the torpor into which they would otherwise relapse.
20   (4) The fourth reason is that children there acquire a praiseworthy self-confidence in public-speaking which is absolutely essential for anyone who has to take up an important position; for nervousness is quite common among people who have been educated in the shelter of a private school, and 25 sometimes it even makes them utterly incapable of reaping any reward from their studies.

All these reasons are very good and others might be added to them to show the value of boarding-schools where the discipline is sound and the number of pupils not ex-30 cessive.

(1) Everything should be regulated—*e.g.* the hours of rising and going to bed, of work and play, of morning and evening prayer, of mass and attendance at the sacraments.

(2) There must be facilities for clearing-up pupils' difficulties and setting their doubts at rest by the giving of lectures and by private tuition.

But in boarding-schools, as elsewhere, there are none the less some disadvantages ; the excessive number of pupils, for 5 example, is no inconsiderable hindrance to their progress both in studies and in good manners. In fact, as Quintilian points out, a good schoolmaster should never take charge of more pupils than he can instruct—just as a good doctor should never attend more patients than he can treat, because 10 this would mean that he would be powerless to help them and be of service to them. This writer, who is one of the most judicious of all the ancients, brings forward the following argument in support of his statement. "A master entrusted with the education of children takes upon himself to develop 15 their intellects ; and he can do this only by strengthening the good qualities which he finds in them, by correcting their defects, so far as he is able, and by making good their deficiencies. Now he can never do this so long as the number of his pupils is too large, since he can scarcely remember 20 their names and distinguish their faces." To make this point still clearer, we must in dealing with children carefully distinguish the memory from the intellect and the judgment ; these are three different faculties all of which the master has to develop to their utmost. He must not set children of entirely 25 different natures all to the same work ; that would be as great a mistake as if a doctor were to give the same medicines to patients of widely-differing constitutions. Now children's memories may be cultivated by making them learn by heart the finest passages from the best authors ; the keenness of 30 their intellect may be maintained by making them read widely ; and their judgment may be developed by questioning them frequently and making them give reasons for everything ; and this is obviously impossible when the number of pupils is too large......... 35

But if an excessive number of pupils is a hindrance to studies, we may say that it is an even greater one to the inculcation of good manners. In truth, just as rivers soon lose their natural freshness when they reach the sea, so children no 5 sooner set foot inside places of this kind [*i.e.* boarding-schools] than they begin to lose that innocence, that simplicity, that modesty which before had made them so dear to God and men alike, owing to an accursed infection which is far more deadly to the soul than the plague is to the body. "I have 10 seen very good children," says S. John Climacus, "who went to boarding-school to gain knowledge and wisdom and to be brought up under a pious *régime*; but who learnt nothing but artfulness and depravity owing to the influence exercised upon them by the other pupils." The amusing dispute, which 15 took place between a father and a philosopher and which is recorded by Lucian in his *Hermotimus*, will serve as another proof of my statements. A philosopher wished to receive a sum of money which a father had promised him in payment for the instruction of his son. But the father refused to give 20 it to him and this is the reason which Lucian makes him put forward in order to excuse himself from paying: "When I put you in charge of my son, I did so that you might endeavour to make him better and more virtuous than before; and yet he is the very reverse. I see nothing but untruthfulness, 25 lack of respect, shamelessness, and other vices; and in them he has made the most marked and disastrous progress. He was far more modest and well-behaved when I put him under your care and I should have been much better pleased if he had learnt to correct one of his faults rather than that he should 30 have learnt the hundred other follies with which he pesters us." This then is one of the chief reasons why Quintilian prefers that children should be educated at home rather than in boarding-schools. He thinks it is even more advantageous from the point of view of study and he calls this a strong argu- 35 ment and one which should appeal forcibly to the mind.

III. *Education in Private Houses, whether in the City or the Country.*

Long ago Erasmus pointed out that, in order to avoid most of these disadvantages, five or six children should be put under the care of one or two reliable men in a private house. He says in the first place that where five or six children live together they will be able to take part in games 5 and so participate in the light-heartedness and playfulness which befit their age; and this is absolutely essential for those who are engaged in study. And in fact tutors employed by persons of high rank find nothing more difficult to deal with than an only child who cannot always be studying and yet has 10 no opportunity for play. The second reason which Erasmus advances is that one teacher is sufficient for the instruction of five or six children; which is as much as to say that it would be impossible for him to give them as much attention as they need if they were more numerous and could not work 15 together. This is why Vives is quite justified in complaining of those schoolmasters who, as he says, are always on the look out for new pupils, who intrigue for them, who entice and cajole them into their school in as large numbers as they can, and to this end resort to every device—plots and stratagems 20 —without caring whether these pupils are fit to profit by their instruction; who think that it is enough to have a number of figure-heads, provided that they can pay the school fees. Such mercenary conduct can hardly be sufficiently condemned and yet it is only too common; for it originates not from love 25 which seeks only the means to please God and to serve one's neighbour, but simply and solely from covetousness—*i.e.* love of glory, desire to rule, or greed of gain. Finally, the third reason which Erasmus advances and which is undoubtedly the most important, is that by this means we shall avoid 30 the corruption of morals caused by too large a number of pupils.

xi

(Fontaine: Mém. sur MM. de P.-R. pp. 393-395.)

M. de Saci, who always had in his hands a copy of
S. Augustine and another of the *Confessions* in his pocket,
sympathised too much with the views of this author to approve of the methods of study which have been established
5 by long custom. How sensitive he used to be on this point!
How often would he groan to see things in Latin authors
which are not in harmony with Christian purity! But the
pious and enlightened persons who had guided him in his
youth had made him read through these books, since they
10 contain the source of latinity; and it would be sad if, on
occasions when it is necessary to defend the Church, the
champions of the truth had not weapons as strong and as
well-polished as those of their adversaries. For these reasons
he found himself—against his own inclinations—obliged to
15 agree that the children also must be made to go through this
course of reading. But with what precautions was his permission given! What care he took to ensure that these tender
souls might be able to draw from these authors what was advantageous as regards the language without being spoiled by
20 what was evil and liable to corrupt their morals! Has not
his love given him the ingenuity for discovering how to render
pure what was most impure? Has it not deprived these
masters of lewdness of the venom by which they poison tender
souls? Has it not so contrived that Terence may be good
25 Latin without being obscene; that Horace may be profitable
without being harmful by his horrible foulness; and that
Martial may innocently stimulate children's minds by his selected epigrams without immersing them in the disgusting
filth from which these have been so industriously removed?
30 How M. de Saci's care in this most important matter warns
those who have charge of the education of children to keep

strict watch over them and to put far from them whatever
might offend their innocent purity ! Dead though he be, the
children still feel the love so pure and tender which he had
for them in striving to his utmost that the white robe of innocence which they had acquired at baptism should not be 5
smirched by any spot and that they should preserve with the
utmost care a treasure which, he knew well, could be recovered
only with the greatest difficulty when one had been unhappy
enough to lose it.

xii

(*Nicole: Epigrammatum Delectus*, 1686, Preface—no
   pagination.   The original of this is in Latin.)

Since in educating the young there are two things which 10
must be kept in view—their studies and their moral character
—I have tried, while engaged in collecting these epigrams,
to pay attention to each.   But I have devoted particular care
to moral character because it is the more important and because I was induced for its sake especially to undertake this 15
task, hoping that I might, to the best of my ability, block up
one of the means of access by which a most deadly contagion
creeps into the souls of many men.

In truth I have always been deeply grieved by the unhappy lot of so many young people who are enticed in the 20
first instance by curiosity into the reading of impure books,
and so receive from this source their first inspiration from
the evil one ; and, when their purity of heart has thus been
lost, throughout the whole course of their after life heap up
by fresh additions the store of vice which they began to ac- 25
cumulate in their early years.

There is only one means of providing against so dreadful
and so pressing an evil—to debar them altogether from these
pestilent books.   But since in these very works there are many
things of extreme elegance and great value (the beauty of 30

which attracts many to read the books to their own destruction), to rob the young altogether of these good things seemed somewhat hard and ill-calculated to draw them away from evil.

5 I have therefore always thought that the best plan was that of those who have taken pains to cut out the indecent passages from the writings of the ancients, and it has been my desire to follow their example and to deserve the gratitude of the young by a similar service. And since I knew
10 no more harmful authors than the writers of epigrams who whet their foulness with wit and humour that it may penetrate more deeply into the mind, I selected this class particularly for expurgation.

With this purpose I took in hand Catullus and Martial,
15 the chief writers of this kind, intending to revise the others afterwards. I must confess that I shuddered when I saw in them so many indecencies and that I felt greatly indignant that such abominable authors should be left in the hands of Christians—not to say of boys; for it were fitting that they
20 had long ago been buried in eternal oblivion and purged by avenging flames.

But as vipers are not altogether harmful but even possess something which conduces to health, so these writers are not everywhere poisonous but are sometimes even harmlessly a-
25 musing; and amid so many deadly herbs there may be seen the most beautiful flowers and the fruits of most noble ideas. These I endeavoured to pluck, lest anyone attracted by their beauty should imprudently abandon himself among so many plagues; I was anxious, too, that virtuous youths should no
30 longer have any colourable pretext for desiring to possess or use these books in their unexpurgated condition.

xiii

(Fontaine : Mém. sur MM. de P.-R. p. 396.)

His [M. de Saci's] opinion was sometimes asked as to the
very wide-spread custom of making children travel; but he
was unable to approve of this, for he had in view their salvation. This it was that he chiefly considered; this it was, in
his opinion, that any sensible person should regard as of the 5
greatest importance. He used to say that travel was but to
see the devil dressed up in all kinds of fashions—German,
English, Italian, Spanish; but it was always the same devil,
cruel everywhere. He used to adapt a text from Isaiah and
apply it to this, saying that just as God hides Himself in the 10
Eucharist for our salvation, so the devil in order to destroy
us hides himself in everything which pertains to the world
and the lusts thereof. Everywhere the evil one wants us to
adore him; everywhere he wants us to bow the knee before
him. He will leave a man alone on no cheaper terms—not 15
even the Son of God Himself.

xiv

(Coustel: Règles, etc. Vol. I, p. 247.)

Travel in foreign countries may form part of the education of children of good family. But in order that such travel
may be of use to them, it is advisable: (1) that they should
have a good knowledge of the map, the history, and even 20
the language of the countries which they propose to visit;
(2) that they should have a good guide who is not content
merely with showing them the position and strength of the
towns through which they pass, or even the beauty of the
churches and palaces, but also the people of merit and learn- 25
ing; (3) that he should point out to them carefully what is
most worthy of note in the laws, manners, and customs—in

a word, the good and bad qualities of the various nations;
(4) lastly, that he should teach them that it is not in their
faults that these nations are to be imitated, but in their good
and praiseworthy qualities. Thus one should not go to Italy,
5 for instance, to become dissolute; to Germany to learn excessive drinking; to Spain to increase one's pride; but one
should try to copy the temperance and prudence of the
Italians, the bravery and patriotism of the Germans, the steadfastness of the Spaniards. Otherwise travel is of little use.

XV

(*Nicole: Visionnaires*, 1683, Vol. I, p. 253.)

It was this passage which gave offence to Racine and was
responsible for his temporary estrangement from Port-Royal (see
Introd. pp. 45 and 49). The person referred to in the extract was
a certain Desmarets or Des Maretz who took an active part in
the persecution of the society.

10 Everyone knows that his first profession was to compose
novels and stage-plays and that by means of them he began
to make himself known in the world. These qualities, which
are not particularly honourable in the eyes of respectable
people, are horrible when viewed according to the principles
15 of the Christian religion and the precepts of the Gospel. A
writer of novels and a stage-poet is a public poisoner, not of
the bodies but of the souls of the faithful; he should consider
himself guilty of innumerable spiritual murders which he has
either actually caused or which he might have caused by his
20 pernicious writings. The more he has tried to conceal under
a veil of respectability the criminal passions which he describes,
the more deadly does he make them and the more likely to
ensnare and corrupt simple and innocent souls. Sins of this
kind are the more terrible in that they are always active, be-
25 cause these books do not perish but continually shed their
poison upon those who read them.

xvi

(*Varet: Éducation, etc.* pp. 182–184 and 187.)

The writer has been quoting from the *Life of S. Theresa* in which the saint from her own personal experience testifies to the undesirable effects of novel-reading.

I do not think, my sister, that I need add anything to what I have said to inspire you with a horror of reading novels, for it reveals so clearly the large number of evil results produced by these fictitious stories which have been devised by the laziness and license of these latter days for the nourish- 5 ment and sustenance of the most dangerous passions. For you see in S. Theresa's words and in her own experience how this undesirable kind of reading fascinates young people and how they become addicted to it owing to the pernicious pleasures, the fatal delights, which it offers them; you see 10 how it leads them to neglect all other occupations in order to devote themselves to this one, until it becomes their one and only pursuit; and how they spend their nights and days, contrary to their own fathers' desires, in satisfying the curiosity thus aroused and kindled in their hearts. You see 15 how novel-reading changes all the good tendencies which nature has given them, how it gradually cools their good desires, and how in a short time it drives from their souls all that is good and virtuous. You see how it makes them love and prize worldly vanity and frivolity; how it teaches them to 20 seek after the means of pleasing the world, of indulging their vanity and adorning their bodies, of ingratiating themselves, of attracting attention and beguiling the beholder; in short, of discovering disguises and cunning devices for hiding the imperfections of the body, and of setting in the best light what- 25 ever can contribute to its being held in high esteem.......

After all, there is now a large number of devotional books, far better written, from which your children may extract much

more eloquence—to say nothing of a knowledge and love of
the Christian verities; and they will even discover in them
every beauty of style without having to seek for these in works
of fiction which serve only to extinguish in them the fire of
5 charity and to kindle in its stead unhallowed flames which
will gradually consume all the pious sentiments with which
you have striven to inspire them.

xvii

(*Varet: op. cit.* pp. 202, 204, 215, 220, 225.)

There is no abuse which the Fathers of the Church have
more often and more zealously resisted than love of the theatre.
10 In a very large number of passages in their writings they give
proofs of their zeal in combating this pernicious tendency
which in those early times began to corrupt the innocence
and purity of the faithful. They regard the stage as an invention of the devil who has had theatres built in every city
15 in order to weaken the hearts of the soldiers of Jesus Christ
and to make them lose their strength and courage. They
deplore the blindness of those who think that there is no
harm in finding pleasure in plays and applauding them, although they derive therefrom nothing but shameful ideas
20 and vicious suggestions. ......

I know quite well that it is asserted that a distinction must
be drawn between the plays of our own days and those which
the holy Fathers condemned in their time; and that if the
plays against which they directed such censure deserved the
25 blame which they gave them, those which are shown in our
modern theatres could not be sufficiently commended because as a rule they never represent anything but examples
of innocence, virtue, and piety. But whatever be the specious
excuses with which the authors of these plays wish to shield
30 themselves and however pure and harmless be their intentions, their works are none the less such medleys and the

saints who are shown on the stage exhibit such weakness as
regards love (which is the principal *motif* in plays) that it is
very difficult not to believe the contrary—that instead of the
stage being hallowed by the representation of the acts of the
martyrs, the sanctity of their sufferings is profaned by the 5
fictitious love interest which is introduced into them. ......

What is there in these stage-plays which can be pleasing
in God's eyes? Is it the splendour and magnificence of the
dresses? Is it the skill of the actors in arousing both in themselves and in others criminal passions? Is it the assiduity 10
with which the actions are suited to the subjects and adapted
so as to strengthen these same passions? Is it the devices
which the poet has found for disguising the truth by mingling
therewith fictitious legends and incidents cunningly enough
contrived? "The Author of truth," says Tertullian, "has 15
no love for falsehood and all that savours of fiction is in His
eyes a kind of adultery."........

But even suppose that there were nothing in stage-plays
which might injure the innocence of young people or arouse
dangerous passions in them; suppose that out of thirty plays 20
there were one which did not openly injure purity and innocence; suppose that there were nothing in the attire (or
lack of it) or attitudes of the actresses which might injure
modesty, but that everything were in harmony with the purity
and piety of the virgins whom they represent; suppose that 25
the other members of the audience were deprived of their
power to inspire young people with that worldly and vain
spirit which appears so manifestly in their apparel, their
actions, their whole personality; suppose that the incidents
of these unhappy plays led to no harm, that the words, dress, 30
evolutions, voices, songs, looks, gestures, instrumental music,
the subjects and intrigues of the plays themselves, in short the
whole spectacle, were free from poison and suggested no impurity—even so you should forbid your children to go to the
theatre. For as S. Chrysostom says, it is not for us to pass 35

our time in mirth and pleasures and delights. That is not
the spirit of those who are called to heavenly life, whose
names are already written in that eternal city, and who have
enlisted in a wholly spiritual warfare; it is rather the spirit of
5 those who fight under the standard of the evil one......

You must then, my sister, inspire your children with a
horror of the theatre, for it is a dangerous pastime and unworthy of a Christian. You must do so because it is very
difficult for them to avoid defiling their eyes, their ears, and
10 their souls at the same time; you must do so because these
spectacles are among those worldly pomps, those works of the
devil, which they have solemnly renounced at their baptism;
you must do so because—even though everything in a play is
pretence—the spectators, as S. Augustine says, none the less
15 share the delight of the lovers on the stage, when by their
devices they have brought their shameless desires to a successful issue, and they commit a sin when they allow themselves
to be touched by a senseless compassion for an actor who
laments the loss of some ruinous pleasure, some miserable
20 happiness. You must do so, lastly—to use the words of the
same saint—because the spectator takes no pleasure in stage-
plays unless he is affected by the romantic episodes which are
shown, and the less he is cured of his passions, the more he
is affected by these. The greater the eagerness then that your
25 children show for the theatre, the less should you let them go
to it; for this very eagerness shows a tendency to luxury,
ostentation, sensuality, fastidiousness, laziness, effeminacy,
and those devices and deceits which form the tinsel of the
stage; and you must do your utmost to expel these from their
30 hearts.

It has been pointed out in the Introduction (p. 26) that the
methods of maintaining discipline in the Little Schools contrasted
very favourably with those employed in the University and elsewhere. In extract xviii we see the general attitude adopted by the
Port-Royalist schoolmasters towards their pupils (refer also to

Part I, extract vi, last paragraph). In xix and xx some details are given as to the punishments which were employed.

xviii

(*Coustel: Règles, etc.* Vol. I, pp. 168–171.)

Since a schoolmaster takes the place of the parents he must try to enter into their feelings and to fill his own heart with that affection and tenderness which nature gives them for their children; or—to put it better—with that love which draws its inspiration from grace and therefore has all the ten- 5 derness of natural affection without its faults and weaknesses. It is this love which will teach him never to treat his pupils with despicable flattery, glozing over faults which he ought to correct, nor to assume a domineering attitude which will prove hateful and intolerable to them; but his manner will 10 always be kind and affable, so that while the children fear him as their master they will respect him as their father and love him as their best friend. It is this love which will lead him to take every precaution to guard them from anything which can do them harm. It is this love which will lead him never 15 to speak to his pupils in a harsh tone which might discourage them, but with that moderation and kindness which inspires them with all the confidence which they should have in him. In fact, just as heavy rains merely run over the surface of the earth without sinking into it and fertilising it, so harsh words 20 make no impression upon the mind into which they do not sink.

Since learning is very difficult for small children, the master's love for them will lead him to seek any method for rendering it more easy. For example, he will tell them the 25 words which they cannot find; he will explain the difficulties which impede their progress and thus facilitate their under- standing of their authors; and he will encourage those of only moderate capacity by helping them to learn their lessons. It will be this love, again, which will help him to endure 30

patiently the hundred little faults which are corrected as they grow older, by very often showing tokens even of the deepest affection for those who are most full of natural imperfections ; in this way he will imitate the behaviour of mothers who, as
5 S. Bernard says, lavish most caresses on those of their children who are weakest.

Nothing certainly is so profitable, alike for master and pupils, as this honourable and affectionate attitude; for it is an infallible means for the master to make himself beloved
10 and thus to dispose his children towards study and right conduct. For since the heart is the spring of all the actions, when you are once master of it you can straightway do whatsoever you please. " Love first, if you would be loved," says Seneca. "Love with all your heart," says S. Augustine, " and
15 then you can treat your neighbour in whatever way you please. If you reprove him and grow angry with him he will not be offended because he knows that you behave thus towards him only because you love him ; and if you even resort to punishment he agrees to it, because he is persuaded that your only
20 object is his own good."

xix

(Lancelot: Mém. de S.-C. Vol. II, pp. 335–337.)

He [M. de Saint-Cyran] did not wish us to have recourse to the cane as a means of punishment except for serious faults and then only after having tried all other methods one after the other. For he wished us first to bear with their faults in
25 order that we might test ourselves in the sight of God and do nothing upon impulse, and also that we might pray to God on their behalf before we reproved them. Next he wished us merely to warn them by certain signs, then by words; and after rebuking them, to use threats, to deprive them for a while
30 of something that they liked—*e.g* their playtime, their lunch or part of their dinner—and to resort to the cane only in the last extremity and for serious offences, especially in the case

of those who could obviously be won over by kindness and persuasion. At the same time he wished us to employ this method of punishment for such as were naturally frivolous and hot-tempered, who were given to telling falsehoods and bursting into laughter on the most solemn occasions. In 5 short, like S. Benedict, he did not wish that they should be forgiven for faults committed in church.

He used to say that to employ punishments without having first prayed long was to act like a Jew and to fail to recognise that everything depends on the blessing of God 10 and on His grace which we should endeavour to draw down upon our pupils by our forbearance towards them He added that sometimes we ought even to punish and chastise ourselves on their behalf, not only because we ought always to be afraid of being partly responsible for their faults, either by our 15 hastiness or our negligence, but also because this is a duty incumbent upon all alike who find themselves entrusted with the charge of others. He used to say that we must keep a constant watch to counteract that kept by the devil, who is always seeking an entrance into these tender souls. He there- 20 fore used to recommend us by our own prayers to assist the prayers of the children under our care ; and thus, since they cannot be expected to be always on their guard, to relieve them of part of this duty. He used to make a point of warning us that in order to train children well we must pray more 25 than scold, and speak more about them to God, than about God to them. For he did not like us to give them long lectures on piety and to weary them with precepts. He wished us to confine such instruction as far as possible to the occasions and opportunities which God brings about, as indicated 30 by the impulse which He gives us and the willingness to hear which He shows us in them ; for the impulse to give no less than the gift itself depends on God and what we say under such conditions would have quite a different result from what we could say on our own initiative.   35

XX

(Coustel: Règles, etc. Vol. II, pp. 128–135.)

When repeated rebukes and warnings have proved fruitless we must at last change our methods and bring to their senses by punishment those whom plain reason has not been sufficient to keep within the limits of their duty; this is parti
5 cularly necessary when they are untruthful or disobedient, when they are guilty of disgraceful conduct or cheating, and when they refuse to apply themselves to their lessons as they should....Scripture supports what I have just pointed out when it says: "He that spareth the rod hateth his son";
10 while to adopt the opposite course is but to follow the example of God Himself, for "whom the Lord loveth He chasteneth." Granting then this maxim that children must be punished when they do wrong, we may next ask what course should be adopted in the event of this regrettable necessity.

15 (1) Recourse should be had to punishment only after the other means which have already been employed have proved useless; in the same way the wise surgeon uses the red-hot iron to cure a wound only when less drastic remedies have failed. We may therefore first of all deprive them of
20 their recreation, keep them in, or make them feel ashamed in front of their schoolfellows or parents.

(2) The cane should be used as seldom as possible for fear lest children should become accustomed and hardened to it.

(3) We should punish them only in a pure spirit of affec
25 tion and with a sincere desire for their true benefit. A father is always a father; and whatever severity he is at times compelled to use towards his child, he can never rid himself of the love which nature has planted deep in his heart. A master as far as possible should be of the same frame of mind.

30 (4) We should never administer punishment in a fit of passion or anger. If we feel our temper rising we should try to calm ourselves and, if possible, defer the punishment to

some other time, for fear of doing anything unadvisedly. For anger should never outstrip reason which is the mistress, but should merely follow it and carry out its orders.

(5) According to S. Bernard, we should never administer punishment save with fear and trembling. "When a fault is 5 so far beyond excuse," he says, "that one cannot be merciful without weakening justice, one should none the less punish only with trembling and grief, being stirred more by the necessity of carrying out one's duty than by eagerness to punish the culprit. For this reason it should always be 10 manifest that one goes to such lengths against one's will."

(6) When children are so incorrigible and hardened that nothing is to be gained by severity and punishments serve to make them worse rather than better, one is considerably embarrassed. Must they be allowed to do whatever they like 15 and must we give up the medicine because our patients are incurable? Moreover, what is the use of giving oneself considerable trouble to no purpose? In such cases it seems that all we can do is to regard them as severe penances imposed upon us by God, and we must endure them patiently with- 20 out ever losing hope that, in His goodness and mercy, they may change for the better ; since with time and trouble even the most savage animals can be tamed.

The Port-Royalists were anxious to spare their pupils all unnecessary difficulties and exerted their ingenuity in discovering methods of simplifying the process of learning. This point is illustrated in detail in many of the extracts which deal with particular school subjects (see Part III) ; but in the following passages (xxi and xxii) the general principle is laid down.

xxi

(*Coustel: Règles, etc.* Vol. II, p. 57.)

Contrive that their studies appear as a kind of pastime or game rather than as a troublesome and tedious employment. 25 This was doubtless why the ancients represented the Muses

with a very cheerful and lively air—some touching a guitar or playing a lute, others dancing or singing, and all disporting themselves in different ways. This again is the reason why the school is called *ludus literarius* and the schoolmaster
5 *ludimagister*. We must not then exact from children while they are of a tender age an application and devotion to study equal to that which we have a right to demand from fully-formed minds. This would mean giving them a dislike for study, which might have undesirable consequences and which
10 also might possibly persist as they grew older.

xxii
(*Guyot: Billets de Cicéron, etc.* Preface.)

Masters must not imagine that what they now take pleasure in knowing their pupils can learn without trouble. On the contrary, they should rather remember their own childhood and the difficulties which they themselves had in acquiring
15 learning. Thus they will adapt themselves to the feebleness of their pupils and will never cause them the least trouble over and above that from which they cannot possibly excuse them. For I cannot agree with those who wish their pupils to become learned only at the expense of toil and trouble
20 and who, instead of relieving them, let them be weighed down by a thousand unnecessary difficulties. I believe, on the contrary, that we ought to give them all the aid we can, and that we should make their work, if it is possible, more pleasant even than their games and recreations. There will
25 always be enough other difficulties—whether they arise from our pupils' intellects or from their inclinations and natural dislike for study—without our adding extra ones of our own by the incompetent manner in which we set about teaching.

It is often said that in the schools of Port-Royal any form of emulation among the pupils was suppressed. This is probably true only to a limited extent. Coustel (Vol. I, p. 63) says: "They

must be induced to work and stimulated to rivalry by offering
from time to time prizes for those who do best"; and again (Vol. I,
p. 112): " In attempting to stimulate them to rivalry we must
take great care to avoid making them feel envious of those good
qualities which they see in their companions, but which they
themselves lack." Of the two extracts which follow, no. xxiii is
taken from Dr Arnauld's plan for the reform of the Faculty of
Arts of the University (see Introd. pp. 6–11); it is based largely
on the actual practice of the Port-Royal Schools and many of the
suggestions which it contains were afterwards adopted by Rollin,
a fervent admirer of Port-Royal, who was Rector of the University of Paris from 1694 to 1696. No. xxiv—an excerpt from
Du Fossé's *Mémoires*—is interesting as giving a personal experience of an old pupil of the Little Schools.

xxiii

(Arnauld : Œuvres, 1780, Vol. XLI, pp. 87–89, 92.)

The examination to which pupils must submit in order
to pass from one form to another should consist simply in
seeing whether they understand thoroughly the authors which
have been set them in the class from which they hope to be
promoted. If they do not they must be, without exception, 5
kept down unless it is quite obvious that they are incapable
of doing better or more work....Places should be given every
month or fortnight simply by examining those who have done
best work in all their exercises, *vivâ-voce* and written translations alike, not from French into Latin, but from Latin into 10
French—at any rate in the four lower forms. For what kind
of Latin can be expected of those who do not yet know this
language ? Setting aside those tests for which rewards are
offered, the chief prizes will be awarded to those who distinguish themselves most in the work of the first six months, 15
or of the whole year if prizes are given only once. By this
means the hopes of the pupils will be stimulated. It must
not be forgotten that the names of those who obtain a *proxime
accessit* should be published and honourably mentioned; but

the chief of all the prizes should be awarded to those who
have shown the greatest piety and whose character is irreproachable. Those who have made attempts to copy them
should also be mentioned. The heart should be rewarded
5 before the mind....

In addition to the yearly tests there should be two more
searching examinations, one for promotion from the Rhetoric
to the Philosophy, and the other for the degree of Master of
Arts. Only such pupils should be promoted to the Philosophy
10 as have satisfactorily answered questions on all the classical
authors; they must show that they have read them and
understand them and they must be able, after an hour's
preparation, to reproduce orally in Latin some story which
they have been given to read for this purpose. They must
15 speak for a quarter of an hour and not confine themselves
to the words or phrases which the author has used. No
one should be granted the degree of Master of Arts who
cannot pass in (1) Classical authors; (2) the whole range of
Philosophy; (3) Ancient and Modern Geography; (4) Chrono-
20 logy; (5) Sacred History; (6) Classical History; (7) French
History; (8) Special set books.

xxiv

(*Du Fossé: Mémoires*, Vol. I, p. 92.)

As our form was composed of those who were most ad-
vinced in studies we used to challenge one another as to
who could recite the largest number of lines of Virgil with-
25 out making a mistake. And it is true that De Villeneuve's
memory outdid us all. I remember hearing him recite whole
books of Virgil almost without making a mistake. However,
this practice stimulated us to do our best and to surpass or to
equal the others. We had, again, another kind of intellectual
30 game or rather a sort of mimic warfare in which each did
his utmost to outdo and triumph over his fellows, the weapon

being not the sword but the tongue. We used to form two sides and the cleverest on each side extemporised Latin verses with which they used to attack or defend. When this ceased to be a game and degenerated into a heated quarrel in which sharp words were used, the masters, who always 5 kept watch on what was going on, were obliged to calm us down and break up the two parties which had shown too much ardour.

Care of the Health, Dress, Games, and Good Manners were all carefully looked after in the Little Schools. The following extracts (xxv–xxix) illustrate these points.

XXV

(Coustel : Règles, etc. Vol. I, pp. 310–315.)

Although the body is but the servant of the soul that is no reason for neglecting it. S. Gregory the Great says : "It 10 is as dangerous to be too harsh and severe with the body as to be too lenient with it. To give it all that it asks is to strengthen the enemy within one's borders ; but, at the same time, to refuse it what it needs is to deprive a loyal citizen of his livelihood." We must therefore take reasonable care 15 of the body so that it may be able to assist the soul in its functions.

(1) Children must early be accustomed to eat anything which is good and nourishing ; they must not be pampered by always being allowed to choose what they like best. For 20 if the appetite is not curbed in early life it becomes the master and then it is very difficult to overcome.

(2) As far as possible, food should not be too varied. This is very prejudicial to health, and to a man in good health a highly-skilled cook is as dangerous as an unskilful 25 physician is to an invalid.

(3) We must accustom ourselves, as Clement of Alexandria says, to eat and drink sparingly and in moderation,

following the example of Jesus Christ when He was upon earth; for to eat even ordinary food with too much eagerness and pleasure is an offence against God.

(4) One may well take a certain pleasure in eating and 5 drinking, but this pleasure should not be the end and object of eating and drinking. Even the heathen were of this opinion. "Nature," says Seneca in one of his letters, " has given us pleasure in this, not that we should be content with the pleasure as if it were the object at which we ought to aim; 10 but that it might afford a relish to make more welcome to us the food without which it is impossible for us to live."

(5) In youth we must wisely lay up stores of health and strength so that some of this may last till old age; for possessions are of little avail to one who is infirm, just as a com-15 fortable bed is practically useless to a man who cannot sleep. A great soul in a feeble body is like a clever pilot in an unseaworthy vessel which he cannot save from shipwreck.

(6) Sleep must be strictly regulated; eight hours are not too much for small children. Since life itself is but a vigil 20 those who are somewhat older should be taught that time spent in the torpor of sleep is wasted.

(7) Pleasing manners and a free and open countenance set off the good qualities of the soul. We must not therefore neglect in our pupils those physical exercises which contri-25 bute to this. For not only do they make a youth strong but they will render him more dexterous and ready for whatever may chance. Dancing helps to make the body graceful; horse-exercise strengthens it; hunting, indulged in with moderation, inures it to the hardships of war of which hunting is a 30 miniature. It is again an advantage to be able to swim well; without it Cæsar would have been lost before Alexandria.

(8) With respect to dress, the age and position of the wearer and the fashion of the country in which he lives must all be carefully considered. A youth who dresses like an old 35 man or an ecclesiastic garbed like a soldier would rightly be

ridiculed. As we do not control the fashions we must per-
force comply with them and we should never make ourselves
conspicuous by affected peculiarities.

(9) If you are wearing your work-a-day clothes, see at
least that they are always clean. A horse is not esteemed 5
for its fine saddle nor a sword for its sheath; so also a man
is not esteemed for his fine clothes.

(10) If your position or noble birth makes it incumbent
upon you to wear fine clothes be careful lest they serve
more to show up your vices and defects than to win you 10
respect.

(11) Again, do not be too proud or vain of your clothes.
The rank that you claim, whatever it be, must in no wise
interfere with your profession as a Christian, which obliges
you to be humble. Moreover those who wish to make their 15
clothes a source of vanity and pride forget that these are
badges of the sin and shame of our first parents. Adam and
Eve were naked in their happy state of innocence; and it
was only after they had lost grace—the adornment of their
souls—that God covered their bodies with the skins of 20
animals. Such then were the first clothes. It is therefore
disgraceful to wish to make a show of something which is
the symbol of our parents' downfall.

xxvi

(Coustel: op. cit. Vol. II, pp. 114–119.)

After speaking of children's study it is proper to say something further about the games and recreations with which it 25
should always be interspersed, so that a little relaxation may
put them in a better humour and make them better disposed
towards work. Ausonius says on this topic that the word
school comes from a Greek word which means game, thus
showing that play and recreation are necessary for children. 30
As a matter of fact we see from experience that games renew

the vigour of the body and maintain that of the mind, whereas excessive application to work soon exhausts and destroys it. Games then are essential to children, just as rest is essential from time to time to soil if it is to continue fertile. Quintilian
5 brings forward yet another reason for the necessity of games in the training of children: they are extremely useful for revealing their intelligence, character, and tendencies.

Given then that games are necessary, we must now consider what characteristics children's games should have.
10 In the first place they must be seemly; they should also be in moderation, for indeed nothing is more harmful to children than the evil practice of letting them do nothing all day long except play and amuse themselves. Cicero lays down these two excellent principles: first, that God has not put us
15 into this world to spend our lives in continual amusement, but that we should employ our time in more earnest and serious pursuits; and secondly that we should use recreation only so far as is necessary for health, in the same way as we use sleep only when tired out after our day's work. In the
20 third place, children's games must be useful—*i.e.* suitable for relaxing the mind and strengthening the body by dissipating the bad humours which are engendered by too sedentary a life. This is a strong reason for forbidding children to play chess, dice, and cards. Mapheus also adds the reason that
25 games of this kind demand too much application and this is harmful to those who are already tired out by intellectual labour. The most suitable games for children are running, walking, tennis, ball-games, and the like. Nevertheless during winter, when one is compelled to some extent to lead a seden-
30 tary life, it is better for children to play at draughts, back-gammon, or billiards, than to stay in a torpid condition round the fire. Or again, they may be told tales of various kinds to make the time pass. We must also try to accustom our pupils, as far as possible, to play like gentlemen—*i.e.* never to cheat
35 or show excessive self-will and anxiety to win.

xxvii

(Du Fossé: Mémoires, Vol. I, pp. 171–174.)

We had among us a Provençal, named Gafareli, who was very good at drawing and understood fortification. De Ville- neuve and I had our heads full of military matters and we often in fancy formed projects and plans for the future. Our great longing was to be able one day to succeed in this pro- 5 fession. We therefore found in Gafareli a means of satisfying in some measure— at any rate by pretence —this great longing which possessed us. We induced him to trace out in the middle of our garden a fort flanked by four bastions with a *demi-lune* in front. We asked permission to do this from 10 M. de Beaupuis who gave it thinking this was quite harmless ; and we began the work in playtimes and on holidays with almost as much zeal as if we had to cope with some formid- able foe. We raised the rampart to the correct height and made the ditches quite properly. But one important thing 15 was lacking to complete our fortification ; this was turf where- with to cover it in default of stones. And since nothing is impossible to zeal and ambition, we took upon ourselves to bring this from a valley in the direction of Gentilly. Thus on holidays we went there to cut sods and each of us brought 20 back one or two under his cloak. It was an incredible labour and trouble ; but we never grew discouraged and we per- severed to the very end to finish completely the work which we had begun ; and it actually turned out to be so well made that one might have gone to look at it as though it had been 25 the real thing.

Then we appointed a governor, subordinate officers, and soldiers to keep guard, and at the same time a general was chosen for the enemy's side with his officers and men for the attack on our fort. As soon, then, as we left the dinner-table 30 to go to recreation, the governor of the fort used to betake

himself thither with his men and gave orders to prevent a
surprise and to offer a vigorous defence in case of attack.
Those of the other side drew themselves up to advance at
once to the assault. I, being by far the strongest of the whole
5 troop, was the first to lead the attack on this place and we
carried out this operation with such enthusiasm that the
game used sometimes to degenerate into a real fight in which
the assailants were knocked down into the ditch or the defenders, finding themselves overpowered, were driven igno-
10 miniously from their position. But when it was at last seen that
a certain amount of bitterness and resentment was involved
in battles of this kind, in which some of the combatants had
even been hurt, we were commanded to make peace. One of
the articles of the treaty was that, since the fort would be a
15 perpetual source of dispute between the two parties and a
cause of fresh quarrels, it should forthwith be dismantled in
order to establish a stable and lasting peace amongst us all.
We were somewhat downcast at this; but since the ambas-
sadors who conducted the negotiations were our masters
20 rather than our agents, we had to make a virtue of necessity.
And since children pass cheerfully from one extreme to the
other we finally pulled down the fort with almost as much
pleasure as that with which we had built it.

Again, once a year we used to have an entertainment
25 which greatly humoured the warlike fancies with which we
were inspired. On Twelfth Night M. de Beaupuis, who was
extremely kind, used as a rule to invite us to a party. As is
usual a cake was served, though the meal itself was on quite a
moderate scale. But after supper the boy, in whose slice the
30 bean had been found, was acknowledged king with due ceremony. A throne was erected and on it he took his seat; at
the same time he chose his officers, his chancellor, his con-
stable, and so on, according to the number of boys available.
Immediately afterwards faction used to arise in his kingdom;
35 and since his term of office was short—ending as it did with

the evening—we used to lose no time in forming powerful
leagues against this newly-crowned sovereign; and before he
could strengthen his hold on his realm, a formidable attack
was launched against him; so that he almost always found
himself dethroned by the time for evening prayers.   5

xxviii

(Coustel: Règles, etc. Vol. I, pp. 357–367.)

How children ought to behave in conversation.

(1) Be always more ready to listen to what others say than
to speak yourself. Indeed, as S. Gregory well says, it is not
by talking much that one learns to speak well. The advantage
to be drawn from silence is that those who can keep it are 10
esteemed—in the eyes of the world at any rate—as very wise,
however ignorant and stupid they may be.

(2) There are times when it is proper to say nothing;
there are others when something should be said; but there
are none when one should say all that one knows.   15

(3) Be very reserved when you find yourself in a company
where there are persons of rank, men of learning, and old men
to whom age has brought much experience.

(4) When you take upon yourself to speak be careful of
three things: of what you speak; to whom you have to speak; 20
how you should speak.

(5) Do not open your mouth until you have properly
thought out and arranged in your mind that which you have
to say, for fear lest your thoughts should appear like those
premature births which have not had sufficient time to be 25
perfectly formed; for when one has difficulty in expressing
oneself, this is usually due to the fact that one has not properly
thought out what one has to say. A man always expresses
himself well when he has properly arranged in his mind all
that he wants to say.   30

(6) When you speak do so neither too slowly nor too quickly; but speak always with the modesty and self-possession of a person who has complete control of himself. You will do far better to restrain yourself—with some violence if
5 necessary—from giving vent to an unkind witticism, than to give your enemies a chance to take advantage of you and to abuse you for having allowed imprudent and inconsiderate words to escape you.

(7) When you address persons for whom you should show
10 great respect, always speak to them *quietly*—without either raising or lowering the voice too much; *intelligently*—so that they may have no difficulty in understanding all that you have to say; *exactly*—without saying anything beyond what they want to know from you; and, finally, always address
15 them *politely*, using the terms "Sir" and "Madam."

(8) Never forestall them when they wish to speak to you and never interrupt them when they are talking to you.

(9) Never take upon yourself to speak of things which are beyond your capacity and do not speak even of things
20 which you think you know best except with great moderation and restraint.

(10) If you wish to pass for a clever man work hard to become so in reality; for time which reveals all things will at last make you appear such as you really are, and there
25 might possibly chance to be someone in the company who would show up your ignorance to your own confusion.

(11) If there occurs an opportunity to relate some story plunge into it at once without stopping to make a tedious introduction; and in telling the tale always use expressions
30 which are well-chosen, natural, and pleasing.

(12) Never mention your own rank or possessions; for if your companions are of vulgar origin you reproach them with their low birth; and if they àre nobles like yourself you give the impression that you wish to dispute the fact with
35 them.

(13) Always try to find an excuse for one of whom evil is spoken and if you cannot excuse the deed for which he is blamed at any rate excuse his intention by saying that he was taken off his guard and that he did not exercise enough forethought. But if you are unable to excuse his intention, 5 attribute his acts to human weakness and the violence of the temptation which might well have overcome others had they been placed in the same situation as he was.

(14) If anyone says anything in bad taste, either pretend that you have not heard it or show by your coolness and 10 silence that you choose to take no part in it.

(15) When one is in society one should neither keep complete silence nor talk continually. The former would be a mark of stupidity or disdain ; the latter of excessive pride and self-conceit. It is right that everyone should contribute 15 to the refreshment of the mind as well as to that of the body.

(16) One's conversation should always be adapted to the place and society in which one moves. Thus it is bad form to play the moralist in the company of ladies or the preacher with people whose only object is pleasure. Again one should 20 never raise points of theology at table or problems which are difficult to solve, but only things upon which everyone can express an opinion without taxing his mind too much.

(17) One should never do violence to the modesty of those to whom one speaks; and to lavish upon them excessive 25 praise, which sometimes they do not deserve, merely entitles one to the name of flatterer.

(18) One must never lie; at the same time it is not necessary to tell every sort of truth—some because they might harm us ; others because they might offend our neighbour. 30

(19) Liveliness contributes greatly to the pleasures of society ; but it ought not to be continual.

(20) If one has put forward an exaggerated or mischievous opinion it is advisable—nay even praiseworthy—to retract it ; on the other hand it would be dishonourable to 35

B   9

alter one's views if they are sincere and accord with the truth. It is but fitting—as S. Augustine says—that persons of enlightenment and judgment, if they have spoken unadvisedly, should repent of it; and as a rule a man gets greater credit
5 if he criticises an opinion of his own which he has put forward unadvisedly than if he had never expressed it or had condemned someone else for expressing it.

(21) Finally, remember that, having the honour to be a Christian, you should always act in a manner becoming to
10 a child of God, and above all you should always acknowledge the truth as soon as you recognise it and not stubbornly oppose it....

We must clearly distinguish innocent joking from that which is utterly detestable; for there is a kind of joking
15 which is not only allowable but which even, as it were, seasons conversation; this is why those who excel in it are everywhere popular. I define a joke as a clever remark which is to the point and causes amusement. To fulfil these conditions it must be :—

20 (1) Refined and subtle; for otherwise the joke and the joker are ridiculed.

(2) The subject of the joke must not be something serious or culpable; for where there is no subject for laughter there is no subject for joking.

25 (3) Marked physical or intellectual deformities should never be made the occasion for joking. Man did not make himself; God made him such as he is, and it is at Him therefore that such jokes are directed.

(4) Joking should be discreet; thus jokes must never be
30 made at the expense of powerful personages. As Quintilian says, we should never attack anyone whom it would be dangerous to offend.

(5) We should never joke about the unhappy for they are worthy of pity. Joking at the expense of the unfortunate
35 is cruel.

(6) In conclusion, joking must be used in moderation; for in excess it is always reprehensible and there is no pleasure in driving people to the end of their patience.

xxix

(Coustel: op. cit. Vol. I, pp. 343–349.)

How children ought to sit and behave at table.

Children should always hold themselves straight without moving their arms and legs and without, if possible, incon- 5 veniencing those who sit beside them. It is very ill-mannered to be continually looking at the dishes and devouring with one's eyes all the food which is being served. One should not be the first to put a hand into the dish nor show impatience before one is served or too much greediness and hurry in 10 eating after one has been served. Take quietly on your plate whatever is given you, bowing your head slightly in order to thank him who serves you, without taking off your hat except to salute persons who are greatly your superiors and for whom you are obliged to show a very special respect. You should 15 never refuse what is offered; for that would imply either finding fault silently because the choice was not good, or else showing that it was not to your taste. It is advisable to grow accustomed early to carving meat properly and to offering it with a good grace—and even to learn which is the best part 20 of a capon, a partridge, a wild duck, etc. If you may take the liberty of putting your hand into the plate, stop at what is in front of you without searching about to the right and left for what may seem a better piece. If there is some good piece, never take it for yourself but offer it to those who 25 have invited you or who are the most important members of the company. Keep your eyes fixed on your plate without letting them wander continually over those of other people

to see what they are eating. Take what is served to you with
a fork and not with your fingers. Do not put too large pieces
into your mouth and do not puff out your cheeks while eating
as if you wanted to blow the fire. Do not break your bread
5 with your fingers but always use a knife for cutting it. Chew
the food which you have in your mouth quietly; this contributes greatly to health because the second digestion does
not correct the faults of the first. Never dip in the dish a
piece that you have already carried to your mouth. Avoid
10 diversity of food as far as possible, for nothing ruins the
digestion more or is so prejudicial to health. Never begin
your meal by drinking; this is too suggestive of the drunkard
who drinks more by habit than of necessity. Also do not be
the first to drink. Wipe your mouth thoroughly and before
15 drinking swallow completely what you have in your mouth.
Always dilute your wine. When it is neat it acts on the body
as oil does on fire, for it enflames it the more, instead of
moderating and diminishing the heat which consumes it. If
anyone does you the honour of drinking your health, thank
20 him humbly. Do not take a pride in drinking to excess. A
barrel has a much greater capacity than the largest stomach.
The custom of forcing other people to drink healths, which
have been proposed, to the detriment of their own is neither
honourable nor praiseworthy. One must be gluttonous and
25 ill-mannered to act in such a way. Equals do not offer each
other anything; to take upon oneself to do this is to take
the lead and act as a superior. It is a mark of excessive
daintiness to complain that the food is ill-prepared or not to
one's taste. If the company stay too long at table, you can
30 withdraw quietly after saluting them politely and courteously.

A record of how the Little Schools were organised is preserved
for us in the two following passages. The first (xxx) is a general
account of the various school groups in the neighbourhood of
Port-Royal des Champs (see Introd. p. 24); it is the work of

Georges Walon, the youngest brother of Walon de Beaupuis, and a former pupil of the Little Schools. The other extract (xxxi) gives a more detailed description of the way in which the group at Le Chesnai in particular was organised.

XXX

(Fontaine: Mém. sur MM. de P.-R. pp. 118–123; also in *Suppl. au Nécr.* pp. 59–60.)

These schools were all organised in the same manner. There was a master in each room with five or six children. The beds were so arranged that the master could see them all from his own. Each had his separate table, and the pupils also were disposed so that the master could see them all, but 5 they could not talk to one another. Each had his drawer, his desk, and the necessary books, so that they were never obliged to borrow anything from their companions. The number of boarders was never large, because a master was never put in charge of more pupils than the number of beds 10 which his dormitory could contain.

They rose at 5.30 and dressed themselves. Those who were too small were assisted by a servant. Prayers were said in common in the dormitory and then each boy looked over his lesson which was from the prose for the morning. About 15 7.0 each said it over to the master, one after the other. Then they had breakfast and in winter warmed themselves. After breakfast they sat down again at their tables and each boy did his translation which they were bidden to write out neatly. When they had finished, they read out their work to the 20 master, one after the other. If there was any time left, they had explained to them the continuation of their author which they had not yet prepared. At 11.0 they went to the refectory and one of them who had been confirmed recited a text from the New Testament in Latin. The boys from one dormitory 25 all sat at the same table with their master who was careful

to help them to the food and even to the drink. During the meal there was a reading. Whenever they left the refectory they always went into the garden for recreation unless it was night-time or the weather was bad. Since the garden was
5 very large and full of thickets and glades, they were forbidden to go without permission outside a space which had been marked out. The masters took their exercise in the same place without ever losing sight of their pupils.

At 1.0 they all went into the big schoolroom until 2.0.
10 There they learnt geography and history on alternate days. At 2.0 they went back to their rooms to learn poetry which they repeated to the master at 4.0; after which they had *goûter*. They then learnt Greek in the same way as the other lessons and repeated it. About 6.0 they had supper at which
15 everything was done as at dinner. The recreation which followed this meal lasted till 8.0, when the boys went back to their rooms to look over their work for the next day. At 8.30 prayers were said and in this all the pupils from the various rooms, the solitaries, and the servants alike took part. When
20 this was over each returned to his room in order to retire. The master in charge of each room was present; thus he was the last to go to bed and the first to get up.

On Sundays at about 8.0 the Superior used to catechise and give instruction. Then they went to parishional High
25 Mass. On returning, if any time remained it was employed in reading devotional books. After dinner which took place at the usual time they went to recreation and this lasted till 2.0, when they went back to their rooms and read some book either aloud or privately. Then they went to parishional
30 Vespers. Their only free time was in the afternoon and this was spent in playing in the garden or sometimes in going for walks to houses in the neighbourhood. ...

They were all dressed in the same manner so that there might be no jealousy among them if some had been more
35 neatly dressed than the others.

xxxi

(Suppl. au Nécr. pp. 54–58.)

Daily Time-table for the Children of the School at Le Chesnai.

Rising. The elder boys always rise at 5.0, winter and summer alike, and the younger at 6.0. As they all sleep in the same room each master has no difficulty in waking his own boys. They rise at once, for it is very dangerous to get accustomed to laziness at the first hour of the day. As soon 5 as they have risen they kneel humbly and worship God. After this they finish dressing and comb each other's hair in perfect silence; for it is very right that their first words should be prayers and thanksgivings to God for having kept them safe during the night. If however anyone has need to 10 leave the room he should ask permission in a low voice.

Morning Prayers. At 6.0 they all go and kneel before the crucifix which is in their room and the usual prayers consisting of the *Veni Creator,* the *Pater,* the *Ave,* and the *Credo,* are recited. Then follows Prime for the elder boys 15 who all remain standing while this prayer is said. After it is finished everyone returns to his table, there to study his lesson and to write his composition; and they stay till 7.0 in perfect silence. At 7.0 lessons are repeated and this lasts till breakfast.   20

Breakfast. They breakfast about 8.0. During this time which lasts a good half-hour they are free to converse together aloud on any subject they please, or to read some history book, to look at maps, etc. However, they do not go out of the room. In winter time they keep close to 25 the fire. After breakfast each goes back to his table in silence to work at his second lesson until 10.0. This in the case of the elder boys consists in saying by heart their Greek lesson which they translate into French, or perhaps in reading their Latin composition. The Greek lesson was 30

usually three large *folio* pages of Plutarch in the morning, and as much again after dinner. For the younger boys the second lesson consists in translating Livy, Justin, Severus Sulpitius, etc. This lesson lasts till 11.0, the hour for
5 dinner.

Holy Mass. They do not attend Mass every day, especially in the case of the small boys, until they are sufficiently advanced for this. For great care is taken that they may always be very well-behaved in church and never turn their
10 heads from side to side. As a rule two are sent to make the responses and they take turns to do this. Since on this occasion they do the office of the angels, they are exhorted to behave with the utmost reverence and to assist at this unbloody sacrifice of Jesus Christ in remembrance of that which
15 He offered to His Father for our sins on the hill of Calvary. If the elder boys commit any fault in church they are reprimanded with the greater severity because, being the most advanced in age, they ought also to be the most sensible and to edify the others by their example.

20 *Prayers before Dinner.* At 11.0 they all assemble in one of the rooms where the examination of conscience is made after the repetition of the *Confiteor* as far as *meâ culpâ*. When the examination is over the rest of the prayer is finished. One of the elder boys repeats by heart a Latin sentence taken
25 from the *Book of Proverbs*. Then they go down to wash their hands and enter the refectory.

Dinner. The boys sit beside and in front of their own particular master, who helps them to what has been served after they have finished their soup, each from his own bowl.
30 We try to accustom them not to cultivate an inconvenient daintiness and always to eat carefully. During dinner all kinds of histories are read—*e.g.* that of the Jews by Josephus; that of the Church by Godeau; that of France; Roman history, and such like. We have found nothing so useful; and
35 it is remarkable how children who are busy eating lose hardly

anything of what is said. On festivals and Sundays certain devotional books are read—as, for example, some of the fine translations which have been made, the *Christian Instructions*, the *Confessions* of S. Augustine, and such like.

Recreation after Dinner. There is always one of the 5 masters who never loses sight of the children, but his presence does not trouble them at all because he allows them perfect freedom to play at any games they like to choose. This is always done with moderation and good breeding and as the enclosure in which they used to remain was very large they 10 were allowed to walk where they pleased. In summer during the heat of the day, as a rule they used to walk in the shady paths in the woods. In winter they used to practise running or betake themselves to a large room ; and since there was a fine billiard table some, after warming themselves, used to 15 stay at it, while others preferred to play at backgammon, draughts, chess, or cards. These cards composed a game which comprised the history of the first six centuries—*i.e.* the time and place at which the chief Councils were held, or at which the Popes, Emperors, chief Saints and profane authors 20 lived, or at which the most memorable events in the world occurred. By virtue of playing this little game most of them had all these events, and the details as to the different times and places at which celebrated men had lived, so firmly impressed upon their minds that no doctor could speak more 25 to the point on these subjects. M. de Sainte-Beuve, after putting them to the test, often used to wonder how these boys, most of whom had not yet reached the age of 16 or 17, had acquired so wide and vast a knowledge of all things, of all countries of the world and all periods of time, that they were 30 able to converse pleasantly with all kinds of people, to take knowledge of all kinds of affairs, and even to explain them. Disputes and disagreements were never heard among them whatever might be the matter. They had been so accustomed to show courteous consideration one for another that they 35

never used the forms *thou* and *thee*, and moreover they were never heard to say the slightest word which they might have thought would appear displeasing to any of their companions. Recreation usually lasted a good hour and a half.
5 On holidays they left the enclosure and went towards Marli, Versailles, and St Cyr (the building of Versailles had not yet been begun). During these walks the children used to converse familiarly and cheerfully with the master on all kinds of subjects, and this developed their minds remarkably.
10 After recreation they alternately repeated the history that they had read or talked about geography. As children have good memories, they used to notice the smallest events in history, so that when the elder boys began to give their account, the younger ones always joined in and said something
15 besides. Thus they grew accustomed to express themselves in good language and to pass a sound judgment on the facts mentioned in the history which had been read. In short, by making them spend their youth in exercises of this kind we used to endeavour to put them in a position to be able to
20 serve God and their fellow-men when they were grown up.

The Return to the Schoolroom after Dinner. On entering they repeated a short prayer to ask God for grace to pass the rest of the day devoutly, and to accustom them to do nothing without beginning and ending with a prayer. When
25 each had taken his place at his table they began their work. Some wrote their copy which was always some sentence taken from Holy Scripture. Others wrote out their commentary on Virgil. Others again looked over their lessons or read some good book. This lasted until *goûter*, which was
30 served regularly at 3.0. It lasted a good half-hour, during which they were again free to converse together, as during breakfast. This meal was considered to be necessary for the younger boys on account of their greater natural energy. The others were excused from it, if they wished. At 3.30
35 they all took their places again at their tables to prepare

the lessons which they had to repeat from 4.0 to 6.0, when they had supper. The recreation was the same as after dinner. In summer the opportunity was often taken of conversing during this time with the elder boys on some point of history or on other useful topics, while the younger ones 5 were amusing themselves with their games. This recreation lasted till 8.0. Then they returned and spent a good half-hour in the schoolroom in looking over what they had to do for the next morning.

Evening Prayers. Evening prayers were said at 8.30. 10 They repeated the *Pater, Ave, Credo,* and *Confiteor* in Latin, the Litanies of the Virgin, *Sub Tuum Præsidium,* etc. After making an examination of conscience each went back to his room in perfect silence.

Going to Bed. After saying his prayers each undressed 15 and got into bed quickly and silently. Thus they were all in bed by 9.0. Since all the exercises of the day were in this way completely regulated and varied, the children had no time to become wearied; and the greatest punishment that could be administered to those who at times showed a 20 somewhat disagreeable disposition was to threaten to send them home, as I have already said.

Rules for Sundays and Festivals. As usual they rose at 5.0. When they were dressed Prime was said. After this they occupied themselves in reading devotional books pri- 25 vately until they all assembled to go to catechism which lasted until the bell rang for Mass. They were always made to learn by heart two or three paragraphs of M. de Saint-Cyran's catechism which is considered to be one of the best books of its kind which have been written. We used always to 30 begin by making the younger boys repeat what had been said the previous time, so as to impress it well on their memory. They always had to hear parishional High Mass; for children of good birth should early be accustomed to submit to the rules which have been laid down by the Church and which 35 have been followed during a long succession of centuries. For one does not sanctify the Sunday by thinking merely of amusements and feasting and paying calls, after first hearing a Low Mass as quickly as possible.

5   It would be necessary here to add the way in which they were taught their lessons and the good and pious maxims with which we tried to inspire them. But since this has already been done to some extent in the *Rules for the good Education of Children*, published by Michallet, it seems un-
10 necessary to repeat them.

III

Reading, Spelling, and Writing (extracts i–vii)

i

(Arnauld and Lancelot: Grammaire générale et raisonée, 1660, pp. 18–23.)

It has already been said that human beings have chosen to express their thoughts by means of sounds and that they have also invented certain signs to express these sounds. But although these signs or characters in the first instance merely symbolise the sounds, we are none the less accustomed 5 to transfer our thoughts from the characters to the things themselves which they symbolise. As a result, the characters can be regarded in two ways—either as merely standing for the sounds or as helping us to grasp the idea for which the sound stands. 10

Regarding them from the first standpoint, we should have to satisfy four requirements to produce a perfect system of spelling. (1) Each sign should denote a given sound—*i.e.* nothing should be written which is not pronounced; (2) each sound should be denoted by a sign—*i.e.* nothing should be 15 pronounced which is not written; (3) every sign, whether simple or double, should denote one sound only; for it is possible to have double letters in a perfect system of spelling, since they simplify it and so render it easier; (4) one and the same sound should never be denoted by different signs. 20

But regarding the characters from the second standpoint (*i.e.* as helping us to grasp the idea for which the sound stands), we sometimes find it advantageous to waive these

rules occasionally—at any rate the first and the last. For
it often happens—particularly in the case of languages which
are derived from other languages—that there are certain
letters which are not pronounced and which therefore are use-
5 less so far as the sounds are concerned, though the sounds
are not sufficient to tell us what the words mean. For example in the words *champs* and *chants*, the *p* and the *t* are
not pronounced, but they are none the less useful to show
the meaning; for we learn from them that the first word
10 comes from the Latin *campi* and the second from the Latin
cantus. From this it can be seen that those who complain
so much because spelling and pronunciation do not always
agree, are not always in the right, and that which they regard
as an abuse is sometimes not without value.

15 The difference between the capital and small letters also
seems an infringement of the fourth rule which is to the
effect that one and the same sound should always be denoted
by the same sign. This difference would indeed be quite
useless if we were to think that the only function of the
20 characters is to mark the sounds; for each capital and its
corresponding small letter alike stand for the same sound.
This is why the ancients did not have this difference—as is
still the case with Hebrew—and many believe that for a long
time the Greeks and Romans used capital letters only.
25 Nevertheless this distinction is of great value for beginning
sentences and for distinguishing proper nouns from the
others.

Again, there are in one and the same language different
kinds of writing—as for example the Roman and Italic type
30 used in printing Latin and various vernacular languages;
and these are of service for bringing out the sense by emphasising certain words or phrases, although thereby the
pronunciation is not at all affected.

These then are the reasons which can be put forward to
35 account for differences which exist between pronunciation

and spelling; but this does not do away with the fact that there are many other differences which are unreasonable and are due entirely to the corruption of language. For example, it is an abuse to pronounce *c* before *e* and *i* like *s*; not to pronounce *g* before these same two vowels in the same way 5 as it is pronounced before other vowels; to soften the *s* between two vowels; and to give to *t* also the sound of *s* before *i* followed by another vowel; *e.g. gratia, actio, action.*

Some people have imagined that they would be able to correct this fault in the vernacular languages (as Ramus has 10 done in his Grammar of the French language), by cutting out all those letters which are not pronounced and by expressing each sound by the letter which best renders its pronunciation—as for example, by putting *s* instead of *c* before *e* and *i*. But they should reflect that, in addition to the fact 15 that this would often be a disadvantage in vernacular languages for the reasons that we have given, they would be attempting an impossible task; for we must not imagine that it would be easy to make a whole nation change the characters to which it had long been accustomed, since the emperor 20 Claudius did not succeed even in introducing one letter which he wanted to make current.

The most reasonable course that could be taken would be to cut out letters which serve no purpose either as regards pronunciation or sense or derivation (this reform has already 25 been begun); and while retaining those letters which are useful, to distinguish them by small marks to show that they are not pronounced or to distinguish the various pronunciations of one and the same letter. A dot in or underneath could serve in the first case—*e.g. temps.* The *c* already has 30 its cedilla which might just as well be employed before *e* and *i* as before the other vowels. *g* with its tail not quite closed could denote the sound which this letter has before *e* and *i*. These cases are given merely as examples.

ii

(*Jacqueline Pascal: Letter to her brother, Blaise Pascal.* Reprinted in Victor Cousin's *Jacqueline Pascal,* 5th edit. 1862, p. 265.)

October 26th 1655.   Port-Royal des Champs.

......Our mothers have asked me to write to you to send me all the details of your method of teaching reading by *be,* *ce, de,* etc., in which it is unnecessary that children should
5 know the names of the letters. I can see quite well how to teach them *Jesu,* for example, by making them pronounce *Je, e, ze, u;* but I cannot see how to make them understand easily that final letters ought not to add an *e.* For naturally, if they follow this system, they will say *Jesusĕ,* unless they
10 are taught that the final *e* is not pronounced unless it really has that value. But I do not see how to teach them to pronounce the consonants which follow the vowels—for example, *en;* for they will say *e, ne,* instead of making one sound *en,* as the French language often requires. Similarly for *on,* they
15 will say *o, ne;* and even if we make them drop the *e* they will not pronounce the nasal sound properly if the pronunciation of *o* and of *n* is taught to them separately.......

No letter in reply to this from Pascal is extant, but the methods which he invented and which were applied at Port-Royal are explained in the two following extracts (iii and iv) :—

iii

(*Arnauld and Lancelot: Gram. gén.* pp. 23–25.)

A new method of teaching how to read easily in all kinds of languages.

This method chiefly concerns those who do not yet know how to read. Beginners certainly find it easy enough merely
20 to recognise the letters; the greatest difficulty is to know how

to put them together correctly. Now what renders this process still more difficult, as things are at present, is that although each letter has its own particular name, it is not pronounced in the same way when it stands alone as it is when combined with other letters. For example, if you make a child put 5 together *f*, *r*, *y*, we make him pronounce *eff*, *ar*, *wy*; which does not fail to confuse him when he proceeds to join these three sounds together to produce the sound of the syllable *fry*. The most natural method then—as certain men of in-tellect have already pointed out—would be for teachers of 10 reading to make children learn to recognise their letters at first only by their value in pronunciation. In teaching them to read Latin, for example, the same value *e* would be given alike to *e* by itself, to *æ*, and to *œ*, because they are all pronounced alike. The same with *i* and *y* and again with *o* 15 and *au* according to their pronunciation in French, for the Italians make *au* a diphthong.

Children again should be taught to name the consonants only by their natural sounds, merely adding to them a mute *e* which is necessary in order to pronounce them. For example, 20 the name which they should be taught to give to *b* would be that pronounced in the last syllable of *tombe*; to *d*, the last syllable of *ronde*; and similarly with the others which have only one value. As for those which have several (*e.g. c, g, t, s*), they should be named from their most natural and ordinary 25 sound; with *c* this sound is *ke*; with *g, gue*; with *t*, the last syllable of *forte*, and with *s*, the last syllable of *bourse*. After this children should be taught to pronounce separately, with-out spelling them, the syllables *ce, ci, ge, gi, tia, tie, tii*; and they should be made to realise that *s* between two vowels is 30 pronounced like *z*; *e.g. miseria, misère*, which are pronounced *mizeria, mizère*.

These then are the most general remarks on this new method of teaching reading which would certainly be very profitable for children. But to develop it satisfactorily, it 35 would be necessary to write a separate small treatise in which instructions would be given for adopting this scheme to all languages.

iv

(*Guyot: Billets de Cicéron, etc.* Preface—no pagination.)

Another fault in the usual method of teaching children
5 to read is that they are shown the letters separately, the consonants as well as the vowels. Now the consonants are called consonants only because they have no sound of themselves but must be joined to vowels and sounded with them. It is self-contradictory therefore to teach the pronunciation of
10 isolated letters which can be pronounced only when they are joined to other letters. For in pronouncing consonants separately and making children name them we always add a vowel—namely *e*—which belongs neither to the syllable nor to the word. The result is that the sound of the letters
15 when named is quite different from their sound when they are joined together. Thus, when a child has correctly named, one after another, all the letters in a word, he is still unable to pronounce them altogether in the same word, because the medley of different sounds is bewildering to his ears and to
20 his imagination. For example, a child is asked to spell the word *bon*, which consists of three letters, *b*, *o*, *n*, and he is made to say them one after the other. *B* by itself he pronounces *be*; *o* alone still makes *o*, because it is a vowel; but *n* alone makes *enne*. How then will the child understand that
25 the sounds which he has to pronounce separately in spelling these three letters one after the other, make only a single sound *bon*? It is something which he can never understand and he learns to take the letters together only because his master himself does so and shouts in his ears over and over
30 again this single sound *bon*.

Again, this unfortunate child is made to spell this further word *jamais* and it is done thus: *j, a, m, a, i, s,* equals *jamais.* Will the child ever imagine that these six sounds which he has been made to pronounce in spelling the six letters make only these two *ja-mais*? For when the letters of this word 5 are spelt they are pronounced separately *je, a, em, a, i, esse.* Here are six or seven sounds out of which the child is told that he ought to form these two *ja-mais.* Would it not be quicker to make the child pronounce only these two syllables *ja-mais,* and not all the consonants and vowels separately? 10 The only result of the latter method is to confuse his mind by this multitude of different sounds out of which he will never make the desired combination, unless you do it yourself and pronounce it for him several times. The same thing may be said of innumerable other and more difficult words; 15 *e.g. aimaient, faisaient, disaient,* etc.

Once more, though you may make a child spell his letters as often as you will, yet you will never teach him by this method how to pronounce syllables and words. He can be made to learn them only by habit and custom from having 20 a given combination of letters shown to him and hearing it pronounced many times with the same sound. But this is because we wish always to be logical with children and to show by rules something that depends entirely upon custom— for custom is the only rule of language. And if the reader 25 will pay attention to what I am saying, he will see that the syllables and entire words are pronounced to children so often that at last they memorise them and remember that to such and such letters in combination such and such a pro- nunciation is given—and one which otherwise they would 30 never have imagined if they spelt the letters one after the other. Consequently it is absolutely useless to make them waste so much time and trouble by this method of spelling when they might have learnt the combinations of letters much more quickly than this multitude of sounds out of which they 35 are desired to make one or two syllables. Thus the ability to read, which children at last acquire, is quite unjustifiably attributed to this method of naming the letters; whereas it is merely the result of their being accustomed to hear syllables 5 and whole words pronounced over and over again; in the same way the rules of Despauter are thought to be the cause of the correctness with which a child does his Latin prose; whereas in composing it he has never thought of them, but has merely followed so much of the Latin usage as he has 10 learnt by reading, writing, and making many mistakes which have been corrected.

First, then, it will be well to show and pronounce to children the five vowels *a, e, i, o, u* and the diphthongs *æ, œ, au, eu, ei*; next, make them look merely at the shapes of 15 the consonants without having them pronounced except in combination as entire syllables, of which a table must be drawn up for the children to learn. This done, they may read entire words isolated one from another; and of these a list should he made containing only those which are com- 20 monest, which they hear spoken most often, and the meaning of which they know. And since they are taught to pray to God from the age of four or five (I assume that they do so in French), we must begin, with the help of their prayers and their catechism which they already know by heart, to 25 teach them to read some continuous narrative, and then break off the thread of it in order to see if they are reading from a knowledge of the letters or if it is merely from memory or by rote. And thus, when they are able to read any part of their prayers or their catechism which may be set to them, 30 we may begin at once to give them books in French.

It was pointed out in the Introduction (pp. 4 and 5) that it was customary in the seventeenth century to use Latin books when giving quite young children their first lessons in reading. As is seen in extracts v and vi, the Port-Royalists unreservedly condemned this practice.

V

(*Coustel: Règles, etc.* Vol. II, pp. 20–23.)

[When children are in the early stages of learning to read]
they must be made to take their time until they arrive at the
point when age and experience have given them the power
to read more quickly and without making mistakes. In
thinking to bring our pupils on we often set them back by 5
hurrying them too much. For when they stumble over every
word they get into the habit of repeating them in a manner
which grates upon the ear and is altogether hateful. They
should be made to pronounce each word clearly and in an
intelligible tone of voice, without stammering and without 10
speaking either at the back of the throat or between the
teeth; for these and similar small faults, if at first neglected,
afterwards become incorrigible. To make their reading pleasant they must be accustomed to observe the stops and
pauses which the sense requires, and to avoid monotony as 15
far as possible; they must likewise be accustomed to show,
by raising or lowering the voice, that they understand the
sense of what they read—especially when this is verse in
which the rhythm should always be marked.

In passing I cannot refrain from quoting a method which 20
I have seen employed by a country schoolmistress for
teaching reading in a very short time to the 30 or 40 little
girls under her care. She first divided them into three groups,
according as they were more or less advanced. Then she
made them read, one after the other, all having in their hands 25
copies of the same book; and while one was reading aloud
five or six lines the other ten or twelve were reading the same
passage and thus profited by what was said to the first. After
this the mistress made another read a similar amount; and
in this way, since each child read in turn, the groups succeeded 30
in reading 60 or 80 lines instead of the 10 or 12 which each
child by herself would have been able to read for an ordinary

lesson. Next, the mistress did the same for the less advanced pupils; and experience proved that in less than three months little girls of six used to learn to read perfectly.

It is better, in teaching children to read, to use French
5 books rather than Latin ones; for since they know their mother tongue they will understand with very much less difficulty what they read in this language than in another of which they have not as yet any idea. In fact it is a general rule that, as far as possible, everything should be made easy
10 for children. We should always proceed from the easy to the difficult, from the known to the unknown.

vi

(*Guyot: Billets de Cicéron, etc.* Preface—no pagination.)

It is a great mistake to begin—as is usually done—by showing children how to read in Latin and not in French. This process is so long and so painful that it not only sets
15 the pupils against all other instruction by inspiring their minds from their tenderest years with an almost invincible disgust and hatred for books and study; but it also makes the masters impatient and ill-tempered because both they and their pupils alike are wearied with the trouble and time (as much as three
20 or four years) which are wasted.........

Is it reasonable then to expect children to learn to read in a short time and with pleasure—or at any rate without excessive trouble—when we begin to make them read in Latin, which is a language of which they know absolutely nothing
25 and which they never hear spoken (for that would be of great service to them, at any rate as regards the pronunciation) except when they are being taught it? Is it not more natural to make use of what they already know in order to teach them what they do not know?· Now children already know French
30 of which they have learnt a very large number of words; why

not then teach them to read first of all in French, since this method would be shorter and less troublesome? They would merely have to remember the shape of the letters and their combinations or groups; and in this the recollection of the words which they already know, together with those which 5 they hear spoken continually in daily intercourse, would help them gradually to call these things to mind. Whereas in Latin they have nothing whatever to help them; everything is new and strange to them; they cannot interest themselves in the letters or groups of letters which are shown to them. As a 10 result, they can remember these only with extreme difficulty and after a long time, during which they have to repeat them hundreds of times before they can call them to mind once; for there is nothing to give them a cue—neither the words, nor the things themselves, nor what they hear spoken day by 15 day.

Since, then, we must make use of what our pupils know already in order to teach them what they do not know (this is an invariable rule which admits of no exceptions whatever in teaching), it would be advisable to teach them to read at 20 first only isolated words of which they know the meaning— *e.g.* familiar objects such as *bread, bed, room*, etc. But before doing so it would be necessary to show them first an alphabet containing the letters and characters which compose these words. But they must be made to pronounce the vowels and 25 diphthongs only—not the consonants, which they should not pronounce except in different combinations with these vowels and diphthongs, thus making syllables and words.

vii

(Coustel: Règles, etc. Vol. II, pp. 23–24.)

It is a good thing to teach children to write well. Nothing is more universally appreciated nor more necessary for people 30 of rank who often have occasion to communicate matters

which they cannot confide even to their dearest friends. For this reason children must be made to practise a fairly large handwriting and to form and finish off their letters properly, always keeping the right proportion and giving special at-
5 tention to everything which can contribute towards making their handwriting clear, legible, and elegant. To accomplish this, use may be made of transparents which afford a means of forming letters over those which are supplied as copies. And since we must skilfully turn to account whatever can
10 contribute to the real good of our pupils, we should always try to set them for their copies some text from Scripture or some fine moral maxim which they may be able to remember all their lives. This is again one of Quintilian's suggestions.

They should be made to notice, as they read, how the
15 words are spelt; this is called *orthography*. Quintilian would have us spell as we speak because spelling is the reflection of words and should always reproduce what we say. However, all are not agreed on this point.

viii

(*Guyot: Billets de Cicéron, etc.* Preface—no pagination.)

As regards writing, great care should be taken to teach
20 children to write well, because this is not only very useful but also is a good method of keeping them busy and preventing them from becoming wearied. For when they can write well they take pleasure in doing so, since we naturally like to do what we can do well and we even desire to excel
25 in it. The best teachers should be selected for this subject, if only they will take trouble and be careful that their pupils hold their pens upright; for that is very important. They must not at first be allowed to write by themselves but under the guidance of the teacher, until they have acquired the
30 proper manner of holding the pen. When they have done

this, they should often pass the dry pen over the lines of their copy, so that the muscles and nerves¹ and the whole hand may acquire the knack and movements which are requisite for good handwriting. I should also desire that they should not be set copies with no particular end in view, but 5 some beautiful lines of French or Latin verse which might help to regulate their minds and their manners. Without realising it they would learn many of these and this would be so much good seed, the fruit of which would appear in due season. It would be advisable for them to continue this 10 exercise for several years and not to let them write either their proses or their translations badly, for in addition to the rule that everything which we do should be, as far as possible, well done, they would soon unlearn what they have learnt with the expenditure of so much time and trouble.   15

The Port-Royalists not only reformed the teaching of reading and introduced methods which have been generally adopted only of recent years, but they were also far in advance of contemporary practice in laying great stress on a study of the vernacular language and literature. In the majority of the public schools of this country no attention was paid to these subjects as late as the middle of the nineteenth century. In the Report of the Public Schools Commission, issued in 1864, the following questions and answers occur:

3530. Q. "What measures do you now take to keep up English at Eton?"
A. "There are none at present, except through the ancient languages."
3532. Q. "You do not think it is satisfactory?"
A. "No, the English teaching is not satisfactory."
3533. Q. "You do not consider that English is taught at present?"
A. "No."

It would seem a fair inference that as regards one of the most important parts of the curriculum, the Port-Royal schools of the seventeenth century were more enlightened than one of the best-known of the English public schools two centuries later. The attitude of the Port-Royalists towards the study of their native language and literature is set forth in the following extract.

ix

(Coustel: Règles, etc. Vol. II, pp. 51–53.)

When children know the most important rules of syntax they are usually made to do Latin prose; this is commonly called "writing themes." This practice might well be censured did not long-established custom lend it such authority that
5 it would be difficult to change it. As a matter of fact, it would seem reasonable to follow the same method in the case of children as is usually adopted with adults, whose mind and judgment are already fully developed, when they are learning a foreign language—*e.g.* Italian, German, or Spanish. Now
10 it is never advisable to make them begin by writing compositions; they should be practised in explaining and translating the simplest authors which are put into their hands, until their minds are full of the finest phrases and best idioms which they find there. They will then be ready to
15 talk a little and to express their thoughts in this language which is foreign to them. It would seem reasonable then to follow the same course with regard to children and not to begin making them do Latin compositions until their memory has been stored with the most classical words and idioms
20 which they have seen and noticed over and over again in good authors. After this they would have no difficulty in modelling their proses on the beautiful style of the faultless originals. To act otherwise and to make children study Latin prose before they have had any practice of expressing them-
25 selves in Latin, does not this mean accustoming them to a jargon which is neither French nor Latin, and teaching them a pitiable gibberish which they will have the greatest difficulty in unlearning afterwards?

Moreover, considering the point of perfection which our language has at present reached, it surely deserves that we should cultivate it a little. As a matter of fact it has never been so rich in its expressions, so noble in its phraseology, so precise and so pregnant in its epithets, so subtle in its 5 turns and circumlocutions, so majestic in its motions, so striking in its metaphors, and in short so natural and withal so magnificent and lofty in its verse as it is at present. It would then be shameful for children to be barbarians in their own country and for them to talk French like Allobroges or 10 Allemanni, when all the nations are striving, one against the other, to learn all the beauties of this language and to perfect themselves in it.

At the same time Port-Royal never lost sight of the importance of a thorough study of the classics—and especially of Latin. This point is illustrated in detail in extracts x–xix.

X

(Domat: Les Lois Civiles dans leur ordre naturel,
1767, Vol. I, p. 118.)

Grammar is useful for learning languages, especially the ancient ones which are the original languages used by the 15 authors of the books in which the wisdom of the sciences and the arts alike is preserved. Among languages the most necessary are Latin and Greek which are the original languages of these authors. They have these advantages that Greek is the original language of the holy books and of all 20 the most ancient authors who have treated of the sciences—comprising under that term even the liberal arts; this means that the greater part of scientific words come from this language; while as to Latin, it is to-day the language of the Church and it has been that of the greater number of good 25 writers of every kind.

xi

(Coustel: Règles, etc. Vol. II, pp. 24–27.)

When children know how to read well and to write fairly
they must learn to decline all the kinds of nouns and to
conjugate all the kinds of verbs, keeping up this practice
until they are perfect in it.   Herein lie the first principles
5 and elements of the Latin language, for the chief constituents
of speech in any language are simply nouns and verbs. This
must not be neglected on the excuse that it is a trifling matter
compared with what must follow.   As Quintilian says, if
we neglect these small things, the great ones become im-
10 possible.

After this they must learn thoroughly the genders, the
principal parts, and the more important rules of syntax. As
soon as they know all their rules fairly they should be given
such books as are thought to be simplest—the *Fables* of
15 Phædrus, the *Captivi* of Plautus, the *Paradoxes* of Cicero,
and the three comedies of Terence.   These authors are
purest in the original and a word-for-word translation of them
is none the less elegant.   Phædrus is certainly a little hard
for beginners, but he is very interesting and amusing.   It
20 could be wished that someone had taken the trouble to edit
the *Colloquies* of Erasmus, for example, which Vives considers
very suitable for beginners.   But we must needs make use of
them in default of others, until something better is available.
When they commence to construe a little they may be given
25 as historians Æmilius Probus, Severus Sulpitius, or Justin.
They should not be disheartened or discouraged if a great
deal is beyond them, because they are not as yet capable
of appreciating the beauty and precision of these authors.

A second or even a third reading will complete what the first
30 has merely sketched out.

xii

(Coustel: op. cit. Vol. II, pp. 28–31.)

Every branch of knowledge has its rules and its method.
By *method* I mean an easy way or manner of learning
thoroughly and in a short time what one does not know.
This method is set forth in rules which should be, as far as
possible, short and clear—short, so as not to overburden 5
children's memories; and clear, since otherwise they will not
help them to understand what they do not know.

These postulates being granted it will not be difficult,
I think, for me to settle the question. Some people maintain
that we ought to employ the Latin rules of Despauter for 10
teaching our pupils the genders, the declensions, etc. They
give as their reason that because their ancestors learnt them
this ancient custom has the force of a law binding on their
consciences. As if in the education of children we should
have any other aims than how we can best help them to 15
progress in their studies! Now to my mind the use of
Despauter neither helps them nor facilitates the learning of
rules; for it is a difficult work, written in Latin and quite
unintelligible in many places. If one were learning Spanish,
Italian, or German, for example, it would be an unheard-of 20
thing to use rules written in Spanish, Italian, or German;
for this would argue that one both knew and did not know
these languages at one and the same time—an obvious con-
tradiction. For if, by means of these rules a man sets out to
learn a language, he apparently does not know it already; 25
and yet he must know it in order to understand the rules
which are couched in this language. If then this method
would never be used in the case of an adult whose mind and
judgment are mature, what course should we adopt with
children whose minds are as yet quite undeveloped and who 30
are often as little able to understand the rules of Despauter
in their present form as Hebrew or Syriac?

On this point it is well to remark that when these rules first came into vogue the Latin language was still in quite common use in France. In the registers of the Parliament of Paris it can be seen that all the public decrees were with-
5 out exception written in Latin down to the time of Francis I. Now Despauter, a native of Flanders, published his work in 1510—*i.e.* five years before Francis I came to the throne. But conditions have entirely changed since then; nowadays everything is done in French and Latin is only for the
10 learned.

Another criticism that must be made is that Despauter's book has been corrected in several new editions and has undergone numerous alterations. This being so, is it not sheer effrontery to tell us that no innovations should be made
15 in methods of instructing children? Besides, it is not wise to reject something because it is new, if otherwise it proves very useful. I should be quite willing, then, to follow the method of our ancestors; but since I have found an easier and more convenient one I shall adhere to it. Those who
20 have laboured in the past to make rules for us are not our masters to compel us to follow them; they are merely our guides and we are obliged to walk in their steps only so far as we find it advantageous to do so.

xiii

(*Nicole: Essais de Morale*, Vol. II, pp. 287–293.)

The necessity and difficulty of learning Latin have led
25 various people to devise means for helping children in this indispensable study. This has given rise to the many and various methods for teaching Latin, each inventor claiming that his own is the best. Other people have concluded, on the contrary, that the best method is to have none at all and
30 to spare one's pupils all the knotty points of grammar by

setting them straightway to reading books. Some think that Latin should be taught by using it as is done with vernacular languages, and to this end children should be compelled to speak nothing but Latin. Montaigne shows that this was the method adopted in his own case and by its means at 5 seven or eight years of age he spoke Latin faultlessly. The French, Dutch, Germans, and Italians have idolised a certain book called the *Gate of Languages* which comprises almost all the Latin words which are used in continuous and connected discourse; and they have imagined that by making 10 children learn this book first they would soon get to know the Latin language without the necessity of reading so many authors.

To put shortly the proper attitude which should be adopted with regard to these different methods of teaching 15 Latin, we may say that it would doubtless be a great advantage if we could teach this language by using it, as is done in the case of a vernacular language. But in practice this method is beset by so many difficulties that hitherto it has proved impossible—at any rate to the generality of mankind; 20 and this is the greatest drawback of all. For in the first place, teachers have to be found who can speak Latin fluently, and that to begin with is a rare accomplishment; and often those who have it are not for that reason the most suited to teach children, because they lack other qualities which are 25 immeasurably more important. It is necessary, moreover, that those with whom the children, who are to be taught in this manner, converse should talk to them only in Latin; and that is inconvenient and difficult to put into practice. There would even arise a danger that, by enforcing this rule 30 upon children who are being educated together and by obliging them never to speak to one another except in Latin when they know practically nothing of the language, this method should prove a means not so much of making them learn how to speak Latin as of making them unlearn how to 35 speak and to think. Thus such constraint would tend to make them stupid owing to the difficulty which they would have in giving expression to their thoughts.

None the less, in matters of this kind we must be guided
5 far more by experience than by *a priori* arguments and theories; and the experiments which very able teachers have made ought to convince all fair-minded people that this method of teaching children is very useful, and that the drawbacks which it entails are either imaginary or at any
10 rate not beyond remedy. But since these teachers by their own skill and care contribute largely to the success of this method and cannot make themselves responsible for a very large number of children, all the difficulties which we have raised still remain in the case of other teachers.

15 We must therefore be content to choose from the other methods those which are most useful. To begin with, common sense shows us that we ought not to employ those in which the grammar rules are set forth in Latin; for it is absurd to set about teaching the principles of a language in
20 the very language which one is going to learn and of which as yet one knows nothing.

Those who have introduced the use of tables seem to have been led away by seeing less words and less pages; from this they have inferred that it would be as easy for the
25 mind to understand and remember the rules as it was for the eyes to see them. But such is not the case. In particular, when learning these charts one encounters the same difficulties as one would find if one were learning the same rules out of a book; and in fact the difficulties would be greater, for the
30 various colours by which an attempt is made to distinguish the different kinds of words are not natural distinctions and do not impress themselves much on the mind. If there were only two or three things to remember, perhaps this method might be of service; but since there is an enormous number,
35 the mind is overwhelmed. It is absolutely necessary, there-

fore, to concentrate the memory upon a few of the most clear and concise rules.

The idea of those who would do away with grammar altogether is merely an idea of lazy people who want to spare themselves the trouble of teaching it. So far from assisting 5 children, this method is a much greater burden to them than the learning of the rules, for it deprives them of a clue which would help them to understand their books, and compels them to learn a hundred times what they might have learnt once and for all. Thus, all things considered, it will be found 10 that the best method for general use is to make children learn accurately their little rules in French verse so that they may go on, as early as possible, to the reading of authors.

Being thus dissatisfied with contemporary methods of teaching languages to beginners, the Port-Royal schoolmasters supplied their own "New Method." These *Nouvelles Méthodes* were written by Lancelot and they were applied to the teaching not only of Latin and Greek, but also of Italian and Spanish. The *New Method for learning with ease and in a short time the Latin language*, which first appeared in 1644, is in essence a translation into French of the Latin rules of Despauter. The following quotations from Lancelot's work show his equivalents for the passages from Despauter which are cited on pages 7 and 8 of the Introduction:

(*a*) Fais toujours accorder ce qu'on nomme *Adjectif*
 En genre, nombre, et cas avec son Substantif.   15
                                                    (p. 357.)

(*b*) 1. Donne au Verbe en Bo, BI, BITUM :

 2. Mais *Scribo, Nubo* font PSI, PTUM.

 3. Sans Supins sont *Scabo, Lambo*.

 4. Tous les Composez de *Cubo*,
  UÏ, ITUM veulent avoir ;   20
  Accumbo te le fera voir.   (p. 242.)

(*c*) There is no exact equivalent in Lancelot for the second quotation from Despauter on p. 8.

B.   11

Lancelot explains and defends his *New Method* as follows:

xiv

(Lancelot: Nouvelle Méthode Latine, 1681, Preface, pp. 17–20.)

For some time it has been widely noticed that the ordinary method of teaching Latin to children is very complicated and difficult, and that it would be desirable to facilitate their access to something so useful as is a knowledge of this language.
5 This has led many people to work at the subject; and although they have all aimed at the same end they have employed very different means. Some, realising that Despauter's verses were often very obscure, have attempted to make other verses in Latin, but clearer and more polished. Others, seeing the
10 trouble which children have in learning any kind of verse in an unknown tongue, have put all these rules into French prose. Others, again, for the sake of abbreviation and in order to reduce the effort needed for learning and remembering have reduced all these rules to simple tables.

15   If I may be allowed to express an opinion on these attempts, I think that those who found the verses of Despauter obscure in some places were quite right; but these critics ought to go one step further and share the views of those who have realised the inconsistency of giving in Latin the
20 rules for learning this language....Since common sense tells us that we must always begin with the easiest things and that what we know already should light the way to what we do not know, it is obvious that we should use our mother-tongue as a means of approach to languages which are foreign and
25 unknown. If this is true with respect to mature adults and if there is not an intelligent man but would think he was being played with if he were advised to learn Greek from a grammar in Greek verse, how much more true is this in the case of children to whom, owing to their age and limited
30 capacity, the most obvious things appear obscure?

With regard to the third proposal which consists in drawing up simple tables, I know that this at first sight is extremely attractive because it seems that one merely needs eyes in order to become proficient in a moment, and that one would know things almost as soon as one had seen them.   But if 5 I am not mistaken this apparent facility arises as a rule simply from the fact that we see in these tables in an abridged form things that we ourselves already know; and this leads us to suppose that it will be as easy for others to learn by means of them what they do not know as it is for us to recall what 10 we have already learnt. For it is certain that since the tables are greatly abridged, they are obscure and are therefore inadvisable for beginners; for in the case of a beginner it is as necessary to aid his power of assimilation by means of explanations as to aid his memory by conciseness. For this 15 reason the only use of such tables as a rule is to show at one glance what has taken a long time to learn....

But although these tables might prove useful to adults in beginning to learn Latin, it is unlikely as a rule that they could be of any service to children. For if they are to make 20 any impression on the mind, the imagination must be blindfolded—and children are but rarely able to do this because they cannot concentrate fixedly on a matter which is of itself very difficult, and because the imagination in children is usually as feeble as the mind. The memory is the only faculty 25 which at this stage is strong and active; and for this reason all that we desire to teach them must be based chiefly upon it.

After considering this whole matter quite impartially I came to the conclusion that we ought to give children the rules of Latin in French and that they should learn them by 30 heart. But I found by experience that another disadvantage arose—namely that when children realised the meaning of the rules and understood the words so easily, they took the liberty of changing the order of the words or the words themselves, taking a masculine for a feminine or one perfect tense 35

for another; and thus contenting themselves with giving the approximate sense of their rules, they thought that they knew them as soon as they had read them. For this reason, while holding fast to the common-sense principle that the rules of
5 Latin must be given in French, which is the only language known to our pupils, I came to the conclusion that in order to aid them to learn by making things clear and intelligible, it was necessary at the same time to fix these rules in their memory by putting them into little French verses; thus they
10 would no longer have a chance to alter the words, since they were bound down to the predetermined number of syllables in each line and to the recurrence of the rhyme which rounds them off and makes them more attractive.

I must confess that at first I thought this would be quite
15 beyond my power for I hoped that, in spite of the trammels of verse, these rules might be almost as short, as clear, and as intelligible as they are in prose. Practice however has made my task somewhat easier. And if I have not succeeded in carrying out the work which I set myself, at any rate I
20 have laboured hard to do so. I do not think that I need ask the reader to forbear from looking for elegant poetry in this book. I hope that those who understand French verse will be so good as to forgive me if I have not adhered to the rule of masculines and feminines, precision of rhymes, and
25 all the other rules which are followed by those who know how to compose poetry in our language. My sole object was to be as concise and clear as possible and for this reason to avoid all those complicated phrases which the rules of poetry involve. Under such conditions it is well to remember the
30 advice of an excellent poet:

Ornari res ipsa negat, contenta doceri.

I have followed Despauter's arrangement as far as I could and have changed his expressions only to insert others which seemed to me clearer and simpler.

The Port-Royalists regarded translation from Latin into French as an invaluable exercise not only for enlarging the pupil's knowledge of Latin, but also for cultivating his power of self-expression in his native language. Extracts xv and xvi deal with this topic. The rules given in extract xvi are of special interest because they were drawn up by Le Maître for the benefit of the young Du Fossé while he was a pupil at Port-Royal.

XV

(Coustel: Règles, etc. Vol. II, pp. 184–189 and 194–198.)

It is not enough to read good authors, to make a choice collection of extracts from them, and if desired to learn their most beautiful passages by heart, if with all this one does not acquire the power of utilising them when chance offers by means of translation; for by it the passages which are beautiful 5 and striking in Greek and Latin books are made to appear so in our language also. It may be said that this is the chief benefit and advantage which can be drawn from study. For out of a thousand people there will not be four who, on leaving school, find it necessary to speak or write in Latin. 10 But everyone should know how to express himself in French; and it is humiliating to be unable to do so in good society. Children then must be practised particularly in translation, because the application which must be employed in pondering the various expressions and for finding the sense of a 15 Latin author exercises their intelligence and their judgment alike and makes them realise the beauty of the French as fully as that of the Latin.

However, translation is as difficult as it is profitable; for it is not an easy task when one has to follow constantly, with- 20 out ever swerving, in the footsteps of another, all of whose thoughts must be faithfully reproduced, while at the same time preserving in the translation the elegance and beauty of the original and imitating the style and diction of the author who is being interpreted....And indeed a large number of 25 factors contribute to the making of a successful translation. In addition to a high degree of intelligence, a reliable judgment, a knowledge of the subject matter with which the author, who is being translated, deals, it is necessary besides to have 5 a thorough acquaintance with the beauties of both languages, *i.e.* that from which and that into which the rendering is being made. The translator must possess a thorough knowledge of the affinities, the resemblances, and the differences which exist between the two languages; and he must also have had 10 plenty of practice and experience. In a word, he must know thoroughly the chief rules of the art of translation. These rules are numerous, but my intention is to turn aside here merely in order to give the most important and indispensable ones.

(1) Firstly, then, an attempt must always be made to 15 preserve the spirit and the genius of the author whom you have undertaken to translate; so that if his style is short and concise your rendering will be so as well, and if on the contrary he is a little diffuse and long-winded the translation will correspond.

20 (2) All the component clauses in a sentence should be properly proportioned as far as possible; *e.g. Ob virtutes certissimum exitium*—to be certain of a tragic end one needed but to be virtuous and eminent.

(3) The beauties of French prose must be clearly dis- 25 tinguished from those of poetry; for the beauty of poetry lies in a fixed number of syllables and in rhyme; whereas the beauty of prose on the other hand lies in the absence of these. It is therefore a general rule that a sentence must never end with a line or half-line of poetry. If the Latin original has 30 some striking feature, an attempt must be made to reproduce this in the French, or to compensate for it if possible by some other beauty.

To sum up, I reduce to this all the other rules which can be given under this heading: translation must be *faithful*, 35 *clear*, and *elegant*.

(4) We have to consider in an author the words and the sense which they express; when therefore I say that a translation must be faithful I do not mean that one must slavishly follow every expression which an author uses and render word for word. But I say that it is enough to render sense for sense; 5 *i.e.* it is enough to express in French, for example, the whole sense of the Latin or Greek original, without being bound down either to the order of the words or to the idioms which are peculiar and natural to each language....

(5) Clearness again is one of the chief *desiderata* in a 10 translation. What is translated therefore must be developed a little; for the beauty of Greek and Latin lies in its conciseness which of itself tends to be obscure; whereas the beauty of French, on the other hand, lies in the exuberance of its phraseology. For this reason it is sometimes necessary 15 to add something in the translation for the purpose of elucidating or embellishing it. Points which are half-understood in the Latin must be explained in the French when this course contributes to the elucidation or embellishment of a passage. Ambiguities—*i.e.* confusions between two separate ideas— 20 must be carefully avoided. Finally, if a sentence is too long and complex, it must be cut up into several shorter parts. By so doing, instead of being obscure and difficult to unravel, it becomes clear and straight-forward; at the same time, instead of being weak and flabby it is strengthened and stiffened.   25

(6) A translation must also show elegance, so that it might be said that if the author on whom one is at work had written in our language, he would have expressed himself thus. Now elegance lies in the words and in the idioms. Every language has its own peculiar words and expressions, and in 30 translation equivalents must be found for these: an emphatic word for an emphatic word; a striking word for a striking word. There are again two kinds of idioms : one kind concerns thoughts and ideas; the other, expression and style. The former consists in setting things forth in a particular way, 35

in a more ingenious or striking or elevated form than is natural; and it may be said that such idioms have the same place in oratory that the arrangement and pose of the figures have in painting. This is what painters usually call grouping. 5 The second kind which concerns merely expression and style is like the colouring of a painting; if I may say so, it serves to brighten and adorn speech. It must always be employed appropriately; for while it is most effective when well managed and well distributed, it becomes ridiculous if it appears over- 10 done or affected. An attempt therefore must be made to render idiom for idiom wherever it occurs.

xvi

(*Du Fossé: Mémoires*, Vol. I, Appendix xi, p. 329; also in *Fontaine: Mém. sur MM. de P.-R.* Vol. II, pp. 176–178.)

(1) The first thing of which one must be careful in trans- lating into French is to be extremely faithful and literal—*i.e.* to express in our language all that there is in the Latin and 15 to render it so well that if Cicero, for example, had spoken our language he would have used the same words as we make him use in our translation.

(2) An attempt must be made to render one beauty by another, one figure of speech by another, to imitate the 20 author's style and to approximate to it as nearly as possible, to vary the figures of speech and modes of expression, and in short to make our translation a picture or vivid reproduction of the piece which is being translated; so that the French may be said to be as fine as the Latin and may be quoted with as 25 much confidence as the Latin original.

(3) The beauties of our prose must be distinguished from the beauties of our verse. The beauties of our verse consist partly in the rhyme, whereas French prose aims at having

none; for it is a general rule that rhymes in prose must be avoided....

(4) In our translation we must neither make long periods nor affect too concise a style. Since our language is naturally more diffuse than Latin and requires more words to express 5 the complete sense, we must attempt to keep the proper mean between too great an abundance of words which would make the style tedious and a brevity which would render it obscure.

(5) All the different parts of a sentence should be so well-harmonised and correspond so closely that, if possible, they 10 counterbalance one another perfectly.

(6) Nothing must be put in our translation which cannot be justified and for the insertion of which no reason can be given. This is more difficult than might be imagined.

(7) Care should be taken never to begin two sentences 15 —and still less, two parts of a sentence—with a conjunction such as *for*, *but*, etc....

(8) When a sentence is too long and involved in Latin or Greek, it must in the translation be cut up into several smaller parts. The result is that, on the one hand, instead of being 20 tedious it is strengthened and runs better; and on the other hand, a passage which would have been full of faults due to obscurity becomes clear and intelligible.

Rules for the explanation of authors :

xvii

(Coustel: Règles, etc. Vol. II, pp. 79–89.)

When we teach geography we first of all show our pupils on a map an epitome of the whole world so as to give them 25 a general idea of the position of its chief parts before going on to the disposition of the empires, kingdoms, and states which it contains. In the same way, before teaching an author to our pupils it is well to give them first a summary and general

idea of him. For example, before beginning the *Æneid* of
Virgil, they should be told in outline what happened at the
siege of Troy, the various battles which took place around its
walls, its capture by the stratagem of a wooden horse filled
5 with armed men, its burning, the escape of Æneas, his
embarkation, his landing in Sicily, the storm which threw
him on the coasts of Africa, the kindly reception which Dido,
queen of Carthage, gave him, his departure from this city, his
arrival in Italy, and finally the great wars which he waged
10 against Turnus on account of Lavinia whom he wanted to
marry. Mapheus Vegius testifies that owing to his master
having adopted this course with him, he was fired with a great
desire to read the *Æneid* thoroughly and the understanding
of it was thus made wonderfully easy for him.

15   A teacher's object in explaining an author should be to
help the pupils to understand him. To this end there is no
need to show off one's skill and ability by straining after
laboured expressions or phrases which are doubtless beautiful
but are too far-fetched and of little value. When children
20 are still backward it is important that they should pay far more
attention to the words than to the general sense of an author.
Thus they must be clearly shown the constructions, the
arrangement of the words in a sentence, the gender of each
noun and how it is declined, the principal parts of the con-
25 jugation of each verb. Quintilian says that it is in pointing
out details of this kind that the duty of a good teacher consists.

The object which all authors have had in the books which
they have left to us has doubtless been to impart to us their
ideas; and this is why they have clothed them with words
30 which manifest them to us. Words may thus be called the
garments of ideas. In order then to recognise and appreciate
the beauty and loftiness of ideas, it is necessary to recognise
fully the meaning and force of every word. A teacher must
therefore consider first of all, in explaining an author, whether
35 a word is simple or compound, original or metaphorical. I

mean by an original word one which signifies the thing which it was primarily intended to signify and which gives us the idea clearly; while by a metaphorical word I mean one which has a meaning remote from that which is natural to it. Secondly, we must consider whether the words are in common use or 5 not. By "words in common use" I mean those which are in accordance with the ordinary methods of expression among the learned; for it is a great mistake in a matter like this to set oneself up against the dictates of good taste. Thirdly, we must see whether words are ancient or modern. By "ancient" 10 I mean those which good authors have employed; for their authority is more binding upon us than reason, and we cannot be blamed for using the language of these great men whom we shall always reverence. By "modern" or low Latin words, on the other hand, I mean such as have been made current 15 by later authors.

Just as isolated stones do not make a palace unless they are arranged in their proper order and symmetry, so words do not form continuous speech unless they are well arranged. Nouns and verbs are the most important parts of a sentence. 20 Nouns are substantive or adjective. Nouns substantive may be compared to persons of rank who usually go with their train and their suite. The adjectives are like the attendants who are obliged to follow their masters wherever they go and who serve to make them appear with greater magnificence and 25 pomp. And so if a noun substantive is masculine or nominative or singular or plural, the adjective has to follow suit. Sentences consist of nouns and verbs combined. To be beautiful and pleasing they should be concise, clear, simple, and harmonious. They are concise when they contain none 30 but necessary words; they are clear when the words are in their usual sense and well arranged; they are simple when the words are such as are in common use; and they are harmonious when their cadence is pleasing to an ear which is qualified to judge of this.... 35

We should not always restrict ourselves to these petty details which may undermine and weaken the intelligence of our pupils; we must alter our methods as they make progress and then pay particular attention to the sense and subject-
5 matter of an author. Excellence in the method of expression must be carefully distinguished from excellence in the subject-matter. Attention must be called to any apt comparisons or beautiful descriptions which occur in authors (*e.g.* descriptions of a storm, a battle, a palace, a garden, etc.), as well as to the
10 various figures of speech, rhetorical touches, fine phraseology, and similar things which our pupils may find useful for their compositions.... When there occurs some fine maxim or good example which may serve to render virtue attractive and vice hateful, a pause should be made in order to turn the light on
15 it and to set it off, if possible, by some fine passage taken from Scripture or from one of the Fathers. There is no need to be afraid of digressions of this kind because they lead to something more useful than what was originally intended. Besides they make all the greater impression upon our pupils'
20 minds in that they were the less prepared for them.... It is not sufficient to make children learn by heart the most beautiful passages from the poets and orators. They must be made to repeat them frequently so that they may always have them ready in their minds for use when opportunity occurs.

Rules for correcting compositions :

xviii
(*Coustel: op. cit.* Vol. II, pp. 89–93.)

25 If we adopt the good custom of making children compose in Latin—*i.e.* what is called writing "proses"—as late as possible, the following rules should be observed.

First stop to correct the bad mistakes—*i.e.* those which break the rules of the declensions, conjugations, and syntax, and which we call "howlers." Next, point out words improperly used and barbarisms, showing that they are not commonly employed—*i.e.* that the authors who have spoken the language most purely have not employed them, either because they are low Latin (*i.e.* used by authors who wrote at 5 a time when the Latin language was declining), or because, though the words are good in themselves, they are badly arranged and, for want of the necessary arrangement, the sentence lacks its proper harmony.

When children have made some progress more time should 10 be spent on the subject-matter; it is not enough simply to say: "This composition is good—or bad." Reasons must be given and details must be gone into; *e.g.* one might say: "This expression, although a good one, is out of place in this context; this might have been put in such and such a way 15 which would have been more elegant and dignified; this explanation is too weak or irrelevant; this phrase is too abbreviated or too long-winded; the various parts of this composition are not properly balanced and related one to another; you plunge into the subject too soon; the narrative is too 20 long; this needs a peroration; you don't prove what you set out to prove; this idiom which you employ would have had quite a different effect elsewhere or if you were to give it a different turn."

As far as possible we should put in place of what is cor- 25 rected other words and expressions which are more classical and elegant, and the same with idioms, so that our pupils may not only see the mistakes which they have made but may also learn how they might have done better. Nothing is more calculated to sharpen their wits and make them fertile in ideas 30 —in a word, to bring them on in a short time. The difficulty is to put this satisfactorily into practice. It is advisable for the master to give them fair copies of their proses from time to time and to call their attention to what is worthy of remark. Quintilian advises a teacher, when he corrects his pupils' 35

compositions, to adopt a pleasant and kindly manner so as to counteract the severity of the remedies which he applies and which are always in themselves rather difficult to take. What he means is that the teacher should commend with appropriate
5 praise the passages which seem good, that he should be indulgent towards such as are tolerable, merely changing the expressions for better ones, and that he should make such additions as would give the composition more beauty and elegance. Above all he strongly advises teachers to allow their
10 pupils to indulge in a somewhat flowery style, because age, a more mature judgment, and experience will always supply the proper restraint; and moreover it is much easier to remedy an excessive abundance than to supply an excessive deficiency.

General rules for teaching Latin :

xix

(Arnauld: Œuvres, Vol. XLI, pp. 90–91.)

When a master sets a piece of French to be put into Latin,
15 he should first of all translate it himself from some ancient author so as to show his class how the author expressed himself. If the boys find the passage, he need not worry about this. The trouble which they have voluntarily undertaken in finding it, being obliged to read much and to disguise the
20 passage when they discover it, will prove a great advantage to them; but they must be blamed if, when they find it, they copy it out without changing anything.

It would be better still to dictate to them the Latin of what has already been dictated to them in French and to make
25 them reproduce extemporaneously the Latin which they have just heard. The model is a sound one; time is economised; and by repeating this exercise quite shortly they get into the way of talking good Latin without ruminating too long over it. Thus in place of one prose badly reproduced by the

ordinary methods they have been led to compose several quite good ones in a very short time; and most of the boys—perhaps all—will take pleasure in bringing them next day.

They must never be made to learn by heart the rubbish contained in the *Methods* which are as a rule badly planned, 5 badly arranged, and very tedious to the young. They should be taught orally and by practice all the so-called rules, and made to recite them, like a little story, only in the lowest forms. Whenever the boys come across a noun or verb which is an exception to the rule, their attention should be drawn 10 to it and they must be made to give an account of it....

It is useless to make them commit to memory whole speeches of Cicero, for it is impossible to remember them and they contain little that is worth committing to memory. In place of this they should learn select extracts from his 15 speeches and particularly from his philosophical works, the *Tusculan Orations, De Officiis*, etc. In addition to these selections from Cicero, it is useful to make them learn speeches from the historians—*e.g.* Sallust, Quintus Curtius, Livy, and above all Tacitus and Pliny's *Panegyric.* In Tacitus, besides 20 the speeches, we may select certain passages which are well worth learning because they contain much wisdom. The same practice may be employed in the case of the poets, with the exception of Virgil and Horace whom it is good to learn in their entirety—especially Virgil's Second, Fourth, and Sixth 25 *Æneid*, and the Fourth *Georgic.* The boys will be made to collect the maxims which they find as they read, and will learn them by heart.

The younger children should be given lessons in grammar and translation, and the elder in composition only to a 30 moderate extent during whatever time is left over after the reading of prescribed authors. This point is more important than one would think, though it is easy to be deceived in regard to it. It is thought that by overwhelming children with grammar lessons and compositions there is much to be gained. 35

Nothing is more mistaken. If they are left to themselves to work exercises, they do not sufficiently realise the importance of time to make use of it. They do not hurry; the clock strikes; then come punishments; they are utterly disheartened
5 and disgusted and as a result all the good that they have gained is nullified. Those who have more facility and a better memory will be induced to do more than the rest by the offering of rewards.

It is usually a waste of time to give boys verse composition
10 as homework. Out of seventy or eighty pupils there may be two or three who gain anything from it. The rest find it an unprofitable or disagreeable task and in the end produce nothing of any value. A subject should be set for those who show taste and ability, and the rest practised according to
15 their capacity. However, all alike may be set to extemporise short verses the theme of which is given. Each pupil should be free to say how he would turn the subject of each verse. Thus from one corner comes one phrase; from another comes an improvement on it. Having obtained permission to speak
20 (which is asked and given merely by a sign to avoid confusion) the pupils judge, criticise, and give reasons for their preferences. Those who have the least enthusiasm exert themselves and all at any rate try to distinguish themselves. The result is an exercise well-adapted to please the pupils and develop
25 those who have any talent.

Greek (extracts xx and xxi).

Lancelot wrote a *Nouvelle Méthode Grecque* on the same lines as his *Latin Method* (see p. 161). The rules of Greek grammar were given in verses which, it was claimed, could be easily committed to memory. The following example will help to give a general idea of the book:

    1. Quand l'Adjectif trois voix admet,
        Oς pur et ρος même α, ον fait ;

2. Tout autre en ος, η, ον veut prendre ;

3. Mais ας par αινα, αν faut rendre.

4. Υς, εια, υ ;   5. Εις, εσσα, εν ;

6. Ως, υια, ος ;   7. Ην, εινα, εν.   (p. 88.)

XX

(Lancelot : Nouvelle Méthode Grecque, 1754, Preface,
p. xxviii.)

Quintilian long ago gave as his opinion that children were 5
made to begin by Greek because Latin was more commonplace and was learnt more easily and almost without effort.
This view may be worth our consideration as well as that of
the Romans. For although our language is not Latin, it is
none the less derived from it and is a kind of dialect of Latin. 10
I do not mean to say that I wish Quintilian's advice to be
taken literally. For since we have to trace our way back it
is certainly advisable to pass through Latin, from which are
derived most of the words in our language, before arriving
at Greek from which Latin is derived. Again, it is certain 15
that the rudiments of the Latin language—the declensions,
the conjugations, and the rest of the grammar—are easier
and more adapted to young children than those of Greek.
Besides, there are many people who want only a little Latin
without wishing to enter upon the other language. But I 20
think that Quintilian's remark is worthy of greater consideration and that often we do not apply children seriously enough
to Greek or else we do not take them far enough in it. For
since the learning of this language is a matter chiefly of the
words, it being easier than Latin as regards the phraseology, 25
and since practically all the necessity and utility of this language lies solely in the understanding of authors and we
hardly ever have need of speaking or writing it, nothing would
seem more natural than that children should be practised in
Greek from an early age. As soon as they have gone a little 30

B.   12

way in Latin we should make them begin Greek and bring them on considerably in it while they are able to act more by memory than by judgment. Meanwhile we must be content merely to keep up their Latin and must reserve for a
5 more mature and judicious age training them in a good style of writing it and speaking it, and in the rules of eloquence.

To facilitate the acquirement of a Greek vocabulary, Lancelot wrote his *Garden of Greek Roots*, in which the principal root-words of the Greek language and their meanings were given in French verse. As judged by the standards of modern philology the work has serious faults, though it has proved its value as a school-book (see p. 38). Its character may be gathered from the following quotation—the first ten lines of the book :

1.	A, *fait un, prive, augmente, admire.*	
2.	'Αάζω, *j'exhale et j'aspire.*	F. σω.
3.	"Αβαξ, *contoir, damier, buffet.*	G. χος, ὁ.
4.	'Αβρός, *lâche et mou, beau, bienfait.*	G. οῦ, ὁ.
5.	'Αβρότη, *nuit, temps où l'on erre.*	G. ῆς, ἡ.
6.	'Αγαθός, *bon, brave à la guerre.*	G. οῦ, ὁ.
7.	'Αγάλλω, *pare, orne, et polit.*	F. λῶ.
8.	"Αγαν, *trop* ou *beaucoup* se dit.	adverbe.
9.	'Αγανακτέω, *je m'indigne.*	F. ήσω.
10.	'Αγαπᾶν, *aimer* te designe.	I. δειν, ᾶν.

The advantages which Lancelot claims for this method of teaching Greek are set forth in the preface to the book. The following passage from it has been selected as being typical of the whole:

xxi

(Lancelot: Jardin des Racines Grecques, 1664, Preface—
no pagination.)

I have found by experience that those who have the least gift for learning by heart can gain some advantage from these verses, provided that they read them over several times. The rhythm of the verse impresses itself imperceptibly on the ear, the lines always begin with the Greek word, and it is of the nature of the memory to pass from what precedes to what follows. If therefore anyone who has read over these verses meets one of the Greek words mentioned in them, it is practi- 5 cally certain that he will at once recollect the meaning which is attached to the word in the verses, even if his memory is not good enough for him to be able to repeat word for word a single one of these lines. It must be well understood that herein lies the great value of this little book—that the lines 10 always begin with the Greek word, and if there are two root-words in a line they always stand before their meaning.... I think therefore that I can claim that there are very few people who could not learn in less than two or three months the chief root-words of the Greek language and who could 15 not with a little care be sure of never forgetting them. For since all the other words are derived from these, which are their origins, all that one reads in this language serves only to impress these root-words more strongly on the mind, and they will develop thereafter into a general knowledge of Greek 20 authors.

The following syllabus, taken from Arnauld's *Règlement* (see p. 43), gives a suggested course of classical reading from the lowest to the highest forms of the schools of the Faculty of Arts (see Introd. pp. 6–10).

xxii

(Arnauld: Œuvres, Vol. XLI, pp. 93–96.)

I take for granted that the time spent in class is two and a half hours in the morning and two and a half hours in the afternoon—*i.e.* five hours a day; and that the pupils can have an equal amount of time for private study. It should be noted 25 that not less than an hour must be devoted to explaining the first author which is introduced to each class ; and after that half an hour should be spent in giving an account of private reading or in exercising the class in oral composition. The rest of the time will be spent as the master thinks most fit.

6th Class.

5   *Morning:* Tursellinus, 1 hr; Latin and French grammar (which will simply be read and explained), ½ hr; historical anecdotes, questions on words in the author, ¼ hr; reading Josephus in French, ½ hr.

Afternoon: Phædrus (difficult for beginners—would be
10 better in the 3rd class), 1 hr; the Enigmas of Luberius, ¼ hr; grammar, ½ hr; historical anecdotes, questions, and reading in French, ½ hr. The pupils in each class might be made to read more particularly about the chief characters in the Bible, so as to give an account of them on the days fixed by the
15 master.

5th Class.

Morning: Cornelius Nepos and Quintus Curtius alternately, 1 hr; select passages from Cicero, ½ hr; correction of written translations, ½ hr; historical anecdotes and principles
20 of geography, ¼ hr.

Afternoon: Terence, 1 hr; Epigrams, ½ hr; repetition of grammar, ½ hr; historical anecdotes and principles of geology, ¼ hr.

Special books: Florus; Eutropius; Justin; Politian's trans-
25 lation of Herodian.

4th Class.

Morning: Second decade of Livy, 1 hr; select books of Cicero, ¼ hr; correction of translations, ½ hr; historical anecdotes and geography, ¼ hr.

30   *Afternoon:* Sallust, 1 hr; second, fourth, and sixth books of the *Æneid*, ½ hr; Greek grammar, ¼ hr; history and geography (which henceforth should be studied together), ½ hr.

Special books: The other two decades of Livy; Cæsar.

3rd Class.

Morning: Tacitus, 1 hr ; select speeches, ½ hr ; correction of compositions, ½ hr ; history, etc., ¼ hr.

Evening: Satires and *Epistles* of Horace, 1 hr ; select passages of Virgil, ½ hr ; Gospel of S. Luke in Greek, dia- 5 logues of Lucian and Æsop alternately, ½ hr ; history and geography, ¼ hr.

Special books : Suetonius ; Ovid *de Ponto* ; the seventh, eighth, tenth, thirteenth and fifteenth Satires of Juvenal.

2nd Class.   10

This class should specialise in Greek and the time hither- to devoted to Latin will now be devoted to this language.

Morning: Herodian, 1 hr ; *Panegyric* of Pliny, ¼ hr ; cor- rection of compositions, ½ hr ; history, etc., ½ hr.

Evening: Plutarch's Lives, 1 hr ; select passages from 15 Lucian and other poets, ½ hr ; Homer, ½ hr ; history, etc., ¼ hr.

Special books : Herodotus, Thucydides, and Xenophon.

Rhetoric.

Morning: Suarez and the *Rhetoric* of Aristotle alternately ; then many passages from Quintilian, constantly comparing 20 one with another, 1 hr ; correction of compositions, ¾ hr ; history, etc., ½ hr.

Evening: Moral philosophy of Plutarch and Seneca, 1 hr ; select passages from modern poets, ¼ hr ; Euripides and Sophocles alternately, ½ hr ; history, etc., ½ hr.   25

Special books : Pliny the naturalist ; Ælian ; speeches of Cicero, Demosthenes, Isocrates, etc.

It should be noted that in the three lower classes more attention is paid to words than to ideas ; in the others the reverse is the case. In the Rhetoric class it is not necessary 30 to explain the whole author in French, but the reader should be made to linger over the fine passages, whether for the purpose of paying special attention to them or of elucidating them.

Although the study of the Classics and the vernacular took chief place in the curriculum of the Port-Royal schools, yet room was found for History, Geography, and—to some small extent— for Mathematics and Science. The following extracts (xxiii–xxix) deal with these points.

xxiii

(*Nicole: Essais de Morale*, Vol. II, p. 236.)

In the education of princes history plays an important part and rightly so, for it can prove of very great use to them if only it is taught in the proper way. But unless we employ the necessary discretion in this matter, it will harm them
5 more often than it is of service to them. For history consists simply of a confused mass of facts. The people of whom it treats are for the most part vicious, careless, or rash. Their actions are often recorded by not very judicious writers who praise or blame at random and who instil innumerable bad
10 examples or false principles into the minds of those readers who are unable to discriminate. A tutor whose judgment is unreliable will render the study of this subject more dangerous than ever. He will pour into the mind of a young prince his own follies as well as those from the books; he will spoil the
15 best things by the undesirable turn which he gives them; and the result often is that by filling his pupil's head with a confusion of facts, the tutor often destroys his pupil's natural gifts of reason and good feeling. Most things are good or evil according to the way in which we present them. The
20 life of a sinner can be as edifying as that of a saint if it is properly dealt with by setting in relief its misery and by inculcating a horror of it. Similarly, the life of a saint can be as dangerous as that of a sinner if it is dealt with in a contemptuous or abusive manner.

xxiv

(*Nicole: op. cit.* Vol. II, pp. 283-286.)

History may be classed among those branches of knowledge which are acquired through the eyes because, as an aid
to memory, we may use various books of portraits and pictures. But even when these are not available, history is of
itself very well adapted to the child mind. And though it be 5
merely a matter of memory it is of great assistance in developing the power of judgment. We must then employ every
device in order to give children a taste for it.

We may first give them a general sketch of universal history, of the various monarchies, and of the chief changes which 10
have taken place since the beginning of the world, dividing
the course of time into different epochs as, for example, from
the Creation to the Flood, from the Flood to Abraham, from
Abraham to Moses, from Moses to Solomon, from Solomon
to the Return from the Babylonian Captivity, from the Return 15
from Captivity to Christ, from Christ to our own times; and
we must join to this general history a general chronology.
We should explain more especially the history of the Jewish
people and should endeavour by means of it to establish our
pupils betimes in the true religion. It is always advisable to 20
treat chronology and geography together with history; we
should point out on the map the places which are mentioned
and always clearly show to which epoch any particular historical event belongs.

In addition to these histories which will form part of their 25
regular studies it would be advantageous to relate to our pupils
each day one separate episode which is not included in the
ordinary curriculum and which would serve rather as a relaxation. It might be called the "story of the day" and we
might give them practice in relating it in order to encourage 30
facility in self-expression. This story should comprise some

important event, some extraordinary occurrence, some striking example of vice, or virtue, or misfortune, or prosperity, or eccentricity. It could include unusual happenings—marvels, earthquakes which have sometimes swallowed up whole cities,
5 shipwrecks, battles, strange laws and customs. By making the most of this little exercise we can teach them what is finest in all history; but to achieve this we must be regular and not let a single day pass without telling them some tale and noting down each day what has been told to them.

10 Again, we must teach them to connect in their minds similar stories so that one may help them to remember another. For instance, it is well for them to know examples of all the largest armies which are mentioned in books, of great battles and slaughters, of great mortalities, of great prosperi-
15 ties and adversities, of great riches, of great conquerors and captains, of favourites both fortunate and unfortunate, of the longest lives, of the signal follies of men, of great vices and great virtues.

XXV

(Arnauld: Œuvres, Vol. XLI, p. 89.)

To cultivate power of expression from the lowest forms
20 upwards it is good to make two boys each day relate a short historical anecdote which they will take from Valerius Maximus or Plutarch or any book they like, the choice being left to them. Those should be marked highest who give their account most freely, naturally, and in the spirit of the author,
25 without restricting themselves to the same words and phrases as he has used. This anecdote should be recounted in French in the three lower forms and French books should be suggested to them. They should be given only a very short passage from an author to reproduce and everyone should be compelled to
30 read every day a given portion of French history and to be ready to give an account of it to the best of his ability.

xxvi

(Racine: Œuvres complètes, Hachette, 1901, Vol. III,
p. 244.)

This essay was written by Racine at the age of about sixteen,
probably while he was still a pupil at Port-Royal.

On Writing History.

In setting out to write history the first thing to do is to
choose a subject which is attractive and pleasing to the reader.
This is an advantage which Herodotus has over Thucydides ;
for Herodotus deals with the war waged by the Greeks against
the barbarians, and the deeds of both sides deserve never to 5
be forgotten; whereas Thucydides has described only a single
war which turned out badly and which we could have wished
had never happened or had been buried in oblivion ; for he
alienates his reader by saying that he is going to tell of terrible
disasters, of cities deserted or destroyed, of deaths innumer- 10
able, of losses, of earthquakes, of eclipses in number un-
paralleled.

The second point which an historian must observe is to
pay great attention to the beginning and end of his work.
Herodotus again has the advantage over Thucydides; for the 15
former starts with the first wrong inflicted on the Greeks
by barbarians and ends with the battle in which the
Athenians were defeated by the Peloponnesians.

xxvii

(Nicole: Essais de Morale, Vol. II, pp. 279–284.)

Geography is a very suitable study for children because
it is largely a matter of the senses and they can be made to 20
see with their own eyes the position of towns and provinces ;
besides it is quite amusing and that again is necessary so as

not to repel them at first; also geography involves but little exercise of reasoning—a faculty which they lack most at that age. But if we are to make this study at once more useful and more pleasant we must not content ourselves with showing the names of the towns and provinces on a map, but we must also make use of various devices to help them remember them. We might have books in which there are illustrations of the largest towns, and show them to our pupils. Children are very fond of this kind of amusement. We might tell them some noteworthy incident connected with the principal towns so as to fix them in their minds. We might point out the battles which have been fought there, the councils which have been held in them, the great men who have come from them. We might say something about their natural history, if there is anything unusual to remark, or the government, size, or trade of these towns; and if they are French towns it is well, where possible, to mention the noblemen to whom they belong or who are their governors.

To the study of geography as a specific subject should be joined a little exercise which is really only an amusement but which does not fail to help greatly in impressing information upon their minds. It consists in never forgetting to locate on the map the scene of any historical anecdote which is told to them. For example, if the *Gazette* is being read they must be shown all the towns which are mentioned in it. Again, they should insert in their maps all the places of which they hear, that thus their maps may serve as a mnemonic for their historical anecdotes, just as the latter in turn should help them to remember the places where the events occurred.

In addition to geography there are several other useful subjects which can be made to enter children's minds through the medium of their eyes. The Romans' war-engines, their forms of punishment, their clothes, their arms, and many other similar things are illustrated in the books of Lipsius and may with profit be shown to our pupils. They may be shown, for example, what a battering-ram was; how the *testudo* was formed; how the Roman armies were organised, the number of men in a cohort and a legion, the officers of their armies, and a large number of other interesting and curious things, leaving out those which are too complicated. Almost an 5 equal profit may be drawn from a book entitled *Subterranean Rome* and others in which there are engravings of what remains of the antiquities of this chief city of the world. To these may even be added the pictures which are to be found in certain voyages to India and China in which the sacrifices 10 and pagodas of these unhappy peoples are described; but the master should at the same time point out the extremes to which men's folly can carry them when they follow their own imagination and the dim light of their own intelligence. The book of Aldrovandus or rather the abridgement of it made 15 by Jonston may also help to amuse children profitably, provided that the master who shows it to them has taken the trouble to learn something about the habits of animals, and tells it not in the form of a lesson but in ordinary conversation. This book may also be used for showing children the 20 appearance of the animals of which they hear whether in their books or in conversation.

An intelligent man has quite recently shown by experiment with one of his children that they are at that age well able to learn anatomy; and it would undoubtedly be useful to explain 25 to them some of its general principles, even if it merely helps them to remember the Latin names for the parts of the human body. At the same time we must avoid raising dangerous curiosity as to certain branches of this subject. It is useful for this same reason to show them portraits of the kings of 30 France, the Roman emperors, the sultans, the great leaders and famous men of the different countries. It is good that they should amuse themselves by looking at these and referring to them whenever they hear these celebrities mentioned. For this all helps to fix the ideas in their minds. We 35 should try to cultivate in our pupils a healthy curiosity for seeing strange and interesting things, and to get them into the habit of finding out the reason for everything. Such curiosity is not a vice at their age since it helps to open their minds 5 and may divert them from many irregularities.

xxviii
(Nicole: op. cit. Vol. II, pp. 237–238.)

Sciences have their uses and their misuses; they can be learnt for base motives as well as for elevated ones. Few people can make the distinction. None the less it is so important to do so that often it is better to be absolutely igno-10 rant of the sciences than to know them basely and to plunge into the futilities which they contain. To few people can be applied the remark which Tacitus made about Agricola: *Retinuitque quod est difficillimum ex sapientia modum.* Most of those who are cleverest at the sciences are least fitted to 15 pass judgment upon them, because they glory not in the usefulness of a branch of knowledge but in its precision. There are very able mathematicians who think that the highest aim in life is to know whether there is a bridge and a hanging arch across the planet Saturn. A prince ought to know what 20 is said about these topics for such information costs but little. But if we do not tell him at the same time that this is but useless curiosity, we are acting wrongly. For it is better to be ignorant of these subjects than to be ignorant that they are useless.

xxix
(Domat: Les Lois Civiles, Vol. II, p. 122.)

25 Before passing on to the other arts and sciences which are taught in schools and of which the chief is geometry, we must here recall what has already been said on the subject

of physics—that although this science deals with bodies and matter, the nature of the parts which compose them, the nature of their properties, and similar subjects, yet it gives us very little knowledge of which we can be at all certain ; whereas geometry, which also deals with bodies and matter 5 but which regards them from a different standpoint, teaches us nothing which is not only absolutely certain, but which does not also rest upon such convincing proof that any mind, which can understand this science, is persuaded of everything which it puts forward just as clearly as everyone is convinced 10 that the whole is greater than its part.

Great attention was always paid to music at Port-Royal and the convent of Port-Royal des Champs, in particular, was cele-brated for the manner in which the offices were sung. It is un-certain whether the teaching of any kind of music ever formed part of the regular curriculum in the boys' schools of Port-Royal; although we have evidence that church singing was taught to the girls who were educated by the nuns (see pages 207 and 218). The general attitude of the community with regard to this subject is illustrated in the following extract.

XXX

(*Domat : op. cit.* Vol. II, p. 124.)

The Church has instituted the custom of singing the divine office in order to touch our hearts and lift them up to ap-preciate the proper meaning of the sacred words which she appoints to be sung. Such words, again, require music which 15 shall be solemn, touching, and easy so that all the faithful alike can join in it. For these reasons the Church has ordained that in all places of worship where the faithful meet to assist at the divine office, a form of singing should be used which contains notes of the same length and harmonies which are 20 not so florid as those of ordinary music. This is what is called

plainsong, the use of which is consecrated entirely to the
Church as being suited by its solemnity to inspire the mind
with the words of which the office is composed, and particularly with those of the Psalms which form its chief part and
5 which were composed in order to be sung. But this plainsong
is not employed as the spirit of the Church requires if those
who celebrate and sing the divine office do not observe
solemnity, decorum, the proper slowness, and the care demanded by the dignity of music which is to give expression
10 to words inspired by the Spirit of God and which are addressed to Him either in praise or prayer—of music, I say,
which is to form part of divine worship in which everything
should be sublime.

IV

THE PORT-ROYAL GIRLS' SCHOOLS

i

(*Racine: Abrégé de l'Histoire de Port-Royal*, Œuvres complètes, Hachette, 1901, Vol. III, p. 34.)

One of the reasons why this convent was held in such esteem and why perhaps it incurred so much jealousy was the excellent education which was given there to the young. There never was a refuge where innocence and purity were more secure from the contaminating atmosphere of the world, 5 nor a school where the Christian verities were more thoroughly taught. The instruction in morals which was given there to the girls made all the greater impression on their minds in that they saw it put into practice not only by their mistresses but also by the whole of a great community, devoted whole- 10 heartedly to the praise and service of God. But it was not enough to instruct them in religion; immense care was also taken to develop their intelligence and reasoning powers, and an endeavour was made to render them equally well fitted to become one day either perfect nuns or excellent wives and 15 mothers. Mention might be made of a large number of girls who were educated in this convent and who have since edified the world by their discretion and virtue. We know with what feelings of admiration and gratitude they have always spoken of the education which they received there; and there 20 are still some who preserve, in the midst of the world or at Court, the same affection for the ruins of this persecuted house as that which the Jews of old preserved in their captivity for the ruins of Jerusalem.

Our knowledge of the organisation of the Port-Royal girls' schools is based chiefly on a passage in the *Constitutions* of the convent and on a more detailed *Règlement pour les Enfans* which is usually found bound up with the *Constitutions*. The first of these was drawn up by Agnès, sister of Angélique and herself for a time abbess of the community. The *Règlement* is the work of Jacqueline Pascal (see Introd. p. 51). In view of the importance of these two documents as affording first-hand evidence, they have both been included almost in their entirety in the present selection of extracts.

ii

(Agnès Arnauld: Constitutions du Monastère de Port-Royal du Saint Sacrement, 1721, pp. 94–102.)

Little girls may be received into the convent to be instructed in the fear of God for several years—not for one year only, for that is not sufficient to form their characters aright, according to the laws of Christianity. Only those shall
5 be received whose parents are willing that they should be instructed in this manner and offer them to God without caring whether they are to become nuns or remain in the world, as it may please God to decide.

The little girls shall have separate quarters from those of
10 the nuns, with a mistress to instruct them in virtue ; she shall be given help for looking after the children and teaching them reading, writing, needlework, and other arts which are useful and do not merely minister to vanity. They will wear the novice's habit, but they will not be compelled to do so at first
15 if they dislike it, until familiarity and the sight of their schoolfellows make them wish for it. But if any child persists in not wanting to wear it, she will be made to wear a secular dress, not of silk, and without any embroidery, so that the others may not feel envious of her. They will attend the choir to
20 sing at certain times when they are old enough to be able to do so and if they ask permission ; so also with the refectory where they will sit at a separate table with their mistress.

Not more than twelve little girls of less than ten years old shall be received, for fear lest the affection which the sisters show them should prove detrimental by taking up too much of their time and attention, and likewise that they may perform their duties more perfectly without, however, failing 5 in any attention requisite for educating their pupils properly. They may be kept until the age of sixteen even though they have no wish to become nuns, provided that they are tractable and well-behaved and that they take no liberties and profit by the instruction which is given them, abounding 10 more and more in the Christian virtues. But if on the contrary their inclinations are vain and worldly, they will promptly be sent home, whatever be their age, for fear lest they should corrupt the rest. If a child has lost her mother and it would be advantageous for her to stay on even after the age of six- 15 teen, the Superior will be asked for permission to keep her and we shall do as seems best to him. The number of the little girls shall not exceed twelve at most, as has been said; nevertheless, when they have passed the age of ten they shall no longer be reckoned as little girls and other younger children 20 can be taken in place of them, even though they live in the convent, because they need far less care and attention than the younger girls. The nuns shall not ask to receive little girls and shall not exert any influence upon their parents to make them give them to us—not even upon those who are 25 related to them; this ought to be the outcome of their own initiative and of a sincere desire for the good education of their children. Special facilities will be granted for the reception of little girls of three or four years who have lost their mothers and they will be affectionately given all the 30 assistance which they need in their weakness; for it should be remembered that such charity is all the greater in that these little orphans are often badly brought up, having no mother to look after them.

Sisters should not imagine that to devote their attention 35

to bringing up children, who as yet are not able to receive
any instruction for their salvation, is an occupation unworthy
of their calling; for in doing so they imitate God Himself
Who first of all formed the body of the first man and then
5 breathed into it the breath of life. Let them then take for
their part the duty of nourishing the small bodies of these
children with all the care which is required, until they reach
that age when they can receive the infusion of grace; by so
doing they become, as it were, mothers to these children,
10 and this will make their virginity fruitful before God Whose
brides they are, even as He is—in the words of S. Paul—the
Father of souls and spirits.

The sisters whose duty it is to look after the children
should regard it as a charitable employment; they should
15 look upon it as altogether an exercise of patience which involves enduring much from these little creatures and being
completely in subjection to them. Still, they should not complain, but devote themselves to the work for the love of Jesus
Christ Who became a child for the sake of us, the servants
20 of these children in whom He Himself abides, humbling
Himself in their weakness. The sisters should also endure
the little whims of their pupils which are often very annoying.
They should never rebuke or correct them in an impulse of
anger, but postpone the punishment until their irritation is
25 past and the children themselves may realise that they love
them no less when they punish them than when they caress
them.

Mistresses will take great care not to favour children,
never showing a greater affection for those who are most
30 pleasant or pretty, so as to give the others no cause for jealousy. They should not pass the time in playing with them
more than is necessary for their amusement if they are not
as yet able to play with the other little girls; and they should
never allow the children to caress them too much or become
35 too attached to them; for this would make them ill-disposed

towards other children who might be put in their charge. This does not mean that they should not try to win their love, but they must be loved in their capacity as mistresses and not as ordinary persons; and although children may not be able to make this distinction, the mistresses must make 5 it and must compel the children to show as much affection towards one mistress as towards another. For example, if a child would not obey one of her mistresses because she likes her less, the other mistress, instead of being pleased that this child liked her the better, will be severe with her and make 10 her show the proper obedience to her colleague. In token that the sisters do not wish to be loved by the children, save for the good of the children themselves, when they are relieved of this duty they will no longer caress the children when they meet them, any more than the other sisters do. The latter 15 again should never amuse themselves thus even with children who happen to be their relations, except so far as the Abbess approves for the purpose of accustoming children to this rule when they first enter. With this exception, or except in certain special circumstances, they will not give expression to 20 any affection which they may have for them and they will sacrifice it to God to obtain of His goodness that these children may profit by the good education which will be given them.

When mistresses take children to the reception-room 25 they will not evince before their parents too great an affection for them, but merely show that they love them as much as they are obliged and that they take all possible care of them. They will never praise children excessively, if some are very pretty, but will merely say that they are extremely tractable— 30 or some similar remark.* On the other hand, they will not blame them for their faults nor accuse them of anything unless the Abbess expressly tells them to do so; and if they are asked whether the children are not bad or tiresome, they will say that much work has still to be done, without showing 35

that they are tired of it or disgusted with it, so as to avoid giving pain to the parents. They will not ask for anything for the children themselves, without the Abbess's permission—not even for toys or books or anything else—so as not to
5 importune the parents and at the same time to avoid affording the other children, to whom nothing is given, an occasion for jealousy. And for this reason it could be wished that they were all equal. We shall therefore continue to undertake their maintenance, as we have done hitherto, so as to obviate
10 the inequality which exists among their parents, some of whom would give liberally while others would deny them what is necessary for them; and this would make the one class proud and give pain to the other. But we remedy this by treating almost all of them alike so far as is consistent with discretion.
15 The little girls will never be allowed in the reception-room alone, neither when they are very young nor when they are older, unless with their father and mother if they wish it —and that only for a very short time. The little girls must never be allowed out of sight for fear lest they fall and hurt
20 themselves. They will not be allowed to play together in a remote part of their room, but they will be watched incessantly so that their little faults may be corrected. The older girls will not be in any way exempt from this supervision; on the contrary, since the ill effects that result may be greater, we
25 shall exercise an equal or greater care that they may never be left without someone to look after them. They must never be allowed to whisper together even for a moment. One of the mistresses should sleep in their room, and when walking about the convent to the choir or the refectory they must always
30 be accompanied, care being taken that they do not keep close together. In short, continual vigilance should be exercised so that, as far as possible, they may not lead each other astray; for that, as a rule, is what most corrupts young people.

The little girls will not be made to go to confession until
35 they have, in some measure, reached the age of reason, that

thus they may do it with the greater reverence for the sacrament; and we shall make them feel apprehensive of not being
sufficiently sincere. In the case of the elder girls, the mistress
will give them very careful instruction on this point and will
try to win their affection so that they may reveal to her the 5
difficulties which they may find in expressing themselves—this
being sometimes a cause of their not telling the confessor
everything. They will not be made to communicate until it
is seen that the fear of God is well-established in them and
that they have a desire to love Him and serve Him. Care 10
will be taken that they may not be inclined to desire this in
order to avoid the humiliation of being deprived of it for a
longer period than other girls. We shall therefore pay more
heed to their conduct than to their words in order to find
out if they are properly disposed towards this.   15

The sisters who are employed in looking after the children
will do so—as has been said—with great affection and great
devotion, yet at the same time with complete detachment,
fully realising that this duty involves so many opportunities
of making mistakes, of becoming too lax, and of losing the 20
spirit of meditation which is difficult to maintain in so busy
an employment. But if obedience none the less binds them
to it they must trust that God will sustain them and that the
charity, which of necessity accompanies this duty, will cover
their sins. Let them know also, for their comfort, that in de- 25
voting themselves to bringing up these children properly they
are recalling before God the years of their own childhood and
youth, which perhaps they employed badly through lack of
such an education.

The following detailed *Regulations* for the conduct of the girls'
schools at Port-Royal are dated April 15th, 1657. They were
drawn up by Jacqueline Pascal in response to a request from
M. Singlin, Confessor of the convent, for an account of the
methods which she employed in educating the *pensionnaires*. The

Regulations are preceded by an *Avertissement*[1] in which it is stated : "[these rules] have been based upon what has been practised at Port-Royal des Champs for many years. It must, however, be confessed that, as far as externals are concerned, it would not always be easy or advisable to put them into force in all their rigour. For it may happen that all the children are not capable of so prolonged a silence and so rigorous a *régime*, without relapsing into despondency and weariness, which must of all things be avoided ; and again that the mistresses cannot maintain so rigid a discipline over them while at the same time winning their affection and their trust—which is absolutely necessary for success in educating them."

iii

(*Jacqueline Pascal: Règlement pour les Enfans*—in *Constitutions du Monastère de Port-Royal du Saint Sacrement*, 1721, pp. 384–415 and 430–432.)

Daily Time-table.

Rising. The eldest girls rise at 4.0 ; the next in age at 4.30; the younger ones at 5.0; and the smallest of all according to their needs and their strength. For, you know, we have children of all ages from four to seventeen or eighteen. We
5 awake them by saying *Jesus*, and they reply *Maria* or *Deo Gratias*. They have to rise at once, without taking time to rouse themselves for fear lest this should give opportunity for laziness. If they do not feel well, they have to inform the sister who wakes them and they are then allowed to sleep on.
10 If one of the elder girls usually needs more rest than the allotted period she is allowed what she requires ; but when the prescribed time comes she gets up at once, for it is dangerous to accustom oneself to laziness at the beginning of the day.

1 This *Avertissement* was not written by Jacqueline Pascal. It was probably added by De Pontchâteau, who was a great-nephew of Richelieu and became a solitary at Port-Royal.

When they wake they say a short prayer appropriate to the hour. As soon as they are up they worship God and kiss the ground; then they all go to the dressing-room and worship God again, kneeling before their oratory and saying the prayers aloud lest anyone should have forgotten them. The elder girls do 5 one another's hair and they should do this in absolute silence, for it is fitting that their first words should be prayers and thanksgivings to God; if any of them have need to say something they should communicate with the mistress so that she may ask for what they want from the girl who has charge of 10 it. This does away with the necessity for any conversation between them during so profound a silence as that of the morning, and since what is said is spoken in very low tones at such a time, there is no danger of their taking the opportunity to say anything which is not necessary and which could 15 not be overheard by the mistress; for this might give rise to the telling of a falsehood if they were asked what they had said. This strict silence lasts till the *Pretiosa* of Prime and it is kept also after the *Angelus* in the evening, even in summer when they walk in the garden.   20

Time allowed for dressing. They are encouraged to do their hair and dress themselves as quickly as possible, so as to accustom them to spend as little time as can be helped on adorning the body which is destined to serve as food for worms, and to atone for the vanity of worldly women in the 25 matters of dress and toilet. As soon as the elder girls are dressed, they dress the little girls and do their hair with the same quickness and in the same silence. Everything has to be finished by a quarter past six at latest, which is about the time when the bell goes for the first Mass. Each older girl 30 takes care to make the younger ones repeat their prayers while they are having their hair attended to.

Morning Prayers. At the first stroke of Prime, or at latest at the *Pretiosa*, they kneel and are ready to begin the prayers when the signal is given by the mistress who is always present, 35 or by the sister who is appointed to help her. First they say their own special prayers and then the great office of Prime. Each week a child is told off to begin the prayers which are said in their room. For this reason I shall refer to her 5 as the monitress for the week. Prime and Compline are said in a moderate tone, neither too high nor too low, with slight pauses. They all remain standing during the whole of Prime and Compline. They are told that they keep in this attitude to show God that they all are ready to fulfil His holy will. 10 All the prayers said in common in their room are recited slowly, clearly, and in a proper attitude. At the end of Prime they make a short pause—the length of about two *Miserere* —to consider in God's sight what they have to do during the day and the chief faults which they may have committed 15 during the previous day ; that thus they may ask for grace from Him to foresee and to avoid the occasions which made them fall.

Making the beds and Breakfast. At the end of prayers they all go together to make their beds and those of the little 20 girls, doing this in pairs, as they have been appointed ; and nobody leaves a room until all the beds in it are properly made, unless the sister in charge allows some of them to go and begin making the beds in the next room, if she thinks she can so station herself as to be able to see both the rooms at the 25 same time, and is also careful that the children whom she sends are those of whose discretion and trustworthiness she is most confident. While the rest are making their beds, one of them gets ready the breakfast, the washing utensils, and wine and water for rinsing out the mouth. When the beds are made 30 they go and wash their hands and then take breakfast, during which one of them reads the passage from the Martyrology appointed for the day, so that they may know which are the special saints whom the Church commemorates on that day, and that they may honour them and put themselves under 35 their protection.

Work. At the end of breakfast—*i.e.* about 7.30 at latest
—all betake themselves to the schoolroom where they must
employ their time well, keeping strict silence. If there is need
to speak it must be in a low voice so as not to interrupt those
who are old enough to commune with God. The little girls 5
also are trained not to talk, but they are allowed to play when
they have tried faithfully to work and be silent; but during
these short intervals when they are allowed to play, they are
made to do so each by herself so as to avoid noise. I have
found that this does not trouble them and when they have 10
become used to it they amuse themselves quite cheerfully all
the same.

The children are taught to render their work profitable by
offering it to God and to do it for love of Him. Subjects are
set them according to the festivals and the seasons, so as to 15
help them to put themselves in the presence of God. From
time to time when the mistress is with them she tells them
some word of God to fortify their minds and to guard them
against vain and useless thoughts. At the same time an
attempt is made not to overdo this by wishing to make them 20
too pious; for as they are so young there are two dangers:
one, that they may take too much trouble and weary their
minds and imaginations instead of uniting their hearts with
God; and the other, that they may grow discouraged when
they see that they cannot attain the perfection which is re- 25
quired of them. We try to accustom the children to mortify
themselves and not to follow their own desires by preferring
one piece of work to another. For this reason they are told
that the less the work which they do pleases them, the more
it pleases God; and that therefore they ought to do with the 30
greatest assiduity and cheerfulness what is most distasteful
to them and to accustom themselves to work in a spirit of
penance. All the same, we do make allowances for them and
give way to them as far as possible, without however letting
them know of this indulgence. 35

They should never be allowed to work in pairs except in case of necessity and then a very good girl should be put with one who is less reliable so that the strong may aid the weak. They should be encouraged not to be too attached to their 5 work but to leave it as soon as the clock strikes, whether it be to go to Office or to recite the private prayers; for they must always be ready to do their duty to God, devoting themselves to that alone. When the mistress is in the room she may take the occasion to make them give an account of how they have 10 understood the Holy Mass; she may thus find an opportunity of explaining in greater detail the ceremonies of the Mass and of showing them how to profit thereby.

When a child has committed a fault, she is rebuked in front of all and the occasion is taken to show them the ugliness 15 of vice and the beauty of virtue. I have found that nothing is so profitable to them and that they remember this much better than the long drawn out homilies which are read to them. We avoid saying too much to them for fear of over-burdening their minds and I have found by experience that 20 religious instruction is much more beneficial to them when they are not at all weary of it. For this reason I think it is well sometimes to allow several days to elapse without giving them any and to let them become hungry, as it were, for this form of nourishment; the result is that they take in better 25 what is said to them.

We are careful to see that they are not negligent, untidy, and careless, that they put things away and do not lose them, and are neat and thorough in all that they do. We also teach them to be fond of needlework and to take it about with them 30 to occupy themselves and not waste any time if some unforeseen opportunity occurs. They also do sewing during the periods of recreation—the elder girls, at any rate—although they are not compelled to do so. They are merely encouraged to form the good habit of never being idle. When they have 35 once acquired it, it is no longer a burden but becomes, on the contrary, a pastime; this by the grace of God is, I see, actually the case with our girls, for as things are they find nothing so tedious as the festival holidays. I have found it a good plan to make them get into the way of putting aside for these occasions some piece of work for which they have a 5 special liking. I have taught our girls to knit woollen gloves and as they have only the periods of recreation for making them, they are very keen on this work.

Throughout the day one of them says aloud and on her knees a prayer which varies according to the season; in Lent, 10 for example, it deals with the Passion. The rest remain seated, but she who is appointed for this duty kneels down as soon as the clock strikes. We are careful to see that they are polite in asking for and receiving what they need for their work, that they hold themselves upright and gracefully, and 15 that they courtesy when entering or leaving the room. For this reason, although they wear a veil, they do not genuflect as the nuns do, except when they are before the most holy Sacrament.

In the interval between breakfast and eight o'clock those 20 elder girls who have rooms to sweep or their cells to tidy do so diligently and in silence. We are careful to see that there are never two at work together except in the case of such as are discreet and absolutely trustworthy. At eight o'clock all those who are busy in the bedrooms must leave them and 25 return to the schoolroom to hear a reading given by the mistress; this lasts till Tierce at 8.30. This reading deals with the subject which Holy Church has taken for the Office of the day. For example, in Advent, the mystery of the Incarnation; from Christmas to the Purification, the birth of our Lord and 30 the adoration of the Magi; in Lent, the Passion; and so on for the rest of the year. Whenever the festival of some noteworthy saint comes round the subject is taken from the life of this saint. This reading should serve as a special topic for the whole day. Whenever they are read to they are always 35 told something which they can apply to themselves or which will instruct them and help them to understand better what they read.

The Office. As soon as Tierce sounds they kneel and ask
5 our Lord's blessing saying *Benedicat nos Deus, Deus noster, benedicat nos Deus et metuant eum omnes fines terræ.* This they do whenever they go out to attend church that they may obtain from God grace to prevent their thoughts from wandering and to behave properly before the eyes of the
10 whole convent. As a rule those who are fourteen years old and sufficiently staid are allowed to attend all the Office on high festivals—even Matins, if they ask permission eagerly and deserve it. They also go to Tierce and Vespers on days which are double or semi-double and on the octaves of the principal
15 feasts. On specially-observed feasts and on Sundays they are also allowed to go to Prime; and all—little girls and elder ones alike—attend Tierce and Vespers on specially-observed feasts and Sundays. They also attend them on Thursdays and certain feasts of the holy Doctors and other
20 saints for whom they have a special devotion, even though these are not regular festivals. None the less, this regulation as to attendance at church on all these days is not observed as a regular custom. Any girl must ask permission according to her devotion; for they should always want to go to church
25 more often than they are allowed to go so that we have the authority to exclude those who are not devout.

We take care that in church they behave with great modesty, not allowing them to raise their eyes and look about; that they sing the whole service if they can; that they always have
30 a book even if they know their Office by heart; that the genuflexions which they make are profound, but that they hold themselves erect. Those who have been favoured by being appointed to take some part in a choir office should put all their devotion into acquitting themselves well, remem-
35 bering that they do the office of angels and that in making

use of them thus a great honour is paid them. They must
know perfectly the part which they have to say alone; and
if they make mistakes they must do penance for them and
recite in the refectory what they said wrongly and in some
cases for several days in succession, if it is through nervous- 5
ness that they went wrong, so that this weakness may be
corrected.

A sister always remains in the schoolroom to look after
those who do not go to Office, even if there are only two of
them. Whenever they go about the convent they walk two 10
and two as in a procession even though there are only a few
of them; and we are careful to avoid putting together those
who might talk to each other. They are always accompanied
wherever they go. As a rule they never go about the convent
singly and still less two or three together. But if there arises 15
a necessity to send them on some errand about the convent,
one of the more discreet and less curious is selected and that
even is done very rarely.

Holy Mass. After Tierce they all attend Holy Mass except perhaps the very little ones or some who are still frivolous 20
and childish, and who are not allowed to go always on weekdays. In this case a sister is left to look after them and she
makes them assist at Holy Mass with as much reverence as
if they were in church. They are accustomed from their youth
to hear Mass kneeling; we have found by experience that 25
this attitude is not so difficult when one is early accustomed
to it. We have decided that it is much better if children are
very young or frivolous to keep them in the schoolroom when
they are under no obligation to go to church, rather than to
let them get into the bad habit of talking or playing during 30
the service.

At the beginning of the *Sub tuum præsidium*, which is
an anthem of the Blessed Virgin and is said immediately
before Mass, they all kneel two by two in the middle of the
choir at a short distance one from another, with their hands 35

ungloved and clasped beneath their scapularies throughout
Mass. They must maintain an attitude of reverence and direct
their thoughts towards God; for this reason we try to give
them full instruction on all the ceremonies and ritual of the
5 Holy Sacrifice. For this they use M. de Saint-Cyran's manual
of instruction on the Holy Sacrifice; and they are taught
how to receive from God the prayers which they must offer,
by being told that whatever they can do will not please God
unless the Holy Spirit inspires it within them; for it is He
10 Who voices our prayers and acts of contrition.

I cannot refrain from saying here that it is impossible to
impress too strongly on children the reverence due to the
church, especially during Mass; and that we must punish
severely faults which are committed there and even prohibit
15 offenders from entering the church (except on festivals) for
as long a time as seems advisable for their good, even in the
case of the elder girls. For the older they are, the better
behaved they ought to be.

The Writing Lesson. After Mass they all have a writing
20 lesson in the same room, after saying a short prayer that God
will grant them grace to do this well; and we try to impress
gently on their minds the pious habit of never doing anything
of importance without beginning and ending it with a prayer.
They say these prayers according to their own devotion and
25 as God gives them utterance. We tell the youngest girls to
say an *Ave Maria* at the beginning and end of everything
of importance which they do. They should redouble their
silence during the writing lesson and they are not allowed to
show each other their papers nor to write anything they please.
30 They simply write their copy or else transcribe something
if they are well advanced and have been given permission.
They never write letters, notes, or sentences one to another
without obtaining permission from the mistress; and when
they have written what they have been allowed to write they
35 put it into the hands of the mistress for her to give it to the

girl for whom it is intended. The writing lesson lasts three-quarters of an hour. The time which remains till Sext is employed in learning to sing at sight.

Prayers before Dinner. When Sext sounds, one of them—the monitress for the week—kneels in the middle of the room 5 to recall their thoughts to God so that they may assist in spirit at this service which is just going to be said in the choir. Although silence is kept by the little sisters all through the day with the exception of lesson and conversation times, there are nevertheless two particular periods when it is more 10 strictly kept. The first is that of the evening and the morning to which I have already alluded, and the second is during the Offices and Masses which are said within the convent, even although the children are not present at them. They ought so to order things and provide for whatever they will 15 need that during these periods they will not have to ask their mistress for anything which concerns their work, nor, if possible, ask permission for anything, so as to commune with God and also to give their mistresses time to say their Office. At other times they may ask with greater freedom for what 20 they need. If one of their lessons—*e.g.* singing or repetition of the Catechism—overlaps the time for an Office, we do not leave off; but we require them to do their lesson in greater silence than usual and that the short prayer should be said at the beginning of each Office which is recited in 25 the choir even if it should be necessary to interrupt a lesson which has been begun. This reminds them that they must recall their thoughts and fix them upon God.

At 11.0 they all examine their consciences after having recited the *Confiteor* as far as *meâ culpâ.* Sometimes during 30 the evening and morning examinations of conscience we remind them of, and make them ask God's pardon for, some fault which apparently they have overlooked and which has been openly committed, that thus they may gently be taught how properly to examine themselves. At the end of 35

the examination they all repeat together aloud the rest of the *Confiteor*; then the monitress for the week asks God to pardon the faults committed and to grant grace that the rest of the day may be better employed. At the end of the examination
5 some of them say Sext privately; this is allowed to such elder girls as show themselves sufficiently devout to perform the Office properly. They are allowed to say from Lauds to Compline.

Refectory. The refectory bell sounds as a rule directly
10 after Sext and they all go to dinner with the same modesty as when they go to church. On arriving they make their reverence two by two in the middle of the refectory and when they pass any sister. They keep modestly in their proper places without talking, waiting till the *Benedicite* is
15 said; they join in this with the sisters in a low voice, with their sleeves turned down over their hands. After the *Benedicite* has been said they seat themselves at table not according to their rank, but as is judged most advisable, placing the best-behaved among those who are not so well-behaved
20 so as to prevent them talking to one another. We take great care not to let them grow dainty; we encourage them to eat anything without preferences and to begin with that part of their helping which they like least, in a spirit of penance, but at the same time to take sufficient nourishment so as to
25 avoid growing weak. For this reason we are particularly careful that they eat enough. They should always keep their eyes lowered without looking about, and should listen quietly to what is being read. Then they say grace with the sisters and go out in the same order as that in which they entered.

30 *Recreation.* After leaving the refectory they go to recreation. Here the little girls are always separated from the elder ones so as to give the latter a chance to converse more quietly and decorously; and this could not be if the little girls were there, because being younger they are allowed to play at
35 games which would prove irksome to their elders. If recrea-

tion takes place indoors the elder girls form a circle round
the mistress and converse unobtrusively yet freely, according
to their ability. They must not be expected to talk on serious
subjects nor to be always speaking about God; great discretion
must be observed in introducing a religious topic, but if it 5
is obviously to their taste it may be continued. They may
be allowed certain harmless games such as knucklebones,
shuttlecock, etc. Not that this is done among us at present; for, with the exception of the very little girls who are
always playing, they all work without wasting their time 10
and they have acquired such good habits that—as I have
already said—nothing is so irksome to them as the festival
holidays.

They are never allowed to be separated one from another
even though it be in the same room, and still less are two 15
or three of them allowed to be together or to speak so that
they cannot be overheard. Everything that they say should
be audible to the mistress and we always keep to the rule
which we have made that, wherever they are, they must repeat aloud what they have said in a whisper, or at any rate 20
that they should say it in an undertone or ask to be allowed
to say it privately to the mistress; for it might possibly be
something which would do much harm if everyone heard
it. For this reason they are privately instructed to say nothing aloud which should have been said quietly because it 25
is evil or might offend or hurt anyone's feelings ; and it would
be counted as great a fault to say such things aloud as to
keep back what they ought to have said. Since one can hardly
expect discretion in children we make them practise this
habit at all times and on all occasions, but especially at 30
recreation when they apparently have the right to talk freely
in their play and relaxation. For this reason their mistresses
are careful to have talks with them with the object of helping
them to say what is sensible and calculated to enlarge their
minds.   35

They are never allowed to speak of what has been said to them in Confession or in private, even if what they would like to say is extremely edifying. For there might be someone to whom such things had never been said and that might 5 give rise to jealousy. They will never talk about the singing of the sisters, saying thàt one sister sings better than another, nor will they speak of mistakes which may have been made in the choir or of the sisters' communions. We are careful to accustom them not to notice these things and not to regard 10 as most devout those who communicate most often nor most remiss those who do so most seldom. They are told when this occurs that each follows the gift of God and the instructions of her Superior and that neither must those be praised who communicate most frequently nor those blamed who do 15 so rarely; but that everything must be left to the judgment of our Lord. Again, they never talk about what happens in the refectory—for example, if some sister has done penance, nor even if they themselves or their companions have done penance. They are also forbidden to speak of the penances 20 for which they usually ask when instruction is given to them, for fear lest they should not perform it seriously, or that one should intimidate another. Moreover they are never allowed to tell the dreams which they may have had during the night, however beautiful and holy they may have been. They must 25 never speak about what has been told them in the reception-room. If there is something that would be edifying and might be told to them all the mistress will not omit to say it, so as to take away from them the desire which they might have for making it known. They are sometimes given information 30 about what is going on, if it does not matter—e.g. about the habit which certain sisters wear, the contents of a notice posted in the choir to ask for prayers for some persons or some pious enterprise or something similar; that thus we may take away from them the desire to find this out by illicit 35 means.

As far as possible they are never rebuked during recreation time, and this opportunity is never taken for telling them
of rules which ought to have been observed in the schoolroom ; for fear lest at such a time they should allow themselves to speak with too much freedom and then it might be 5
necessary to rebuke them ; and that must always be avoided
as far as possible. This does not mean that if they commit
grave faults during recreation time nothing is said ; on the
contrary, they are rebuked with an equal if not greater severity
than if the faults were committed at some other time, for 10
fear lest they should get into the way of not caring and of
following their inclinations too freely under pretext of amusing
themselves. All I say is that we keep the small faults for
another occasion and that we never mention during recreation faults committed at some other time.   15

We encourage them not to talk all at once, so as to avoid
a loud noise, but to listen one to another and when anyone
has begun a sentence not to interrupt, which we tell them
is extremely impolite. We tell them never on any occasion
to say anything uncharitable and to beware of the slightest 20
utterance which their sisters would not like to have said about
them even if what was said were not at all ill-intentioned ;
for they should be able to gather from another's silence that
she would prefer that the subject were changed. We exhort
them also to show a holy and courteous consideration one 25
for another, a habit which nothing save affection can produce.
They avoid all kinds of familiarity one towards another—
e.g. caressing, kissing, or touching one another on any excuse
whatever. Even the elder girls do not show these marks of
affection towards the little ones. If such things are forbidden 30
during recreation time they should all the more be prohibited
at other times, for then they are never allowed to speak to
one another except in the presence of their mistresses and
then only when it is necessary.

Recreation ends with a prayer to the Blessed Virgin that 35

she may ask of Jesus Christ, by the intercession of His Holy Mother, to give them grace to spend the rest of the day without sin.

Instruction. At the end of recreation they are drawn up in two rows in the middle of their schoolroom in readiness to receive instruction. They kneel and say together the *Veni Sancte Spiritus* and the mistress who is to instruct them says the collect and the little versicle. After the prayer they all sit down and any girl who has the devotion to make mention of her faults aloud may do so; but no one is obliged to do this; on the contrary, they are given to understand that this is allowed them as a favour but not commanded. None the less they are in the habit of doing so with real sincerity. They must listen with great attention to the admonition which is given them and which should always be kindly. For they must fully realise that they are reproved only for their own good and that no one of them is spared more than another. They must recognise that the mistress is not animated by any unworthy motive, whether it be her own feelings or interest; but that this does not prevent her from rebuking them severely so that they may be thoroughly humiliated and ashamed. For if this practice became perfunctory or they did it merely in order that it might be thought that they were very religious to confess their faults, the whole thing would become a mockery and hypocrisy; and this must be avoided at all costs. For this reason they are given a penance for all the important faults of which they accuse themselves; and I have not noticed that on this account they confessed them any the less freely. They never confess their faults in this way—*i.e.* before their sisters—on festivals or Sundays.

As soon as the confessions are over (this always lasts more than a quarter of an hour) the rest of the hour is spent in giving them instruction and in repeating what was said the day before. This repetition consists in making three or four children tell what was said to them on the preceding day.

They are not asked in order, so as to take them by surprise. First one is put on, and then another, but not all of them for that would take too much time. But if the confessions have taken a full half-hour another three-quarters is spent over the repetition and instruction.   5

On days which have a special Gospel—*e.g.* on specially-observed feasts, Ember Days, and the eves of Sundays, all stand with clasped hands and listen reverently to the Epistle and Gospel. After the Gospel has been read it is explained to them as simply as possible. On the other days when there 10 is no special Gospel they have the Catechism or the Christian Virtues explained to them. They are also taught how to make their confession, to communicate, to examine themselves, and to pray aright. We do not pass lightly from one subject to another, so as to give them time to understand 15 properly what is said to them. The explanation of the Catechism must needs take a long time, for we begin with the sign of the cross, then the articles of our faith, the commandments of God and of the Church ; the chief mysteries are reserved for the time immediately preceding those days 20 when they are commemorated by the Church. I will tell you the method I have followed for the last four years. During the first year I spoke to them about the creed, the sign of the cross, holy water, and the ten commandments. In the second year I tried to make them thoroughly under- 25 stand the explanation of the Holy Mass which is displayed in the new choir ; for even though it is fully explained there, they do not understand it at all because they read it by rote without thinking—at any rate most of them do, and especially the newcomers. I have done the same with the morning and 30 evening prayers, self-examination, and the other duties of a good Christian. Since then I have spoken to them on the virtues, using for this purpose S. John Climacus. The present year I have employed so far in dealing with penance, using the *Tradition of the Church* and laying particular stress 35

on those passages which show how important it is for
Christians to preserve the innocence given them at baptism
and how hard it is to recover when once it is lost. My intention now is—if God gives me grace—to explain most
5 carefully to them the *Catechism* of M. de Saint-Cyran, so as
to give them instruction on their duty to God and their
neighbour, and on morality.

Instruction ends with the prayer *Confirma hoc Deus*. This
exercise is over about 2.30. They do needlework during
10 this instruction provided that they have no questions to ask ;
for if a girl has need of anything she does nothing sooner
than disturb herself or the rest.

Employment of the time between None and Vespers. Between None and Vespers a catechism lesson is repeated, the
15 girls taking turns day by day in asking and answering ; she
who asks one day answers the next ; and at the end they
repeat a hymn in Latin or French. These repetitions cause
no disturbance and waste no time because while they are in
progress every girl stays in her place and does not leave her
20 work. Children's memories must be given plenty of practice
for this develops their intelligence, occupies them, and prevents evil thoughts.

The time that is left after instruction and before Vespers
is passed in working in absolute silence, except that at this
25 time and in all the intervals we make some of the moderately-
advanced girls read if their reading still needs improvement.
The girl who is put on to read in the schoolroom ought to
be able to do so reasonably well so that all may profit by
what is read. As for the little girls we have found that they
30 learn to read far more easily when they are alone. For this
reason the elder girl who is chosen to teach them to read
does so in a separate room during all the intervals throughout the day. We always employ for this duty one of the elder
girls who intends to become a nun, and even so it is necessary
35 to take care that she is well-behaved, sensible, and gentle,

and that she does this duty to the best of her ability and for the love of God.

About 3.30 a light meal is served to the little girls and those who are moderately advanced. We readily exempt the elder girls if they ask, as this meal is not very 5 necessary to them because we dine late and sup early; and it is noticed that those who do not partake of this extra meal enjoy the best health. Girls of fourteen years and over may be given permission to go without this meal except in cases where it is thought necessary; for in such cases girls would 10 be compelled to take a little food. We do not so readily exempt the younger ones, even though they beg us to do so, for fear lest they should ask permission only out of hypocrisy and in order to be thought grown up.

At this same time if those elder girls who are best-behaved 15 express a desire to go and say their prayers [in the convent church], a mistress accompanies them thither and remains with them until they have finished their prayers. Permission to pray thus is granted only to those who—as far as we can judge—are prompted to ask for it by a sincere desire to 20 please God, and who derive benefit from it.

Vespers and employment of the time until Refectory. At 4.0 the eldest girls go to Vespers if they deserve this favour. During this time also the youngest girls are instructed; for even though they are present at all the 25 instruction that is given in the schoolroom they do not listen to it, and unless they are spoken to privately, one by one, they understand nothing. At the end of Vespers one of the elder girls reads aloud until it is time for refectory. As often as possible the head-mistress should be present 30 at this. The reading continues until the bell sounds for refectory to which they go in the same order as in the morning.

Evening Recreation and Prayers ; Going to Bed. After this comes recreation—the same as in the morning except 35

that during the summer they go out into the garden in the evening and during the winter in the morning. The children are separated one from another in the evening as in the morning. We do our best that there may be two nuns with
5 the elder girls if some of them are not well-behaved ; and it is the duty of one of these nuns to walk behind the girls so that she may discover those who, pretending to be indisposed, lag behind so as to talk together in a low voice. Evening recreation lasts till the first stroke of Compline except during
10 the hottest part of summer when it will end later, due regard being paid to the needs of the pupils and to letting them stay out in the fresh air. However, recreation never ends later than 7.30 so that evening prayers may begin then. In the hottest part of the year the girls may say these kneeling
15 in some secluded spot ; there they proceed to say Compline in the same tone of voice as that used at Prime in the morning. They may walk whilst reciting the Psalms provided that they halt in order to perform all the ceremonies of the Office. When the heat is not so great they begin prayers at the first
20 stroke of Compline so that they may be able to be present in the choir when the anthem of the Virgin is sung ; they assist at this all the year round with the exception of about three months when it is hottest (*i.e.* from the Octave of Corpus Christi to the end of August), so as not to interrupt
25 the walk which is thought to be beneficial to them at that hour of the day.

On leaving the choir or the garden they go straight to their rooms where they undress quickly and in perfect silence, so that, winter and summer alike, they must all be
30 in bed at 8.15 ; each has a separate bed—a rule which is never broken under any circumstances. As soon as they are in bed they are all without exception visited—those in the cells and those in the dormitories alike. Each bed must be visited separately to see that its occupant is covered up
35 with proper modesty and also that she has sufficient bed-

clothes in winter. After this all the lights are extinguished except one lamp which is left alight all night in one of the dormitories for use if need arise during the night. In each dormitory a sister sleeps or else one of the elder girls who is absolutely trustworthy. 5

This then is the daily routine, although of course altera-tions in the time-table are sometimes made for special reasons—*e.g.* on fast-days appointed by the Church and in Lent, when the morning is much longer than the after-noon. 10

[Here follow the Morning and Evening Prayers which were used in the school.]

Time-table for Festivals.

On festivals the whole of the day is filled up with little exercises so that our pupils may not waste any time and may thus avoid boredom and the foolish behaviour which inevitably results if children are not kept occupied; for they have not sufficient strength to devote all their time to the 15 service of God.

They rise and dress at the same time as on working days. At 6.0 if the little girls are nearly dressed, the elder ones who have the devotion to go to Prime may do so if they ask permission, which is not given unless it is recognised that 20 they ask out of a sincere desire to please God and to sing His praises. This is the case with attendance at all the canonical hours. After Prime the first Mass is said; at it all are present—younger and elder girls alike. After Mass they go and make their beds and have breakfast. This lasts till 25 about 8.0 when they all gather in the schoolroom to hear the reading which takes place as on working days. At 8.30 most of them go to Tierce and all of them to High Mass. After High Mass there is about three-quarters of an hour interval until Sext. This they spend in learning by heart the passages which they ought to know—*i.e.* all the *Familiar Theology*, the *Exercise of the Holy Mass*, and the *Treatise on Confirmation*. After this they learn all the French 5 hymns in their Book of the Hours, and then the Latin ones from the Breviary. Thus many of those who come to the convent quite young learn the whole of their Psalter. They do not find it very difficult if they are given encouragement and helped on a little. At Sext they make their examination 10 and then those who have permission to say their Office repeat Sext. After Sext comes refectory, and then recreation until 1.0. From 1.0 till 2.0 the eldest girls learn arithmetic; meanwhile the younger ones write copies and the youngest of all say their catechism. From 2.0 till 2.30 the 15 elder girls teach arithmetic to the younger ones and at 2.30 they say None privately until 3.0. At 3.0 the eldest girls practise plainsong and one of them teaches the younger girls; even though they need only learn their notes this employs their time and prevents them becoming 20 wearied and at the same time they gradually learn to sing. At 4.0 they all go to Vespers and the Adoration which follows it. After Vespers those of the elder girls who are inspired with great devotion and have been granted permission stay behind to pray until refectory. If, there 25 is less than half-an-hour left all the rest are taken to the schoolroom and spend their time at their devotions or in reading their *Imitation* or in repeating something that they know by heart. The rest of the day is spent as on working days.

The second part of Jacqueline Pascal's *Regulations* deals with the attitude which the mistresses were to adopt with regard to their pupils.

iv

(*Jacqueline Pascal: op. cit.* pp. 433–458 and 472–479.)

The spirit in which we should do service to our pupils. Mistresses' Meetings. General rules for their conduct, particularly with regard to the younger children.

I believe that if we are to be of service to our pupils we must never speak to them nor do anything for them without 5 first looking to God and asking Him for grace, hoping to find in Him all that is needful for instructing them in the fear of Him. We must feel great love and affection for them, never neglecting any of their spiritual or bodily needs and showing them continually that we set no limits to the services which 10 we can render them and that we do it affectionately and whole-heartedly because they are children of God and we feel ourselves constrained to leave nothing undone to make them worthy of this holy estate. It is essential that we devote our-selves wholly and unreservedly to them and that, except in 15 cases of unavoidable necessity, we never leave their quarters. We shall thus always be present in the schoolroom where they work unless we are employed in talking to them or in visiting such as are sick or in performing some other duty which con-cerns them. We must never mind missing the whole Office 20 unless the elder girls assist at it; for it is so important to keep a constant watch over the children that we ought to prefer this duty to all others if our obedience requires it of us, and still more should we set it above our own inclinations even though they concern things spiritual. The love with which we 25 do them all the services which will be of use to them will not only cover many of our faults but also will take the place of many things which we might think would be profitable for our own perfection.

There will be one sister on whom reliance will be placed and who will never be relieved from her charge. If possible
5 this sister who is told off to help us must be on duty in the schoolroom as often as she can. For this reason it would be desirable to have two, both animated by the same zeal and the same sympathy with children. As often as possible they should both be in the schoolroom together, even when the
10 headmistress is there; so that when they see the respect which the children show to her they may both have the right to require in her absence the same respect as is shown when she is present. We must do our utmost that the children may notice a perfect harmony, an absolute agreement and con-
15 fidence, between us and the sister who is told off to help us. For this reason we must never countermand any order or act of hers, so that the children may never notice any disagree- ment; but we must wait and tell her of it in private. For it is important—nay, almost essential—for managing the children
20 properly that the sister who is assigned to help us should be ready to acquiesce in whatever is told her. Otherwise the Superior should be informed. But if her opposition to us merely thwarts our own private whims but does not harm the children in any way, we must ask God for grace to rejoice in
25 that we have an opportunity of being thwarted. We must pray often that God will give the children a great respect for the sisters who help us. We must at the same time give to these sisters great authority—especially to her who ranks next to us. It is advisable therefore to show the children—and
30 even on occasion to tell them—that she has a deep regard for them, that she loves them, and that it is we who compel her to give an account of whatever goes on in the schoolroom; and on the other hand to tell her in front of the children that she is compelled both by her duty and by her regard for them
35 to report to us not only their more serious faults but also their

slightest failings, so that they may be helped to overcome them.

We confide in any sister who helps us so far as to tell her the dispositions of the children, especially of the younger ones and of those elder girls who might create some disorder, 5 so that she may the more easily keep watch on them. We must not however go so far as to tell her what the children say to us in private (unless such a step is obviously necessary for their good) for fear lest, without thinking, she should give them a hint of it. I realise that it is extremely important that 10 the children should understand that we keep their secrets, even though what they tell us be of no great importance at the time; for it may happen that they will have important things to tell us at another time, especially when they grow older, and they would be reluctant to tell them if they had discovered 15 that we had not been faithful to them in small matters. Important as it is that we should have a perfect agreement and understanding with the sisters who are told off to help us, it is still more important that these sisters should act only in accordance with the regulations which they find drawn up 20 and that they should so conform to the ideas of the headmistress that they speak only with her mouth and see only with her eyes; that thus the children may notice no inconsistencies among their mistresses. But if the sisters have anything to say against the behaviour of the headmistress they 25 should tell her, if they have sufficient confidence in her and have been given permission by the Superior. If God does not give them this confidence they should inform the Abbess for fear lest, without intending it, they should betray some sign of their dissatisfaction before the children.   30

If there are two nuns in the schoolroom when the hour for Office strikes they can say it one after the other, so that there may be one to supervise the children; but she will say nothing of the faults which she sees committed, unless they are serious, until her companion has finished her Office, so as to 35

inspire the children with great reverence when they see anyone praying. But as soon as the Office is said (and it does
not take long when it is repeated in a low voice) they must
be punished according to the magnitude of their fault and
5 with greater severity than when prayers are not being offered
to God. If the mistress is alone she need have no scruple
about keeping watch over them, but she should say nothing
whatever to them until she has finished the Office. We have
found by experience how profitable this is for them; for if
10 we are particular about not speaking to them and not rebuking
them during prayers this makes them in turn much more
reverent when they pray and much more afraid to interrupt
us. We cannot too thoroughly impress reverence for God
upon the young, by our example as much as by our words.
15 We shall therefore be very particular about saying Office at ·
the times when it is said in the choir, stopping whatever we
are doing at the second bell for Office and never letting ourselves be induced to finish anything in which we are interested.
This does not mean that if an occasion arises when it is
20 necessary to do some service to the children we ought not to
prefer it to our Office; but it is good that the children and
our own consciences should clearly realise that we act for God
alone. It is by our example that we can best instruct them;
for the devil gives them memory to make them bear in mind
25 our slightest faults and he takes it from them to prevent them
from remembering the small amount of good which we do
perform.

We cannot therefore too often pray to God or humble
ourselves or keep watch over ourselves, that thus we may do
30 our duty by the children since our obedience enjoins this upon
us. I regard it as one of the most important obediences of
the convent and we cannot be too diffident about fulfilling it,
though there is no need to be afraid; but we must put our
whole confidence in God and induce Him by our lamen-
35 tations to grant us that which we do not of ourselves deserve

but which we ask of Him through the blood of His Son, shed
for the innocent souls which He has put into our charge. For
we must always look upon these tender souls as a sacred trust
which He has confided to us and of which He will demand
an account from us. Therefore we should speak less to them 5
than to God on their behalf. And since we are obliged to be
always with them, we must so behave that they may not find
us inconsistent or capricious, treating them sometimes too
indulgently and sometimes too severely. These two faults
usually result one from the other; for if we allow ourselves 10
to lavish on them little endearments and blandishments and
leave them free to follow their own inclinations as much as
they please, the inevitable result is that they will have to
be rebuked; and so arises this inconsistency which is far
more distasteful to children than being always kept to their 15
duty.

    We must never make ourselves too familiar with them
nor show them too much confidence—even in the case of the
elder girls; but we should always evince true affection and
great kindness in all that concerns their needs and even 20
anticipate these. We must always treat them very politely,
always speak to them with respect, and give way to them where
possible. This helps greatly to win them over. It is advisable sometimes to make concessions to them in matters which,
from our point of view, are not important, so as to win their 25
confidence. When it is necessary to find fault with them for
frivolity and disobedience they must never be mimicked or
pushed roughly, even though they are out of temper. On the
contrary, we must speak to them very gently and reason with
them so as to convince them. This will prevent them be- 30
coming embittered and they will thus take very well what is
said to them.

    We should often pray to God that He will make the
children straightforward; we must co-operate with Him by
putting far from them all evasions and subterfuges; but we 35

must do even this straightforwardly lest we render them evasive by exhorting them to be straightforward. I think therefore that we must not let them suspect that we consider that they are sly. For sometimes we make them evasive by dint 5 of telling them not to be so and they make use of all that was said to them during the time when they had not this vice when, on some subsequent occasion, they want to use evasion to hide faults which they do not wish known. We must therefore keep unfailing watch over the children, never leaving 10 them alone wherever they may be, whether they be well or ill. But we must not let them know that we are so particular about this lest we encourage in them a suspicious attitude and they be always on their guard. For thus they would get into the habit of doing little naughtinesses in secret—particu- 15 larly the little girls. I think then that our watch should be always a kindly one and that we should show them a certain confidence which makes them the rather realise that we love them and that it is only to look after them that we are with them. They will thus like watchfulness instead of being afraid 20 of it. The youngest girls even more than the others we must train and nourish, if possible, like little doves. Little should be said to them when they have committed a serious fault which deserves punishment; but if we are perfectly sure about it we must punish them without saying a word, not 25 even giving the reason of the punishment until it is over. Then it is good to ask them, before saying anything else, if they know why they have been punished; for as a rule they do not fail to have realised it. A punishment of this kind, administered promptly and silently, prevents them telling 30 falsehoods in order to find excuses for their faults, a habit to which little children are much addicted; and I find that they rid themselves of their faults much better because they are always afraid of being taken off their guard.

I think also that in the case of their less serious faults 35 they ought to be warned; for insensibly they grow accustomed to being continually spoken to. For this reason in the case of one out of every three or four faults we should pretend not to notice; but afterwards for a while we must take them by surprise and make them pay the penalty on the spot. This corrects them far better than any amount of talk. If there are little 5 girls who are thoroughly obstinate and disobedient, they must be forced to make amends three or four times in the same way. This completely subdues them when they realise that we do not grow wearied. But if we do this one day and forgive them or take no notice the next, this makes no impression 10 on their minds and it will be found needful to resort to more drastic methods than those which would be necessary if employed consistently. Telling falsehoods is very common among small children. We must therefore do our utmost to prevent their acquiring this bad habit; and to this end I think 15 we should warn them with great kindness in order to get them to confess their faults, telling them that all that they have done is clearly seen and that if they confess of their own accord they must be pardoned or their punishment mitigated.   20

Even children who are very young—*e.g.* four or five years old—must not be left without anything to do all day. But their time must be split up into short periods, they should read for one quarter of an hour, play for another, and then work for another short period. These changes keep them 25 amused and prevent them from getting the bad habit (to which children are very subject) of holding their book or their work and playing with it, or of sitting awkwardly and continually turning their heads about. But if we ask them to work hard for a quarter of an hour or half an hour and promise them 30 that if they persevere with their lesson or their work they will be allowed to play, they will work quickly and hard for this short period so as to win the reward afterwards. But even if they play in spite of this promise which has been made to them before they begin to work, nothing should be said to 35 them; but at the end when the time is up and they are thinking of going out to play, they should be made to begin another period of work. They should thus be shown that we do not want to be always speaking to them, but that since 5 they have merely been wasting time they must start again. This takes them by surprise and teaches them to be on their guard another time.

The objects which we set before them in general conversation and on the occasions when they give us an opportunity of speaking 10 *to them and warning them.*

They are made to understand that perfection does not consist in performing a number of private acts, but in carrying out what they do in common properly—*i.e.* with all their heart and for the love of God, with a sincere desire to please 15 Him and to fulfil always His holy will with joy. We teach them to prize those little opportunities which God sends them of suffering something for His sake—*e.g.* any little slights from their sisters, any ungrounded accusations which are made against them, any thwarting of their wills and inclinations, 20 any occasion for forgoing their own desires, whether it arises on the part of their mistresses or from some other source. We beseech them to take these things as the gifts of God, as a proof of His deep love and of His care in sending them day by day opportunities of perfecting themselves. They 25 should frequently be told of the pleasure and satisfaction that there is in giving oneself unreservedly to God and in serving Him in simplicity and truth, holding nothing back from Him. They must be taught that nothing is irksome when we do it out of sheer love; that unquestioning response 30 to God's promptings draws down upon us ever fresh supplies of grace; that some will gain heaven and others will merely deserve punishment in virtue of one and the same action according to the motive which inspires it and the purity or impurity of the intention. It is well to make them realise this by resorting to little examples ; *e.g.* a good action, done for the love of God and with a desire to please Him and to fulfil His holy will, leads us to heaven ; whereas the selfsame action, done in a spirit of hypocrisy and vanity and simply with the desire to win the applause of men, would deserve 5 nothing but punishment. For if we have done nothing for God we ought not to expect any reward, but merely chastisement as payment for our hypocrisy.

We should strongly exhort the children to know themselves, their inclinations, their vices, their passions, and to 10 strike at the root of their faults. It is well too that they should realise their natural proclivities, that thus they may restrain what would be displeasing to God and transform their natural tendencies into spiritual ones. We should tell them, for example, that just as they should transform their love 15 for themselves and for their fellow creatures—if they are of an affectionate disposition—into a whole-hearted love for God, so also should it be with their inclinations. We must point out from time to time that one of the greatest faults of youth is disobedience, which is perhaps natural ; but that if they 20 do not guard against this vice it will destroy them by making them unamenable to any kind of admonition ; and that this is a fault peculiar to a spirit of pride. For this reason they will often be told that they ought to welcome harsh treatment and that by the meekness with which they receive the ad- 25 monitions which are given them they show their willingness that everything within them which can displease God should be destroyed. We exhort them never to be ashamed of doing good ; for sometimes those who have been badly-behaved are ashamed of doing right in front of those who have seen 30 their misbehaviour. They should be told to pray to God that He may give them strength to do the right fearlessly ; and if at first they often relapse, they must even more often and more steadfastly recover themselves. This advice should be given to them all alike, even at times when none of them behave 35

badly, so that this may serve for another time and those who are
best-behaved may apply it to their own needs. We tell them
that the difficulties which they encounter in the path of virtue
are due to the fact that as soon as there appears some vice
5 to overcome or some virtue to acquire they have recourse to
themselves; they consider their own inclinations and caprices,
their self-esteem, their weaknesses and the trouble which they
have to overcome them; whereas, instead of enfeebling themselves by such human considerations, they ought to have
10 recourse to God in Whom, even in their weakness, they would
find all power. For to be devoid of hope that He will deliver
them by the power of His holy grace shows a lack of confidence in His goodness. If they were told to escape from
their troubles and weaknesses by their own power they would
15 have every cause to despair; but since they are told that
God Himself will take away all their difficulties they have
but to pray, to hope, and to rejoice in God to Whom they
should always look for aid. They must be induced to welcome
and desire help for overcoming the weakness of their corrupt
20 nature; they should not be pestered, but induced gently to
bear without complaint slight humiliations and rebukes administered in the presence of the other girls, so as to accustom
them by degrees not to be too sensitive and to confess their
little faults from time to time in public that thus they may
25 grow used to penance and humiliation. We try to impress
upon their minds that a virtuous intention counts as nothing
in God's sight if it is not followed out in action when opportunity occurs; and that it will avail us little at the hour of
death to have spent our life in continually forming impulses
30 if we have not put them into practice; for so far from
being rewarded for them we should justly be punished by
God.

We should not predispose them towards the religious life
—especially in our talks with them all together—nor should
35 we show them all that we believe concerning how few people

win salvation in the world. It is enough to show them the
great difficulty of winning salvation there, and to make them
realise the responsibilities which they bear as Christians and
the promises which they made at baptism. They must also
be shown all that they should avoid if they return to the 5
world. Occasionally it is good to tell them some of our own
personal feelings on this subject and not hide from them our
joy, our contentment, and our peace of mind. If they themselves introduce the subject of the religious life and give
their own views, we may well profit by the opportunity to 10
tell them something of the happiness of a good religious
who lives truly after her vocation, her constant consolation
being to reflect upon those great means—obedience and
humility—which God has given her for loving Him and winning for herself everlasting bliss; for there is no other way 15
than this to heaven for all Christians, and especially for religious. We must therefore make them understand that the
religious life is not a burden but one of God's greatest gifts
and a relief for those who wish throughout their life to keep
their baptismal vows; that God does not grant this grace to 20
everybody nor even to all who wish for it; and that since it
is so excellent a gift we must ask God for it with all the
greater humility and prepare to receive it by good works.

It is sometimes advisable to show them that we love them
for the sake of God and that this is why we feel their faults 25
so much and find them so painful to endure; and that it is
the intensity of this love which sometimes renders so harsh
the words which we use when we rebuke them. At the same
time we shall assure them that whatever we do we are inspired solely by the love which we bear them and by our 30
desire to make them as God would have them be; that there
ever remains in our hearts a great tenderness for them, that
our severity is directed only against their faults, but that in
such cases we exert our utmost strength, although we would
far rather treat them with kindness than with severity.   35

How children should be spoken to in private.

The custom of talking privately to children is of the greatest assistance in managing them. It is by such conversations that we comfort them in their troubles, put ourselves
5 on their level so as to induce them to wage war against their faults, and show them their deeply-rooted vices and passions; and I venture to say that when God gives them perfect confidence in their mistress great things may be expected, for I have never seen a confidence which was perfect and which
10 has not succeeded. These conversations which we have with them should be very serious; on such occasions we should show them great affection but no familiarity, and if we find a girl who obviously is seeking to talk merely for the sake of amusement she must be treated more coldly than the others.
15 It is necessary therefore to exercise much discretion not only as to the conversation itself but also as to how often it should take place. I think about once a fortnight is sufficient except in case of special needs about which no rule can be laid down.

20 We must carefully guard against being deceived, and it is a great advantage when children are given to understand that we know all their slyness. This makes them desist from it and reduces them unconsciously to a simple and straightforward frame of mind without which we cannot possibly do
25 them any benefit. It is therefore essential that we should never be taken off our guard and we cannot avoid this without God's continual help. For this reason we shall never speak to them without first praying to God and even forecasting in His presence what we think they are likely to say
30 and the answers which we think He would have us make to them. We shall with tears and lamentations implore that His divine majesty may illumine our darkness and that the light of His grace may help us to discover what the children would hide from us; and if in conversation they tell us some-

thing and we are not perfectly sure of the right answer we shall tell them that we are going to spend a short time in praying to God before replying, and that they on their part also must pray that He may dispose them to receive with a heart absolutely free from worldly considerations all that we 5 tell them on His behalf for their well-being. We shall employ this same delay in answering, directly we realise that they would be irritated by what we might say to them or that they would not take in the right spirit any rebuke that we are about to administer. We might tell them that we see 10 plainly that they are not well-disposed to listen to us or that we perhaps are not properly enlightened, and that if we both pray to God—if we do so humbly—He will doubtless have pity on us. Such little acts of condescension as these should not be shown to all, but they are extremely valuable in the 15 case of the older girls and those who are intelligent. Great discretion must be exercised so as to speak to them at a suitable time and place. I therefore repeat—what I cannot repeat too often though I do it not enough—that we must pray more than speak; and I believe that our hearts and 20 minds must ever be lifted up on high so that we may receive from God all the words which we ought to say to the children.

We must always be on the watch to study them and to find out their inclinations and caprices, that thus by studying 25 them we may discover what they have not power to reveal to us of themselves. It is good to anticipate them if we see them shy in confessing their failings; and to give them greater freedom in revealing these it is advisable at first to keep back from them many truths which we feel would be 30 too strong for their imperfect state. In proportion as God opens their hearts so that they speak to us with some measure of sincerity, we can speak to them with the greater plainness and show them the obligation which they are under to do penance in cases where we see there is need of it. We must 35

also show them how narrow is the way which leads to heaven
and tell them that it is only the courageous and the violent
who take heaven by force.

If they ask for many special penances to perform, only
5 very few or none at all will be granted to them; but we shall
show them that it is not by these that they will please God
unless they come from a heart truly touched by love of Him
and by a sincere desire to please Him and to do penance;
and that, as far as we are concerned, we shall judge them not
10 by these acts, but by the fidelity with which they carry out
the smallest schoolroom rules, by the help which they give to
their sisters, by the affection with which they serve one another
in their needs, by the care which they show in mortifying
their bad habits; that it will be these things which will make
15 us believe that they wish to serve God, and not a number of
special acts; and that for this reason they must not be disappointed if we do not permit these, because we desire to
promote their well-being and not to help them to deceive
themselves. We shall tell them these things although some-
20 times we shall not hesitate on other occasions to grant what
they ask without taking any notice or making any account of
it. On the contrary, when they ask for something out of the
ordinary we shall pretend to pay no attention to them, though
we do not fail to notice more carefully than at other times
25 all their actions, so as to call their attention to these afterwards when opportunity arises. By adopting this attitude
towards them we shall soon discover if they make their
requests out of hypocrisy. For if they make them only to
attract attention, when they see that no regard is paid to them
30 they will not fulfil what they asked for and will not make the
request again. For the same reason we must be very strict in
making them carry out the duty for which they have asked,
not letting them see that we know their dispositions until
some other time when we find them better disposed; then
35 we shall make them realise their condition and the danger

there is in wishing to do unusual things from purely worldly motives.

Should there be some girls who are badly-behaved but whom the Superiors for good reason think should be retained in the school, we should implore them, when they are in their 5 best moods, to be reconciled to our not indulging their failings; and we should show them with all possible affection and kindness their obligation to lead a Christian life. But if it is obvious that these admonitions do not profit them at all, they must be given to understand that we shall not put up 10 with their faults and that the more we see that what we do for them and say to them is useless, the more steadfastly shall we, for the unburdening of our consciences, continue to warn them and compel them to expiate their faults by penance. Thus we shall not allow them to acquire bad habits; and 15 besides God wills that we compel them to make reparation before their sisters for the bad example which they set, lest their failings should harm the rest. It is advisable to show them that our consciences compel us to act in this way.

The Penances, both public and private, which may   20
be imposed on them.

They must be made to ask the pardon of any of the sisters or of their schoolfellows whom they have displeased or to whom they have spoken rudely or set a bad example. This pardon may be asked in various ways according to the mag- 25 nitude of the fault—either in public or in private, in the refectory or during instruction. They may also be ordered to kiss the feet of their comrades whom they have offended. Great care must always be exercised that if the fault was observed by only two or three or four people, the offender 30 should make satisfaction for it in private—at least, if it is of small consequence; for it is very dangerous to make a mistaken attempt to edify those who have not seen the faults

of others. I say the same as to the faults of special girls who have some influence; when a number of girls have committed these faults we must wait and reprove each of them in private or all the offenders together, lest we fail in an attempt to edify
5 the weaker ones.

They may be made to wear a grey cloak, to go to refectory without a veil or scapular or even to stand at the door of the church in this garb. Sometimes, again, they may be forbidden to go to church for one day or several days, accord-
10 ing to the magnitude of their fault; or they may be made to stay at the door of the church or in some place apart from the rest. It is particularly necessary to take care that being forbidden to go to church is not a matter of indifference to them The youngest and middle-school girls can be made to
15 wear labels which show their fault and which should be inscribed in large letters; it is enough that there should be one or two words; *e.g.*: *Idle*; *Careless*; *Story-teller*; etc. Or again they can be made to ask the sisters in the refectory to pray for them, explaining the fault into which they have
20 fallen or the virtue which they lack. In the case of the older girls we should make them fear for the love of God and through dread of His judgments; and when occasion arises we can impose on them some of the penances which the younger girls are made to undergo—*e.g.* going without a veil or asking
25 the sisters in the refectory for their prayers. But we must be very careful that this will benefit them and not do them harm by embittering them; and this means that we must pray unceasingly to God that He will enlighten us and in everything guide us for His own glory and salvation of the souls
30 which He has entrusted to us.

Here follow four sections dealing with (1) Confession; (2) Holy Communion; (3) Confirmation; (4) Prayer. Before a pupil is admitted to the sacraments of Confirmation or the Eucharist the mistresses are to be assured of her worthiness to receive them. Great care is to be taken that those who are too young or of a frivolous disposition shall not be confirmed or allowed to communicate. It was customary at Port-Royal for the pupils to be confirmed before making their first communion —a rule which is still prescribed in the rubric of the English Office, although in the Roman Church the first communion usually precedes confirmation. In the fourth section, in spite of the numerous prayers which are enjoined upon pupils by the Regulations, Jacqueline Pascal recognises that the spirit of prayer— an habitual attitude of mind—is more to be desired than the punctual repetition of routine formulæ. It is recommended that particular devotion should be shown to the Blessed Virgin (Notre-Dame de Port-Royal), to the guardian angel, and to certain special saints.

Reading.

The books which we use for instructing the children are the *Imitation*, the *Sinner's Guide*, the *Philothée*, *S. John Climacus*, the *Tradition of the Church*, the *Letters of M. de Saint-Cyran*, the *Familiar Theology*, the *Christian Maxims* 5 which are in the *Hours*, the letter of a *Carthusian Father* (recently translated), the *Meditations of S. Theresa on the Lord's Prayer*, and other books the aim of which is to form a truly Christian life. The morning readings at eight o'clock I have specified in the daily time-table. For the reading 10 which one of them gives after Vespers other books can be used—*e.g.* some of S. Jerome's letters, *Christian Almsgiving*, some passages in S. Theresa's *Way of Perfection*, and also the historical outlines from the *Lives of the Desert Fathers* and other lives of saints which are to be found in special 15 books. We ourselves always read when the whole school is present with the exception of the reading after Vespers; but we are always present at the latter to explain what is read and to talk about it. Our aim should be to accustom the children not to listen to reading in a spirit of diversion or 20 curiosity but with the desire of applying it to themselves; to this end our manner of making them understand it should

be directed far more to rendering them good Christians and inducing them to correct their faults than to making them learned. They must be told to ask of God grace to profit by the readings which they hear and also that He may
5 put into our minds what will be most helpful to them in making daily progress in the way of perfection.

With regard to the readings which we do not give in person, we show them what they have to read and they are not allowed to change either the passage or the book; for
10 there are few books in which there is not something to be passed over. At the reading after Vespers they are allowed —or rather, bidden—to ask questions continually on whatever they do not understand, provided that this is done respectfully and humbly; and in answering we show them
15 how to apply what is read to the correction of their own conduct. If while reading we notice that they do not ask any questions on some point which, we think, most of them do not understand, we ask them if they understand, and if we see that they cannot answer they will be rebuked for remaining
20 in ignorance after having been bidden to ask for information about anything of which they are ignorant. As soon as the reading is over the book is taken back; for we never leave any books in their private possession except their *Hours*, the *Familiar Theology*, the *Words of Our Lord*, an *Imitation*, and
25 a Psalter in Latin and French. All their other books are in the mistress's charge; and they are quite agreeable to this arrangement because they themselves recognise that it is more beneficial for them, and that the most sacred readings are useless if they are performed out of curiosity—and this
30 is what almost always results when they have books in their private possession and at their own disposal. They are never allowed to open a book which does not belong to them or to borrow them one from another without the mistress's permission—and that is given rarely so as to avoid the many
35 small disturbances which borrowing entails.

The Sick and their bodily needs.

Very great care must be taken of those who fall ill. They must be attended to carefully and regularly at the proper times. The doctor should be sent for if the illness requires it and all his orders for the relief of their sickness must be 5 exactly carried out. We do our utmost to be present when the doctor pays his visit and it is well always to speak to him before he visits the invalids, to give him an account of their illnesses and how they take their medicine and food. He should be asked to say little in their presence for fear of 10 depressing them or giving them occasion to be sorry for themselves. After the doctor has visited them he should be asked what must be done for their relief. We accustom them not to make any fuss over taking even the most unpleasant remedies. On such occasions we are always present to speak to 15 them some word of God to encourage them and to make them offer their illness to God. We exhort them never to complain of the doctor's orders because in their illness he takes the place of God in regard to them. They must therefore obey him as if he were God Himself, abandoning their life, their 20 health or sickness, to the disposal of Divine Providence which avails Itself for our benefit of the good or ill success of the remedies which are applied. Whatever unpleasantness therefore is to be endured, the fault must never be laid on the doctor or his remedies; but in silence and humility the 25 authority which divine goodness exerts over us must be adored; and in order to ensure that the sick should adopt this attitude I presuppose that we should always have, if possible, doctors who are good Christians and good doctors.

There will always be a room set apart for the reception 30 of the sick; into it the other children will not be allowed to enter except in case of great necessity and with their mistress's permission. During the recreation hours one of the most reliable girls may be sent there to cheer the invalids. The sister who looks after them must never leave them unless 35

there are elder girls—*e.g.* such as are ready to enter the noviciate and in whom absolute confidence can be placed—who can watch them and even look after them if their illness is not severe. If there are many invalids another sister must
5 be told off besides her who acts as nurse; and these sisters must be wise and kind—wise, so as to keep them in the path of duty lest in their illness they lose all that they have so laboriously acquired during health, and also so as not to humour their caprices or the dislike which they have of taking
10 the prescribed remedies and of abstaining continually from certain foods which would be harmful to them. But at the same time they must be kind so that by the affectionate way in which they treat their patients and by their gentle words they may mitigate all the refusals which must be made for
15 health's sake.

We give great attention to the invalids even preferring to leave those who are well, partly in order to give them the proper treatment but also to keep them in the right path and teach them to bear their illnesses like Christians. Thus they
20 do not so soon become unruly. Besides this attention and these general visits, on special occasions we visit each privately if there is more than one invalid. These visits are made with the greatest possible kindness and affection whether it be to hear what they have to say or to encourage them to endure
25 their sickness in patience and to offer it to God in honour of our Lord Jesus Christ and for love of His sufferings; and although they must be treated gently and affectionately they must not for all that be allowed to show bad temper or a fastidiousness which would make it difficult to attend to them.
30 On the contrary, they must be made to yield to all our wishes with a virtuous intention.

In cases where the illness is serious the advice of the Mother Abbess and the doctor must be taken as to the administration of the sacraments, according to the age and
35 capacity of the patient; and we for our part must redouble all our care and assistance whether spiritual or bodily so as

to give them perfect contentment and take their minds from
thinking about themselves; that thus they may think of God
rather than of their illness, if their age and devotion enable
them to do so. At the same time, we should never urge them
too much—on the contrary, we should be particularly careful 5
that our conversation is not burdensome to them. For this
reason we may sometimes visit them merely for the purpose
of cheering them, but as we find them disposed to talk about
God we may introduce into our conversation some pious
remarks. 10

As soon as children have recovered they will be sent back
to be with the others for fear lest they should become unruly.
This is to be feared in the case of young people whose chief
desire, as a rule, is freedom. But even though they have
returned to the schoolroom great care will be exercised to 15
see that they are given as much nourishment and rest as is
necessary for their restoration to perfect health.

For the slight indispositions to which they are subject
they will be given whatever is necessary but they must not be
pampered too much; for there are children who sometimes 20
pretend to be ill. I have seen some of this kind though, by
the grace of God, it is long since such a thing happened among
our children. But if this happens we must not show them
that we think they wish to deceive us; on the contrary, we
should sympathise and say they are really ill and at once 25
put them to bed in a separate room with a sister who looks
after them but says nothing to them; for they must be told
that talking to them is bad for them and that they need rest.
They are put on a diet of broth and eggs for a day or two.
If the illness is real this treatment is very good for them, and 30
if it is not it is certain that next day they will say that they
are quite well. Thus we cure their deceitfulness without
giving them cause to murmur as they would do if we told
them that they had not the illness of which they complain
and we might even expose them to telling falsehoods and 35
carrying their pretence even further.

APPENDIX. SOME TYPICAL

	The Little Schools of Port-Royal	The Oratorian Schools	Lancelot's Regulations for the Princes de Conti
a.m.			
5.0	Elder boys rise		—
		5.30. Rise. Prayers	
6.0	Younger boys rise. Prayers Prime (for elder boys). Preparation	Preparation	Rise as soon as they wake
7.0	Repetition of lessons	Preparation 7.45. Breakfast	Prayers
8.0	Breakfast 8.30. Lessons	Preparation	Breakfast Recreation
9.0	Lessons	Lessons Mass	Lessons
10.0	Lessons	Lessons	Lessons
11.0	Dinner 11.30. Recreation	Dinner Recreation	Lessons 11.30. Recreation
12.0	Recreation	Recreation 12.30. Preparation	Dinner 12.30. Recreation
p.m.			
1.0	Lessons	Preparation	Recreation
2.0	Lessons	Lessons	Recreation
3.0	Goûter 3.30. Preparation	Lessons	Recreation 3.30. Goûter
4.0	Preparation	Lessons 4.30. Goûter	Lessons
5.0	Preparation	Preparation	Lessons
6.0	Supper 6.30. Recreation	Preparation 6.30. Prayers	Recreation
7.0	Recreation	Supper 7.30. Recreation	Supper Recreation
8.0	Preparation 8.30. Evening Prayers	Reading Prayers	Recreation
9.0	All in bed by 9.0		Bed (winter) 9.30. Bed (summer)
		9.30. Bed	

TIME-TABLES

A modern French *lycée*	The Port-Royal Girls' Schools	The Girls' School of Saint-Cyr
Rise 5.20. Preparation	4.0—5.0. Rise Prayers and silence	—
Preparation	Prime Making of beds	Rise 6.30. Domestic duties
Breakfast 7.30. Recreation	Breakfast 7.30. Lessons (some girls clean the rooms)	Domestic duties 7.30. Breakfast
Lessons	Reading of the Scriptures 8.30. Tierce	Mass 8.30. Preparation
Lessons	Mass (for some of the girls)	Preparation
Recreation 10.15. Preparation	Writing lesson Singing lesson	Lessons
Preparation	Confession. Sext 11.30. Dinner	Lessons
Dinner 12.30. Recreation	Recreation	Dinner 12.30. Recreation
Recreation	Lessons	Recreation
Lessons	Lessons 2.30. None	Lessons
Lessons	Catechism 3.30. Goûter (for younger girls)	Lessons
Goûter 4.15. Recreation	Vespers	Preparation
Preparation	Reading	Preparation
Preparation	Supper 6.30. Recreation	Supper 6.30. Recreation
Supper 7.30. Recreation	Recreation 7.30. Compline	Recreation
Bed (for younger boys)	All in bed by 8.15	Recreation
Bed (for elder boys)	—	Bed

NOTES

p. 58, l. 5. **S. Monica** (A.D. 332–387) was the mother of S. Augustine. She was a Christian and it was largely owing to her influence that her son became a Christian.

p. 58, l. 10. **the fifth chapter of the First Epistle to Timothy,** verse 10; "well reported of for good works; if she have brought up children."

p. 58, l. 21. **Take ye heed, etc.** Mark xiii, 33.

p. 59, l. 2. **the first Church.** See Acts ii, 41–47.

p. 59, l. 28. **Vincennes.** See Introd. p. 22. Vincennes is about a mile and a half to the west of Paris. In the keep of the castle, which still stands, state prisoners were formerly confined. John Evelyn the diarist visited it on Feb. 8th, 1644—a year after Saint-Cyran was set free. He says: "The Bois de Vincennes has in it a square and noble castle, with magnificent apartments, fit for a royal court, not forgetting the chapel. It is the chief prison for persons of quality. About it there is a park walled in, full of deer; and in one part there is a grove of goodly pine trees." The castle seems to have been rather a place of detention than a prison in the usual sense, but Du Fossé tells us that Saint-Cyran was treated "avec des derniers rigueurs." He was forbidden to see any of his friends and it was with considerable difficulty that he even maintained a correspondence with them.

p. 60, l. 4. **a prophecy in Isaiah**—see chapter xxviii, verse 9.

p. 60, l. 20. **Pelagians.** See Introd. p. 15. Pelagius was born in Britain about the middle of the fourth century A.D. He afterwards lived at Rome and at Carthage. His doctrines were formally condemned and he had to leave Rome in 418. Of his after life nothing definite is known.

p. 60, l. 20. **the Church's ceremony of breathing upon the infant.** At the beginning of the Roman baptismal office the priest breathes three times upon the face of the person to be baptised, saying, "Depart from him, thou spirit of evil" (*Exi ab eo*, etc.).

p. 61, l. 22. **young D'Andilly,** elsewhere named De Villeneuve (see pp. 87, 120, and 125). He was one of the sons of Arnauld d'Andilly, the eldest brother of Angélique, Agnès, and Dr Antoine Arnauld. He died young.

p. 61, l. 22. **De Saint-Ange**—also known as D'Espinoy (see p. 87) —was the second son of the Baroness de Saint-Ange who was a friend of Arnauld d'Andilly and of Saint-Cyran. She eventually became a widow and entered the convent of Port-Royal in 1652.

p. 63, l. 30. **any absolution.** Saint-Cyran held strict views on the subject of absolution; they had brought him into conflict with Richelieu and probably formed one of the reasons for his imprisonment. The Cardinal in a Catechism which he had drawn up for the use of his diocese of Luçon had stated that *attrition*, an inferior degree of mental sorrow for sin arising chiefly from fear of punishment, is sufficient for acceptable penance and sacramental absolution. In opposition to this view Saint-Cyran asserted the necessity of *contrition*—true and real repentance arising out of a love of God—before sin could be forgiven. Saint-Cyran's views were elaborated in Arnauld's treatise *De la Fréquente Communion* (see Introd. p. 23).

p. 64, l. 30. **these responsibilities and delusions.** Le Maître about the year 1634 had entertained the idea of marrying but afterwards abandoned his intention.

p. 67, l. 3. **Pharaoh......a type of the devil himself.** The same idea is found in the modern Roman Catholic devotional manual known as *The Garden of the Soul.* In the instructions for Communion we read: "that lamb was first offered in sacrifice for our eternal redemption from the bondage of the infernal Pharao." Cf. also *Constitutions*, pp. 16–17.

p. 68, l. 3. **greater love, etc.** John xv, 13.

p. 68, l. 31. **by the Prince of the Apostles.** The reference is to 1 Thess. v, 19: "Quench not the spirit."

p. 69, l. 4. **children of seven or eight years old.** Lancelot (*Mém. de M. de S.-C.* vol. I, p. 133) tells us that Saint-Cyran during his captivity occupied himself with educating the two sons of the prison governor. He also taught the son of a poor widow; and it is obviously to these children that reference is made in this passage.

p. 69, l. 16. **Erasmus** (1466–1536) was a Dutchman by birth and became one of the greatest of the humanist educators. He paid several visits to England and was a close friend of Thomas More, Linacre, Colet, and other English scholars. Refer to Woodward, *Erasmus concerning Education* (Cambridge, 1904).

p. 70, l. 21. **It is good, etc.** Lamentations iii, 27.

p. 70, l. 22. **S. Gregory** (c. 540–604), surnamed the Great, was the first pope of that name. He is the hero of the possibly apocryphal incident, recorded by Bede, relating to the English boys in the slave-market at Rome. At any rate, he sent Augustine to evangelise Britain.

p. 71, l. 25. **confined to memory work.** Nicole's recommendations here would seem to be not altogether sound. If a child has a weak memory it would surely be advisable to exercise it and so strengthen it, rather than to set the child exclusively to tasks for which the memory is but little required.

p. 74, l. 33. **too many pupils.** A feature of the Port-Royal educational system was that each master was put in charge of a group of not more than five or six pupils. For this reason their system in its entirety could never have become general.

p. 75, l. 21. **S. John Climacus** (flourished c. 605 A.D.) was one of the last of the Greek Fathers. He was a solitary of the desert and was chosen by the monks of Mt Sinai to be their abbot. He owes his title to his chief work *The Holy Ladder of Perfection.* It was highly esteemed by the Port-Royalists and was used as a reading-book in the girls' schools (see p. 235).

p. 77, l. 7. **industry.** "Mot aimable," Sainte-Beuve calls it. See *Port-Royal*, vol. III, p. 484.

p. 77, l. 17. **In the day, etc.** Gen. xxxi, 40.

p. 77, l. 31. **they offered their pupils every day to God.** As was but natural, the Port-Royalists unanimously enjoin that the schoolmaster should continually pray for those who are put into his care. Cf. "Those who had charge of the children were careful to ally prayer with their labour and to offer them every day to God, remembering that those who plant and water are nothing but that it is He alone, possessing all power, Who giveth the increase." (Fontaine, *Mém. sur MM. de P.-R.* p. 391.)

p. 78, l. 26. **A Father of the Church.** Jerome (c. 331–420 A.D.) was an opponent of the Pelagians (see p. 15). His chief work was a translation of the Scriptures into Latin. He also wrote a letter to a lady named Læta in which he advises her upon the education of her daughter. It is from this letter that the passages here quoted are drawn. The references are *Ep. ad Lætam*, § 9 and § 4; they will be found in Migne, *Patrologia Latina*, xxii, pp. 875 and 871.

p. 79, l. 5. **it is this which M. de Saint-Cyran used to advise.** It was customary for girls to be educated in schools attached to convents (see Introd. p. 32). Saint-Cyran wished that schools for boys also should be set up within the precincts of monasteries or special houses. In one of his letters he says: "I think I could do a great deal for children......if only I could make them spend their early days in a country house or monastery where they would be permitted all the pastimes proper to their age, but where they would be allowed to see only good examples of good living in those who would assist me."

p. 79, l. 14. **a little girl.** There are some charming passages in Saint-Cyran's letters to his little niece and god-daughter, whom he sometimes calls "la petite Prédestinée." She is probably the "little girl" here referred to. In one place he says: "I am sending you this little pot

only to serve as a remedy for your cough; for otherwise God would not have approved of my sending you sweetmeats, which little souls that belong to Him ought to hate. But since illnesses leave certain after-effects, you may eat these sweets so that your cough may not come back."
(*Lettres chrestiennes*, vol. II, p. 26.)

p. 80, l. 28. **Duchesse de Guise...M. de Guise.** The Guise family came from Lorraine. The Duchess here mentioned was the wife of Charles IV of Lorraine who had served under Henri IV and was banished by Richelieu in 1631. Her son, "the present M. de Guise," is better known as Henri II of Lorraine (1614–1664). He had been made Archbishop of Rheims in 1629.

p. 80, l. 33. **anxious to see persons of high rank well educated.** See Introd. p. 45.

p. 82, l. 23. **Thou therefore, etc.** Romans ii, 21.

p. 83, l. 23. **Keep thy heart, etc.** Proverbs iv, 23.

p. 84, l. 15. **In heaven their angels, etc.** Matthew xviii, 10.

p. 85, l. 21. **If ye have judgments, etc.** 1 Cor. vi, 4.

p. 85, l. 25. **one of the great successors of the Apostles.** S. Gregory the Great; see p. 88 and refer to note on p. 70, l. 22.

p. 86, l. 5. **one of whom teaches us.** S. Paul. The reference is to 1 Cor. i, 25.

p. 86, l. 17. **a Father of the Church.** S. Augustine (354–430 A.D.); see *Confessions*, Bk I, c. 16. I have quoted the passage from Pusey's translation, but the word *lignum* (here translated *cross*) might obviously refer either to the Cross or to the Ark.

p. 86, l. 31. **his nephews.** Sons of Mme de Barcos, Saint-Cyran's sister, and younger brothers of Martin de Barcos (see Introd. p. 39).

p. 87, l. 9. **M. d'Espinoy and M. de Villeneuve.** See *supra* notes on p. 61, l. 22.

p. 87, l. 16. **M. Singlin.** Antoine Singlin (1607–1664) came under the influence of Saint-Cyran and was made Confessor at Port-Royal. He was a man of no great education but of considerable common sense and marked humility. He gained a reputation as a preacher. Du Fossé (*Mémoires*, p. 94) tells how, when a pupil at the rue Saint-Dominique, he was taken every Sunday to Port-Royal de Paris to hear a sermon given by Singlin.

p. 87, l. 21. **M. de Barcos.** A whole-hearted disciple of Saint-Cyran. At his uncle's death he succeeded him in his abbey (see Introd. p. 39).

p. 87, l. 22. **M. d'Andilly.** See Introd. p. 18.

p. 87, l. 24. **M. de Saci.** See Introd. p. 40.

p. 87, l. 26. **two admirable letters.** Unfortunately they are not included in the *Lettres chrestiennes et spirituelles*.

p. 87, l. 30. **I was busy at that time in church.** Lancelot acted as sacristan.

p. 87, l. 31. **M. Arnauld**—*i.e.* Dr Antoine Arnauld. Refer to Introd. pp. 42–44.

p. 88, l. 3. **the greatest man of recent years.** Saint-Cyran. In a letter of his which appears in the *Supplément au Nécrologe* (p. 47), he says, in reference to the duty of educating children : " Those who were most religious in the order of S. Benedict found this penance the most severe of all...For myself I have always regarded this occupation as so burdensome that I have never employed for it anyone to whom God had not given special gifts."

p. 88, l. 5. **S. Gregory.** See *supra* note on p. 70, l. 22.

p. 88, l. 16. **the greatest conqueror the world has ever seen.** Alexander the Great. His tutor was the philosopher Aristotle. The anecdote is related in Plutarch (*Vita Alex.*).

p. 88, l. 19. **Theodosius I** (c. 346–395 A.D.), emperor of the Eastern Roman Empire. He appointed **Arsenius** (354–450) to be tutor to his sons Honorius and Arcadius. Arsenius afterwards retired to an Egyptian monastery.

p. 88, l. 25. **S. Ambrose** (c. 340–397 A.D.), born at Trèves, became Bishop of Milan in 374. He opposed the Arian heresy and wrote a number of hymns.

p. 90, l. 3. **the art of cultivating.** This comparison of the educative process with that of cultivating the ground is a commonplace with the Port-Royalists—as indeed it is with almost all wise writers on education. Such a comparison implicitly condemns "cramming" and any undue attempt to estimate the value of the education, which pupils have received, by their success in public examinations.

p. 90, l. 20. **Quintilian** (c. 40–118 A.D.). A famous Roman rhetorician. His chief work was a treatise *De Institutione Oratoria* in which he deals with the education of those who are to enter the profession of rhetoric (refer to Monroe, *History of Education*, pp. 201–203, and A. S. Wilkins, *Roman Education*). Coustel's writings abound in quotations from Quintilian ; the present passage is from *Inst. Or.* Bk II, ch. 2.

p. 90, l. 31. **S. Chrysostom** (c. 345–407 A.D.). Archbishop of Constantinople, a great preacher (*chrysostom* = golden-mouthed), an opponent of the Arians, and a voluminous theological writer.

p. 91, l. 7. **the University statutes.** Cf. " The heads of colleges shall receive and admit masters and professors whose conduct and teaching are equally praiseworthy, so that in teaching literature to children they may at the same time inculcate good morals" (*Laws and Statutes of the University of Paris, promulgated by order of Henri IV* (1600)—Art. 1).

p. 91, l. 8. **Pliny the younger** (62–c. 114 A.D.). A Roman orator and author who had studied rhetoric under Quintilian. He has left ten books of letters ; the reference for the passage here quoted is Bk III, letter 3.

p. 91, l. 12. **The first Council of Milan.** 343 A.D. A synod of Latin Bishops at the time of the Arian Controversy.

p. 91, l. 20. **Erasmus.** See *supra* note on p. 69, l. 16. **Vives** (1492–1540). Spanish scholar and educationalist ; see Introd. p. 9. **Juvenal** (c. 60–c. 140 A.D.). Roman satirist.

p. 91, l. 23. **every author**—*i.e.* all the classical authors whose style is considered worthy of imitation.

p. 91, l. 24. **Quintilian.** *Inst. Or.* Bk II, ch. 3.

p. 92, l. 23. **It is somewhat astounding, etc.** It is indeed remarkable that, at any rate so far as secondary school teaching in this country is concerned, Coustel's criticisms are as worthy of application to-day as they were when they were written 250 years ago.

p. 95, l. 3. **Le Fèvre.** The passages quoted in this extract form the only account of Le Fèvre that we have in any of the writings of the Port-Royalists. Moreover, these passages do not occur in the earlier editions of Du Fossé's *Mémoires*, but only in the complete edition published at Rouen by F. Bouquet in 1876.

p. 96, l. 22. **De Bohebert.** He apparently made no lasting reformation in spite of Le Fèvre's influence. When he grew up he had a disagreement with a neighbour over "un certain droit de dixme." The dispute led to a violent quarrel in the midst of which De Bohebert shot his adversary.

p. 97, l. 9. **the country.** The surroundings of Port-Royal des Champs, although described by Mme de Sévigné (letter dated Jan. 26th, 1674) as a "hideous desert," are in reality very charming and not unlike parts of Buckinghamshire and Oxfordshire. It was indeed an ideal neighbourhood for a school and afforded innumerable opportunities for "nature study." The writer was struck particularly by the profusion of wild flowers in the valley of the Rhodon and by the great variety of butterflies which the whole district affords.

p. 97, l. 18. **Education at Home.** Coustel's remarks on the education of children by a private tutor in their own home are of special interest because, after the dispersion of the Little Schools, he himself acted in this capacity to the nephews of Cardinal de Furstenberg, bishop and prince of Strasbourg (see Introd. p. 47). From what is said in this passage one is tempted to infer that his experiences as a private tutor were not altogether pleasant.

p. 98, l. 23. **the servants.** Cf. Locke, *Thoughts concerning Education*, § 69.

p. 100, l. 9. **Quintilian.** *Inst. Or.* Bk I, ch. 2.

p. 100, l. 21. **self-confidence in public-speaking.** It should be remembered that Quintilian speaks as a rhetorician and that the study of oratory was of far greater importance to an educated man in his day than it was in the time of Port-Royal or is at present. At the same time, it is to be regretted that so very little attention is given in the curriculum of the average English school to teaching boys how to express themselves orally with clearness and confidence. In this respect our English practice compares very unfavourably with that of French or American schools.

p. 101, l. 7. **Quintilian.** "Sed neque præceptor bonus maiore se turba, quam ut sustinere eam possit, oneraverit." *Inst. Or.* Bk I, ch. 2. At Port-Royal, as has been said, no master had charge of more than five or six pupils.

p. 102, l. 10. **S. John Climacus.** See *supra* note on p. 75, l. 21.

p. 102, l. 16. **Lucian** (c. 120–c. 190 A.D.). A Greek satirical writer. His *Hermotimus* is a dialogue dealing with the Stoic philosophy; its general conclusion is that the study of philosophy is not worth the trouble involved.

p. 103, l. 1. **Erasmus.** See *supra* note on p. 69, l. 16. The passage to which reference is here made comes from his *Treatise on Christian Marriage*.

p. 103, l. 16. **Vives.** See *supra* note on p. 91, l. 20.

p. 104, l. 2. **S. Augustine.** See *supra* note on p. 86, l. 17, and Introd. p. 15 *et passim*.

p. 104, l. 17. **What care he took, etc.** A number of translations from Latin authors were made for school use by various Port-Royalist writers. De Saci himself rendered Phædrus, Terence, and two books of the *Æneid* into French; and in every case the original was most carefully expurgated.

p. 104, l. 27. **selected epigrams.** A reference to the *Epigrammatum Delectus*, which was drawn up by Nicole and Lancelot with the help and advice of De Saci (see Sainte-Beuve, *Port-Royal*, vol. III, p. 537). Refer to the next extract (no. xii, p. 105).

p. 105, l. 17. **means of access.** The word in the original is *otium*; but as this makes no satisfactory sense and is apparently a printer's error I have taken the liberty of emending it to *ostium*.

p. 106, l. 22. **vipers.** In former times preparations made from vipers, and especially viper broth, were in great request as medicines. The simile was probably suggested to Nicole by the following passage in S. Gregory Nazianzen's *Panegyric on S. Basil*: "As we compound healing drugs from reptiles, so from secular literature we receive principles of inquiry and speculation, while we reject their idolatry."

p. 107, l. 9. **a text from Isaiah.** Probably a reference to Is. xlv, 15.

p. 109, l. 3. **evil results produced by these fictitious stories.** At first one is tempted to smile at what might seem the puritanical narrowness of these remarks. It should be remembered, however, that the novel as we now understand it had not yet come into existence and that such works of fiction as were available in Varet's time were extremely unsuitable for children. Vives in his *De Institutione feminæ christianæ* (1540, p. 216) gives a long list of contemporary works of fiction and emphatically asserts their unsuitability as reading for the young. The whole problem is still insistent and still unsolved. We are always debating as to whether the influence of the cinematograph is beneficial or the reverse to our pupils; while the wide-spread circulation of "halfpenny comics" and "bloods"—to say nothing of periodicals of an even more pernicious type—is still causing considerable searching of heart to all who are interested in the good education of children.

p. 109, l. 7. **S. Theresa** (1515–1582). A Spanish nun who founded a community of the Carmelite order. Its discipline was of the strictest. The order, which showed a tendency towards mysticism, was introduced into France by Cardinal de Bérulle in 1604. S. Theresa was always held in honour at Port-Royal. Refer also to pages 44 n. and 235.

p. 110, l. 9. **the theatre.** The Port-Royalists unanimously condemn the theatre in spite of the fact that they lived in the most brilliant epoch of the French stage and had educated the most eminent of French playwrights. Their attitude, however, was that of the Church as a whole from its earliest ages; and there are still large numbers of Christians who can find nothing but condemnation for the theatre and all that it implies.

p. 111, l. 4. **the representation of the acts of the martyrs.** Possibly an allusion to Corneille's *Polyeucte*.

p. 111, l. 15. **Tertullian** (c. 160–230 A.D.). The earliest of the Latin Fathers.

p. 111, l. 35. **S. Chrysostom.** See *supra* note on p. 90, l. 31.

p. 112, l. 14. **S. Augustine.** See *supra* note on p. 86, l. 17. The reference is to his *Confessions*, Bk III, ch. 2.

p. 114, l. 5. **S. Bernard** (1090–1153). Cistercian monk, preacher, and theologian. He founded the monastery at Clairvaux near Dijon; when the abbey of Port-Royal was built in 1204 it was put in charge of the monks of Clairvaux.

p. 114, l. 14. **Seneca** (3 B.C.–65 A.D.). Roman statesman and philosopher. The reference for the quotation—"si vis amari, ama"—is *Ep.* 9.

p. 115, l. 6. **S. Benedict** (480–543). An Italian monk; founder of the Benedictine order.

p. 116, l. 9. **He that spareth, etc.** Prov. xiii, 24.

p. 116, l. 11. **whom the Lord loveth, etc.** Heb. xii, 6.

p. 117, l. 4. **S. Bernard.** See *supra* note on p. 114, l. 5.

p. 118, l. 4. **ludus literarius.** In Rome the school was called *ludus*—*i.e.* play or game—a similar idea to that contained in the Greek word σχολή (=leisure). It thus became customary in the middle ages to refer to the school as *ludus literarius*—the literary game—and to the schoolmaster as *ludimagister*—the master of the game. Wolsey in his plan for a great grammar school at Ipswich says that the pupils must be led to regard the school as a *ludus literarius* (see Foster Watson, *The Old Grammar Schools*, p. 18). In 1612 also John Brinsley published a book called *Ludus literarius or the Grammar Schoole.* As a matter of fact, the schools of the middle ages had greatly belied this title. Rodolphus Agricola (1443–1485), an eminent Dutch classical scholar, says: "If there is anything which has a contradictory name it is a school. The Greeks called it σχολή (leisure, recreation), and the Latins *ludus literarius*. Aristophanes named it φροντιστήριον—*i.e.* place of care and trouble—and this is the name that suits it best."

p. 118, l. 12. **learn without trouble.** Ideas similar to those which are expressed in this passage from Guyot will be found in chap. v of Fénelon's *De l'Éducation des Filles.*

p. 119, l. 7. **Places should be given, etc.** The system here advocated by Arnauld is still to a large extent in vogue in the modern French *lycée*. Places are taken regularly on the results of a formal test known as a *composition*.

p. 120, l. 8. **the degree of Master of Arts.** Refer to Introd. p. 10.

p. 120, l. 17. The curriculum at the present time for the classical *Baccalauréat*, which nearly corresponds to the Master of Arts degree here referred to, comprises French, Latin, Greek, Modern Languages, Ancient and Modern History, Geography, and Mathematics; in the second part of the examination Philosophy, elementary Science, and contemporary History and Geography are included.

p. 120, l. 25. **De Villeneuve.** See *supra* note on p. 61, l. 22.

p. 121, l. 10. **S. Gregory the Great.** See *supra* note on p. 70, l. 22.

p. 121, l. 19. **they must not be pampered.** Saint-Cyran was of the same opinion. In Fontaine's *Mém. sur MM. de P.-R.* (p. 192) he is reported as saying: "Accustom your pupils to eat vegetables of every kind, cod, and herring"—*i.e.* the very salt dry and unpalatable fish which was all that could be obtained on fast-days before the era of quick transit by railway.

p. 121, l. 27. **Clement of Alexandria.** A Greek Father who flourished about 150 A.D., but of whom few details are known. He wrote a book called Παιδαγωγός or *the Tutor*, which however is not a treatise on education but a theological work in which the Church is compared to a school, Christ being the Tutor or Pedagogue.

p. 122, l. 7. **Seneca.** See *supra* note on p. 114, l. 14. The passage quoted occurs in *Ep.* 116, § 3.

p. 122, l. 18. **Sleep.** According to the time-table of the Little Schools (see p. 240) eight hours was the usual time allowed for sleep.

p. 122, l. 31. **Cæsar would have been lost before Alexandria.** The incident is described in Plutarch (*Vita J. Cæs.*). During a sea-fight near the isle of Pharos Cæsar, seeing his men hard pressed, leapt into a boat to go to their assistance. But being attacked by the Egyptians he threw himself into the sea and with much difficulty escaped to his galleys by swimming. See also Suetonius, *Div. Jul.* § 63.

p. 123, l. 28. **Ausonius** (310–c. 390 A.D.). Latin poet. He was made tutor to Gratian, son of the emperor Valentinian.

p. 123, l. 28. **the word school.** Refer to note on *ludus literarius* (p. 118, l. 4). The use of the phrase in this sense is at least as old as Plautus.

p. 124, l. 4. **Quintilian.** *Inst. Or.* Bk I, ch. 3.

p. 124, l. 13. **Cicero.** The reference is to *De Officiis*, chap. XXIX, § 7.

p. 124, l. 24. **Mapheus.** Mapheus Vegius wrote a book *De Educatione liberorum et eorum claris moribus*, which was published in 1511. It contains advice on the education of children even from the period before birth, and physical, intellectual, and moral welfare are all dealt with. See also p. 170.

p. 124, l. 30. For the indoor games at Port-Royal see p. 137.

p. 125, l. 1. **Gafarell.** He is not mentioned in the *Nécrologe* or in any other of the Port-Royalist writings. Du Fossé elsewhere calls him "un fort joli garçon."

p. 125, l. 11. **M. de Beaupuis.** See Introd. p. 46.

p. 125, l. 19. **Gentilly.** The school at the time of which Du Fossé is speaking was established inside Paris in the rue Saint-Dominique d'Enfer. Gentilly is now a suburb of Paris, just outside the fortifications and due south of Port-Royal de Paris.

p. 126, l. 24. **an entertainment...On Twelfth Night.** The Epiphany festival which is here described was widely celebrated in this country as well as in other parts of Europe until within relatively recent times. In France the person whose slice of cake contained the bean was called the "King of the Bean" (*le Roi de la Fève*). From this has originated the proverbial phrase for good luck: "Il a trouvé la fève au gateau." A full history of this custom and a description of the ceremonies connected with it will be found in Chambers' *Book of Days*, vol. I, pp. 62–64.

p. 127, l. 8. **S. Gregory.** See *supra* note on p. 70, l. 22.

p. 130, l. 30. **Quintilian.** *Inst. Or.* Bk VI, ch. 3.

p. 131, l. 13. **without taking off your hat.** It was considered polite to wear one's hat at meals. Saint-Simon in a chapter describing *la Mécanique de la Vie de Louis XIV*, says: "Aux repas tout le monde étoit couvert; c'eût été un manque de respect dont on vous auroit averti sur-le-champ de n'avoir pas son chapeau sur sa tête. Monseigneur même l'avoit; le roi seul étoit découvert. On se découvroit quand le roi vous parloit ou pour parler à lui."

p. 132, l. 7. **the second digestion**—*i.e.* that which takes place through the action of the gastric juice in the stomach; the first digestion is accomplished by the saliva in the mouth.

p. 133, l. 19. **translation**—*i.e.* Latin into French.

p. 134, l. 3. **the garden.** The abbey of Port-Royal des Champs was and still is surrounded by woods and glades. Racine wrote some descriptive odes dealing with the abbey and its neighbourhood; they are collectively known as *Paysage ou Promenade de Port-Royal des Champs.*

p. 134, l. 13. **goûter.** A light meal served in the middle of the afternoon and corresponding somewhat to "tea" with us. *Goûter* is still taken by children in France though not usually by adults.

p. 134, l. 24. **parishional High Mass**—*i.e.* Mass said in the church of S. Lambert in the parish of which Port-Royal des Champs was situated. S. Lambert is a hamlet at a distance of about a mile from the convent. The village church is still standing. It was in the churchyard here that the remains which were exhumed from the cemetery of the abbey when it was demolished in 1710–13 were re-interred. Their resting place is now marked by a plain but massive monument.

p. 134, l. 33. **They were all dressed in the same manner.** It is, of course, still customary for the pupils of a French *lycée* to wear a uniform dress.

p. 135, l. 7. **comb each other's hair.** As can be seen in almost any contemporary portrait, it was usual at this time for men—especially laymen—to wear their hair long. The custom is well illustrated, for example, in the picture of Le Maître which has been beautifully reproduced as the frontispiece to Mrs Romanes' *Story of Port-Royal.*

p. 136, l. 3. **Justin,** usually known as Justin Martyr (c. 100–c. 165 A.D.). Christian apologist.

p. 136, l. 3. **Severus Sulpitius** (363–410 A.D.). Ecclesiastical historian.

p. 136, l. 12. **they do the office of the angels.** Cf. the Preface from the English Communion Office (which is translated from the Roman *Ordo Missæ*): " Therefore with angels and archangels and with all the company of heaven, we laud and magnify Thy glorious name." Refer also to p. 204, l. 35.

p. 136, l. 22. **Confiteor.** The prescribed formula for confession. " I confess to Almighty God...that I have sinned exceedingly in thought, word, and deed through my fault, through my most grievous fault" (*meâ culpâ, meâ maximâ culpâ*).

p. 136, l. 32. **Josephus** (37–c. 100 A.D.). Celebrated Jewish historian.

p. 136, l. 33. **Godeau.** Antoine Godeau (1605–1672) was an ecclesiastic who won some contemporary fame as a poet and *littérateur*. He was appointed Bishop of Grasse by Richelieu, but he remained friendly to Port-Royal.

p. 137, l. 3. **Christian Instructions.** I have been unable to trace any contemporary work bearing this title; but in the original the name is not spelt with capital letters, and therefore the reference may be not to any special book but to a certain part of some devotional or instructional manual such as Saint-Cyran's *Catechism*.

p. 137, l. 26. **M. de Sainte-Beuve.** Doctor of the Sorbonne and friend of Port-Royal. He must, of course, be clearly distinguished from the illustrious nineteenth-century literary critic, Charles-Augustin Sainte-Beuve, to whom we owe what is at once the most interesting and the most complete account of Port-Royal.

p. 138, l. 5. **Marli, Versailles, and St Cyr** all lie to the north of Port-Royal des Champs at a distance of about eight or ten miles. The palace of Versailles owed its origin to a hunting château built in 1624. In 1668 huge additions to this structure were begun and Louis XIV transferred his residence thither in 1682. S. Cyr afterwards became famous as the site of Mme de Maintenon's school for girls (see Introd. pp. 33–36) and Napoleon's military school.

p. 138, l. 29. **goûter.** See *supra* note on p. 134, l. 13.

p. 139, l. 11. **Confiteor.** See *supra* note on p. 136, l. 22.

p. 139, l. 12. **Sub Tuum Præsidium.** " We fly to thy patronage, O holy Mother of God, etc." An anthem which occurs in the Litany of the Blessed Virgin.

p. 139, l. 28. **M. de Saint-Cyran's catechism.** A handbook, entitled *Théologie familière*, which had originally been written by the Abbé for the two sons of M. Bignon, who were among the earliest pupils at Port-Royal. It was published in 1643 but, owing to Jesuit intrigue, was condemned by the Archbishop of Paris.

p. 139, l. 33. **parishional High Mass.** See *supra* note on p. 134, l. 24.

p. 140, l. 8. **Rules for the good Education of Children.** This refers to Coustel's *Règles de l'Éducation des Enfans, où il est parlé en détail de la manière dont il se faut conduire pour leur inspirer les sentimens d'une solide piété ; et pour leur apprendre parfaitement les belles lettres.* The work was published in 1687 by Estienne Michallet. This fact is of importance because, taken in conjunction with the present passage, it shows that Coustel's *Rules* were not mere theories of his own invention, but a *résumé* of the practice of the Little Schools.

p. 142, l. 7. **champs and chants.** These two words are, of course, pronounced in exactly the same way. The phonetic equivalent is ʃɑ̃.

p. 142, l. 23. **for a long time the Greeks and Romans used capital letters only.** One may assume that there arose early a distinction between cursive handwriting (used for business purposes or private study) and the formal alphabet (used for inscriptions or literary purposes). But the earliest surviving examples of minuscules, or small letters, are to be found on wax tablets discovered at Pompeii and bearing dates ranging from 15 to 62 A.D. Later these small letters are found mixed with uncials, or capitals, in formal writing (inscriptions and manuscripts). The earliest specimens of this admixture date from the third century A.D.

p. 143, l. 10. **Ramus** (1515–1572) or Pierre de la Ramée. Professor of Philosophy at the Collège de France and the greatest educational reformer of his day. He made a praiseworthy, though not very successful, attempt to popularise the vernacular as a subject of instruction. In order to effect this he wrote a "Gramere" of the French language. It was first published in 1562 and its orthography anticipated in a remarkable way the reforms suggested in more recent times by the advocates of simplified spelling. The following quotation from the 1587 edition of this book (the spelling system of which differs slightly from that adopted in the first edition) will help to convey some idea of Ramus' proposals:

Enfans oyez une leçon.	Énfans oëies unę lęson.
Nostre langue a ceste façon	Notrę langę a sętę fason
Que le terme qui va devant	Kę lę tèrmę ki va dęvant
Volontiers regit le suivant....	Volontièr rějit le suivant....

(pp. 104–5)

The work as a whole is still of great interest because of the light which it throws upon the pronunciation of French in the sixteenth century.

p. 143, l. 21. **Claudius** (Roman emperor 10 B.C.–54 A.D.), as a matter of fact, invented three new letters. The inverted digamma (Ⅎ) stood for the consonant or semi-vowel V; the antisigma (Ɔ) for the combination *bs* or *ps*; and the sign Ⱶ for the sound between *u* and *i* which occurs in

NOTES 255

such words as *optumus* (*optimus*), etc. ⊦ was also used to represent the Greek Τ. The symbols are found in contemporary inscriptions.

p. 143, l. 29. **A dot in or underneath.** A dot (called dagesh) is placed in certain Hebrew letters for the purpose of slightly changing their value.

p. 144, l. 9. **Jesusë**—*i.e.* for Jésus, with the final *s*.

p. 144, l. 13. **en.** A simple nasal sound. In phonetic script it is written ã.

p. 145, l. 9. **certain men of intellect**—*e.g.* Blaise Pascal; see *supra* extract ii, p. 144. As a young man Pascal had been a member of a scientific club in Paris which was the forerunner of the *Académie des Sciences*. At its meetings numerous subjects were discussed, and among them was phonetic spelling (see Mersenne, *Questions Inouïes*, Paris, 1634). It is quite possible that Pascal's ideas on reformed methods of teaching reading date from this period.

p. 145, l. 33. **this new method of teaching reading.** It should be noticed that the "syllabic" and "look-and-say" methods of teaching reading, which are adumbrated in this and the following extracts, have been widely adopted within recent years.

p. 146, l. 27. **bon** = bõ.

p. 147, l. 5. **jamais** = ʒamɛ.

p. 147, l. 16. **aimaient** = ɛ·mɛ; **faisaient** = fəzɛ; **disaient** = di·zɛ.

p. 148, l. 6. **Despauter.** See Introd. pp. 7 and 8.

p. 150, l. 4. **French books rather than Latin ones.** See Introd. pp. 4 and 5.

p. 151, l. 21. **isolated words of which they know the meaning.** This rule of method in teaching is so obvious that it might seem unnecessary to state it. We have doubtless made considerable advance since the days of Guyot; but even yet we do not always follow his advice. The writer, for example, for some time after beginning to learn Latin with the aid of a primer which has had an enormous vogue, was well aware that *agricola* meant "husbandman"; but what a "husbandman" might be neither he nor the other members of the class had any idea.

p. 152, l. 7. **transparents.** They were copies in thick black type which would show through a superimposed page of white paper. The sheet of ruled lines, supplied with the modern writing-tablet, serves a somewhat similar purpose; or one may compare with this device the ground-glass slates under which is placed a picture to be copied.

p. 152, l. 11. **some text from Scripture.** See *supra* p. 138, l. 26.

p. 152, l. 13. **Quintilian.** *Inst. Or.* Bk 1, ch. 4.

p. 155, l. 10. **Allobroges.** An ancient Gallic tribe occupying the districts of Savoy and Dauphiné. **Allemanni.** A confederacy of German tribes living between the Danube, Rhine, and Main. The French words *Allemagne* and *Allemand* are derived from this name.

p. 156, l. 8. **Quintilian.** *Inst. Or.* Bk I, ch. 4.

p. 156, l. 21. **Colloquies of Erasmus.** See Introd. pp. 8 and 9. Luther, like Coustel in this passage, recognises the value of Erasmus' work, but points out the unsuitability of much of it for children. Such chapters as that, for example, entitled *Adolescentis et scorti colloquium* render the book, in an unrevised state, quite impossible for school use ; and it is for this reason perhaps that the work was not only criticised by the great Protestant reformer, but was also condemned by the Sorbonne and put upon the *Index* at Rome.

p. 156, l. 25. **Æmilius Probus.** A Roman historian who edited and abridged the biographies written by Cornelius Nepos.

p. 156, l. 25. **Severus Sulpitius, or Justin.** See *supra* notes on p. 136, l. 3.

p. 157, l. 10. **Despauter.** See Introd. pp. 7 and 8. The criticism which Coustel makes in lines 16 to 32 is echoed by Malebranche who says : "Is it not obvious that we must make use of what is known in order to learn what is unknown, that it is but trifling with a Frenchman to give him a grammar in German verse to teach him German ? Yet to teach children Latin we put into their hands the Latin verses of Despauter, which are utterly unintelligible to children who have difficulty in learning even the easiest things. Reason and experience are manifestly contrary to this practice, for children take a long time to learn Latin badly. None the less, it is considered rash to venture to find fault with it. If a Chinaman were to hear of this practice he could not forbear laughing at it, but in the part of the world which we inhabit the wisest and most learned cannot withhold their approval from it."

p. 159, l. 4. **Montaigne.** The reference is to *Essays*, Bk I, ch. 25.

p. 159, l. 8. **the Gate of Languages,** or *Janua Linguarum*, by John Amos Comenius, first published in 1631. It achieved an immediate and wide-spread success and was translated into fourteen foreign languages. It comprehended a thousand sentences dealing with the things of every-day life ; the Latin phrases with their German equivalents were given in parallel columns. For details see S. S. Laurie's *John Amos Comenius*.

p. 160, l. 18. **the grammar rules are set forth in Latin.** It was customary in English schools until well into the nineteenth century to make children learn their Latin grammar rules in Latin. The *King Edward VI Latin Grammar* was typical of this system ; as an example one may take its rule for the construction of a conditional sentence : "Conditio, si nude dicitur, ponitur in indicativo ; si opineris eam vel

veram esse vel verisimilem, in præsente subjunctivi ; si minus veram aut
minus verisimilem, in perfecto subjunctivi." An edition of this book "for
the use of schools" was published as late as 1864.

p. 160, l. 29. **the various colours.** This is doubtless a reference
to the Oratorian De Condren's *Latin Method*, which he composed for
the pupils of the Collège de Juilly (see Introd. p. 27). For example, it
gives the plural of *hic, hæc, hoc* as follows :

Nom.	Gen.	Dat.	Acc.	Abl.
hi	*horum*		*hos*	
hæ	**harum**	HIS	**has**	HIS
HÆC	HORUM		HÆC	

Here the masculine forms are shown in red, the feminine in green,
and the neuter in YELLOW. Forms which are common to all three
genders appear in BLACK. A somewhat similar method has recently
been employed by Prof. H. G. Atkins in his *Skeleton French Grammar*.
The preface to this book explains that "red ink has been used to represent pictorially the points on which the greatest stress is to be laid and
to give the means of revising at a glance the main features or the
particular difficulties of any chapter."

p. 164, l. 23, **the rule of masculines and feminines.** Words which
end in a consonant are said to have a masculine ending, while those that
terminate with a mute *e* have feminine endings. It is a rule of French
prosody that the alternate rhymes must be masculine and feminine. Any
passage of French poetry will illustrate this rule. As an example we
may take De Saci's prologue to Lancelot's *Jardin des Racines Grecques* :

> Toi qui chéris la docte Grèce
> Où jadis fleurit la sagesse,
> D'où les auteurs les plus divins
> Ont empruntés leurs termes saints...

p. 164, l. 31. **Ornari res ipsa, etc.** "The subject lends itself naturally
to instruction, not to ornament." The line occurs in Manilius, *Astronomica*.

p. 166, l. 21. **ob virtutes, etc.** Tacitus, *Hist.* Bk I, ch. 2.

p. 170, l. 11. **Mapheus Vegius.** See *supra* note on p. 124, l. 24.
He particularly recommends the study of Virgil. The passage to which
reference is here made by Coustel is in *De Educatione Liberorum* (1511),
Bk II, ch. 19.

p. 170, l. 25. **Quintilian.** *Inst. Or.* Bk I, ch. 4.

p. 173, l. 35. **Quintilian.** *Inst. Or.* Bk I, ch. 5.

p. 174, l. 15. **he should first of all translate it himself from some
ancient author.** Cf. Ascham, *Scholemaster* : "For translating use you
yourself...some part of Tully...and translate it you yourself into plain
natural English and then give it him to translate into Latin again."

B. 17

p. 175, l. 5. **Methods.** See *supra* Part III, extracts xii–xiv.

p. 175, l. 19. **Quintus Curtius** Rufus. Roman historian who lived towards the end of the first century A.D. and wrote a history of Alexander the Great.

p. 175, l. 20. **Pliny's Panegyric.** Pliny (see *supra* note on p. 91, l. 8) wrote a Panegyric on the emperor Trajan.

p. 175, l. 24. **Virgil.** Cf. " Virgil may be excepted from the number of authors from whom extracts only are to be learnt; at any rate, the second, fourth, and sixth books of the *Æneid* should be learnt in their entirety " (Nicole, *Essais de Morale*, vol. II, p. 295).

p. 176, l. 9. **verse composition.** This was an important part of the curriculum in contemporary Jesuit schools. It flourished in the public schools of this country for many years after Port-Royal had demonstrated its futility in the case of the average boy, although there were not wanting those who from time to time protested against the practice. Compare, for example: " There are few boys who remain to the age of eighteen or nineteen at a public school, without making above ten thousand Latin verses—a greater number than is contained in the *Æneid*; and after he has made this quantity of verses in a dead language, unless the poet should happen to be a very weak man indeed, he never makes another as long as he lives....The prodigious honour in which Latin verses are held at public schools is surely the most absurd of all absurd distinctions." (Sidney Smith—review of Edgeworth's *Essays on Professional Education* in *Edinburgh Review*, 1809). D'Arcy Thompson also has some scathing remarks on the subject; see *Day Dreams of a Schoolmaster*, ch. II, pp. 19–25.

p. 177, l. 5. **Quintilian.** *Inst. Or.* Bk I. ch. 4, init.

p. 180, l. 5. **Tursellinus** or Orazio Torsellino wrote a treatise *De Particulis Latinæ Orationis* (Lugd. Batav. 1609) and a number of other works.

p. 180, l. 8. **Josephus.** See *supra* note on p. 136, l. 32.

p. 180, l. 10. **the Enigmas of Luberius.** After considerable search I have been unable to trace any book of this name. It is just possible that Luberius is a misprint for Lubinus—*i.e.* Eilhard Lüben (1565–1621), a forerunner of Comenius and a classical scholar who was known chiefly for his commentary on Horace. Mr G. H. Wheeler, of the Bodleian Library, who very kindly helped me in the investigation of this point, suggests that the title may have been merely a fanciful name to distinguish this from any similar collection of enigmas. At any rate it was customary, especially in the Jesuit schools, to set riddles to be guessed more particularly as a holiday exercise; cf. " About the middle of sommer there is a small time of feriation in which there is provided and set up an enigma, which whosoever expoundeth receiveth a book...as an honorarium" (quoted in Corcoran, *Studies in the History of Classical Teaching*, chap. xv). Again, in the Jesuit Jouvency's *De ratione discendi et docendi* (1711, pp. 140 ff.), there is a whole chapter devoted to the art of composing enigmas. Mr Wheeler also informs me that with a number of 16th and 17th century editions of Phædrus, preserved in the Bodleian Library, there are bound up collections of Latin enigmas. It seems obvious, therefore, that this riddle-guessing exercise was widely employed in the teaching of elementary Latin; but as to the particular collection of enigmas here attributed to Luberius, I can discover nothing definite.

p. 180, l. 17. **Cornelius Nepos** (99–24 B.C.). Roman historian.

p. 180, l. 17. **Quintus Curtius.** See *supra* note on p. 175, l. 19.

p. 180, l. 24. **Florus** (contemporary of emperor Trajan) and **Eutropius** (secretary of emperors Constantine and Julian). Roman historians. **Justin.** See *supra* note on p. 136, l. 3.

p. 180, l. 24. **Politian's translation of Herodian.** Herodian was a Greek historian who flourished in the third century A.D. His work was translated into Latin by Politian or Angelo Poliziano (1454–1494) who was a famous Italian classical scholar. He was tutor to the children of Lorenzo de' Medici and professor at the University of Florence.

p. 181, l. 19. **Suarez.** Francisco Suarez (1548–1617). Spanish theologian and philosopher. Amongst his voluminous writings is a treatise on rhetoric.

p. 181, l. 26. **Pliny the Naturalist** (23–79 A.D.). Uncle of Pliny the younger (see *supra* note on p. 91, l. 8); author of a *Naturalis Historia*.

p. 181, l. 26. **Ælian** flourished at the end of the second century A.D. and wrote a natural history in Greek.

p. 181, l. 27. **Isocrates** (436–338 B.C.). Celebrated Attic orator who kept a school of rhetoric.

p. 182, l. 1. **history.** Coustel (*Règles*, etc., vol. II, p. 237) also recommends the study of history—not merely biblical and ancient history, but that of France and modern nations; he specifies Italy, Spain, Hungary, Turkey, Poland, Sweden and Denmark. He also distinguishes between reading an historian to find out what he says, and reading him to find out the truth as to what really happened. It would seem then that the critical study of history was not unknown in the Little Schools. It is surely not without significance that some of their most illustrious pupils afterwards became historians. De Tillemont won fame as a church historian; Du Fossé is the author of a *Lives of the Saints* and of a *Mémoires pour servir à l'histoire de Port-Royal* to which frequent reference has been made in this book; while Racine, although best known as a poet, was also historiographer to Louis XIV and wrote an account of his master's campaigns as well as a *Histoire abrégée de Port-Royal.*

p. 183, l. 29. **the "story of the day."** An interesting modern application of this idea will be found in the *Year Book of English History* (Year Book Press, 1916). An historical fact is selected for each day of the year and it is suggested that "a daily five minutes talk on them might sow the seeds of method, interest and research."

p. 184, l. 21. **Valerius Maximus.** Roman historian of the time of the emperor Tiberius.

p. 186, l. 1. **geography involves but little exercise of reasoning.** It is only within the last twenty years that geography has ceased to be mere rote-work and has developed into a most valuable exercise of the reason.

p. 186, l. 7. **books in which there are illustrations.** A wealth of beautifully illustrated geography text-books has been produced within recent years. In the teaching of geography more use might profitably be made of exercises based on carefully-selected pictures.

p. 186, l. 24. **the Gazette.** The first weekly newspaper in France. It was first published in 1631 and consisted of four quarto pages. It was an official record of current events and was under the control of the government; it was therefore only to a moderate degree representative of public opinion. There is a good account of it in D'Avenel, *Richelieu et la Monarchie absolue.*

p. 186, l. 34. **Lipsius.** Justus Lipsius, or Joest Lips, was born in 1547 near Brussels and educated at Louvain. He spent two years in Rome and wandered over Europe, supporting himself by teaching. He won great fame as a classical scholar and died at Louvain in 1606. In 1604 he had acted as one of the judges appointed to consider an Essay on Scholastic Philosophy, the work of Saint-Cyran who was at the time a pupil at the Jesuit College (see Introd. p. 15). Lipsius' chief work is entitled *Roma Illustrata, sive Antiquitatum Romanarum Breviarium—opusculum ad instar commentarii in Romanarum rerum scriptores* (Lugd. Batav. 1645). This book is ornamented with interesting woodcuts and is much like a modern "Companion to the Classics" or "Handbook of Roman Antiquities."

p. 187, l. 1. **testudo** or tortoise. A sort of penthouse of shields, formed by Roman soldiers when attacking a fortification.

p. 187, l. 6. **Subterranean Rome** or *Roma Subterranea novissima, in quâ antiqua Christianorum illustrantur* (Rome, 1651). The author is Paulus Aringhus and the work is a large folio volume containing many illustrations, copies of inscriptions, etc.

p. 187, l. 15. **Aldrovandus.** Ulissi Aldrovandi (1522–1605), an Italian naturalist born at Bologna. He studied medicine at the university

NOTES

of his native city and in 1560 became professor of natural history there. He wrote numerous books about insects, plants, fishes, animals, birds, natural phenomena, etc. His work shows laborious and patient research, but little use of the critical faculty.

p. 187, l. 16. **Jonston.** Joannes Jonstonus (1603–1675) was a Pole of Scottish descent. His chief works are a *Thaumatographia Naturalis* (1630) and a *Historia Universalis* (1634). He also makes little attempt to discriminate the true and the fabulous; for example, his *Thaumatographia* gives a detailed account of the barnacle goose.

p. 188, l. 13. **Retinuitque, etc.** "He retained from philosophy the quality of moderation, and that is a very difficult accomplishment." See Tacitus, *Agricola*, ch. IV, § 5.

p. 188, l. 19. **Saturn.** The shape of this planet was for long a puzzle to astronomers. Formerly it was supposed to be like a vase; hence the name *ansæ* or "handles," which was given to its rings. In 1655, however—shortly before Nicole wrote this passage—a Dutch astronomer, named Huyghens, ascertained the true shape of the planet and published his discovery in the form of a Latin anagram.

p. 188, l. 26. **geometry.** This branch of mathematics was always held in special honour at Port-Royal. Pascal was, of course, a geometrician of extraordinary brilliance and Dr Arnauld also composed an *Éléments de Géométrie* for use in the Little Schools.

p. 189, l. 15. **music which shall be solemn, etc.** A Franciscan, Father Comblat, who visited Port-Royal des Champs in 1678, says: "The nuns sing the ordinary Roman plainsong, according to the Paris use, as they belong to this diocese; but they never make any trills or runs in a frivolous or affected manner which might give an impression that the singer wished to show off her voice. What one hears as a rule is an entirely admirable method of singing which elevates the listener; and the psalms and anthems, when they are finished, die away in a sighing manner which is extremely affecting." Cf. also *Constitutions du Monastère de Port-Royal* (pp. 109–110): "The nuns will sing plainsong which they will learn with great care, adapting their skill and the harmony of their voices to the reverence which they owe to God, Who should be served faithfully in all things, and to the edification of the hearers, and not in a vain spirit of self-satisfaction." It should be noticed that church-singing was the only form of music to which Port-Royal gave its approval. Music as the handmaid of religion must thus be carefully distinguished from music as a society accomplishment. The latter was considered to be a dangerous dissipation and almost as undesirable for children as novel-reading or theatre-going. The Port-Royalists were not unique in holding these views, for many other contemporary educationalists took up an almost equally exaggerated attitude. *E.g.* Fénelon in his treatise *De l'Éducation des Filles* (1753, pp. 247–248) quotes with approval Plato's strictures on "Lydian harmonies" and includes such music among "divertissemens empoisonnés." So also Rollin (*Traité des Études*, 1745, p. liii) says: "It is proved by almost universal experience that the study of music has an extraordinarily dissipating effect upon girls and inspires them with a distaste and aversion for all other occupations." Locke again asserts that "Musick...wastes so much of a young Man's Time to gain but a moderate skill in it; and engages often in such odd Company, that many think it much better spared" (*Thoughts on Education*, Quick's edition, p. 174). Quotations of this kind from writers of the period could be multiplied almost indefinitely. Modern opinion would hardly endorse these views; but they do remind us that music may have greater effect than we sometimes realise upon the character of those who are susceptible to its influence, and that therefore much care should be exercised in the choice of the music which we give our pupils to study or allow them to hear.

p. 191, l. 15. **perfect nuns or excellent wives and mothers.** Racine's enthusiasm has perhaps led him to give too favourable a judgment on the girls' schools of Port-Royal. Anyone who takes the trouble to read Jacqueline Pascal's *Règlement* (pp. 198 to 239) will see that the education given in them was more suitable for a conventual than for a domestic career. Refer to Introd. p. 33.

p. 191, l. 17. **edified the world.** The excellence of the moral education given at Port-Royal was proverbial. Cf. Boileau, *Sat.* x:

L'Épouse que tu prends sans tache en sa conduite
Aux vertus, m'a-t-on dit, dans Port-Royal instruite,
Aux lois de son devoir règle tous ses désirs.

p. 192, l. 13. **the novice's habit.** The novices at Port-Royal wore the *petit habit*. It was a white dress, such as was worn by the professed nuns, but the latter were distinguished by the wearing of a long black head-dress and a scarlet cross on the front of the scapulary. The novice's habit can be seen in the picture of Marguerite Périer (see Introd. p. 25) in the village church at Linas near Montlhéry; while the nun's costume is well shown in the representation of the miraculous healing of Sister Sainte-Suzanne, which is preserved in the Louvre. Both these pictures were painted by Philippe de Champagne, who was one of the "amis du dehors" of Port-Royal and to whom we owe portraits of many of those who were connected with the abbey.

p. 192, l. 14. **they will not be compelled to do so.** In one of Saint-Cyran's letters to his little niece (Letter xviii in the 1744 edition) he advises her to wear the *petit habit* now that she is a *pensionnaire* at Port-Royal.

p. 194, l. 11. **S. Paul.** See Hebrews xii, 9.

p. 195, l. 25. **the reception-room.** The *parloir* was the room in the convent where parents were interviewed and where nuns were allowed, under special conditions, to receive visits from their relatives. Detailed rules for such interviews and visits are given in ch. xxiii of the *Constitutions du Monastère de Port-Royal.*

p. 196, l. 7. **it could be wished that they were all equal.** The children at Port-Royal came largely, but by no means exclusively, from the "upper classes." Besoigne in his *Histoire de Port-Royal* (vol. I, pp. 412-413) gives a list of the *pensionnaires* who were turned adrift in 1662. It includes the daughters of a Parisian lawyer, of a merchant *rue aux Fers*, of the Duc de Luynes, and of Maignart de Bernières who was a *maître des requêtes* and a member of the *Conseil Privé*, the highest judicial court in the country.

p. 196, l. 13. **treating almost all of them alike.** Distinctions of rank were more marked in the age of Louis XIV than they are to-day. Thus, in spite of the evident desire at Port-Royal to treat all the children alike, we find that special arrangements had to be made for special cases. For example, Mlle d'Elbœuf (a grand-daughter of Henri IV and Gabrielle d'Estrées), who entered the school at the age of nine, was served first at meals and her ordinary food was different from that of the other boarders. At thirteen she had a room to herself and a sister to wait upon her (see *Vies intéressantes des Religieuses de Port-Royal*, vol. III, p. 183). She afterwards became a novice and atoned for the indulgence shown to her in the past, by learning to cobble the nuns' shoes.

p. 198, l. 5. **Deo Gratias.** Thanks be to God.

p. 199, l. 1. **a short prayer.** The set prayers which were repeated at regular intervals throughout the day are given in the *Règlement pour les Enfans* (*Constitutions*, pp. 415-430); but they have not been included in the present selection of extracts because their interest is hardly educational.

p. 199, l. 4. **their oratory.** The *Constitutions* (pp. 129-130) prescribe that there shall be no oratory of any kind in any part of the convent, "except in the children's room."

p. 199, l. 18. **Pretiosa.** In the Office of Prime, after the martyrology there follow this versicle and response :

V. Pretiosa in conspectu Domini
R. Mors sanctorum eius.

(*I.e.* Precious in the sight of the Lord is the death of His Saints.— Psalm cxvi, *v.* 15.)

p. 199, l. 18. **Prime.** Frequent allusions will be found, throughout these Regulations, to the Canonical Hours. The recitation of these

Offices at intervals throughout the day is incumbent upon all religious and persons in Holy Orders in the Roman Church. The Hours are Prime at 6.0 a.m.; Tierce at 9.0; Sext at noon; None at 2 or 3 p.m.; Vespers about 4.0; Compline about 7.0; Matins and Lauds at midnight or daybreak. The exact times at which they are recited vary somewhat according to the time of year and to particular circumstances (see time-table for the girls' schools, p. 241). The Offices consist chiefly of psalms and it is from this source that the English Matins and Evensong have derived their canticles and the regular recitation of the Psalter.

p. 199, l. 19. **the Angelus.** A short devotion in honour of the mystery of the Incarnation. It is recited three times during the day. The name is derived from the introductory words of the angelic salutation to the Blessed Virgin, with which the Office begins: *Angelus Domini nuntiavit Mariæ...*, "the angel of the Lord declared unto Mary...."

p. 199, l. 31. **the younger ones repeat their prayers.** Eton boys in the fifteenth century repeated the Matins of the Blessed Virgin before five o'clock in the morning, while they were making their beds. See Foster Watson, *The Old Grammar Schools*, p. 84.

p. 200, l. 12. **Miserere.** The fiftieth Psalm.

p. 202, l. 29. **needlework.** An interesting commentary on this passage is furnished by a contemporary print of a conference of the nuns in a part of the grounds at Port-Royal des Champs known as the "Solitude." Every one of the twenty nuns shown in the picture is busied with some form of needlework, knitting, or spinning.

p. 203, l. 17. **they do not genuflect**—*i.e.* although they wear the religious habit, they do not make the special kind of reverence which is appropriate for professed nuns; instead they courtesy in the manner prescribed by the usages of polite society.

p. 204, l. 5. **Benedicat nos, etc.** "May God bless us and let all the ends of the earth fear him." Psalm lxvii, 7.

p. 204, l. 14. **double or semi-double, etc.** In the Roman Church the various feasts are divided, according to their rank, into doubles, semi-doubles, and simples. Certain great feasts also have octaves—*i.e.* they are celebrated throughout eight days and with particular solemnity on the last. For example, the festival of the Circumcision is a double, the Epiphany is a double with an octave, and all the days within the Octave of the Epiphany are semi-doubles.

p. 204, l. 15. **specially-observed feasts.** These are festivals which are kept by the Church as a whole but which are celebrated with special solemnity by certain particular religious communities, just as an individual might specially celebrate the day of his patron saint or a church the feast of the saint to whom it was dedicated. In the case of Port-Royal, for example, the festivals of S. Theresa and of S. Martin, pope and martyr, were specially honoured because the community had a particular devotion for these saints. The festivals of S. John Chrysostom, S. Athanasius, S. Gregory Nazianzen, S. Basil, S. Agnes, S. Agatha, S. Cecily, and S. Lucy were also specially-observed feasts.

p. 204, l. 35. **do the office of angels.** Cf. *supra* note on p. 136, l. 12.

p. 205, l. 32. **Sub tuum præsidium.** See *supra* note on p. 139, l. 12.

p. 206, l. 5. **M. de Saint-Cyran's manual of instruction.** The *Théologie familière.* See *supra* note on p. 139, l. 28.

p. 207, l. 8. **the little sisters**—*i.e.* the *pensionnaires.* This term is illustrative of the conventual aspect with which the girls' school was always regarded.

p. 207, l. 11. **that of the evening and the morning**—*i.e.* before the *Pretiosa* and after the *Angelus.* See *supra* p. 199.

p. 207, l. 30. **Confiteor, etc.** See *supra* note on p. 136, l. 22.

p. 208, l. 14. **Benedicite**—*i.e.* the grace before the meal.

p. 209, l. 24. **privately instructed.** This private instruction of individual girls was a recognised part of the educational system of the convent. It was, of course, confined to questions of religion and morals. See *supra* pp. 230–233.

p. 210, l. 16. **what happens in the refectory, etc.** It was customary to make nuns expiate their faults by doing public penance in the refectory during mealtimes. The following forms of punishment are specified on p. 158 of the *Constitutions de Port-Royal* : eating one's meal off the ground, asking a sister's pardon publicly, saying prayers in a prostrate position, wearing a bandage over the eyes, and kissing a sister's feet. The last of these penances was sometimes applied in the case of the *pensionnaires*—see p. 233, l. 28 and note.

p. 211, l. 25. **to show a holy and courteous consideration one for another.** Practically the same phrase—"se prévenir d'honneur les unes les autres (avec une sainte civilité)"—occurs in the *Suppl. au Nécr.* p. 56, in the Regulations for the boys' schools. See *supra* p. 137, l. 35.

p. 212, l. 7. **Veni Sancte Spiritus.** "Come Holy Ghost, our souls inspire." This hymn is included in the English Ordination Office.

p. 213, l. 6. **specially-observed feasts.** See *supra* note on p. 204, l. 15.

p. 213, l. 33. **S. John Climacus.** See *supra* note on p. 75, l. 21.

p. 213, l. 35. **the Tradition of the Church.** *Tradition de l'Église sur la Pénitence et la Communion.* The author was Antoine le Maître. It consisted largely of quotations from the Fathers and other ecclesiastical writers.

17—5

p. 214, l. 2. **the innocence given them at baptism, etc.** This emphasis on the inestimable importance of preserving baptismal grace is particularly characteristic of Jansenism (see Introd. pp. 15 and 19–20).

p. 214, l. 5. **the Catechism of M. de Saint-Cyran.** The *Théologie familière*. See *supra* note on p. 139, l. 28.

p. 214, l. 8. **Confirma hoc Deus.** An antiphon from the Confirmation Office: "Confirma hoc, Deus, quod operatus es in nobis, a templo sancto quod est in Jerusalem" ("Confirm, O God, that which Thou hast wrought in us, from Thy holy temple which is in Jerusalem").

p. 215, l. 24. **are instructed.** "Instruction" was a technical term at Port-Royal. See *supra* note on p. 209, l. 24.

p. 216, l. 16. **the same tone of voice.** Cf. "Prime and Compline shall be said with shorter mediations than the other Hours" (*Constitutions*, p. 110).

p. 218, l. 2. **the Familiar Theology.** See *supra* note on p. 139, l. 28. The other two works were evidently devotional or instructional handbooks for the use of children.

p. 218, l. 7. **learn the whole of their Psalter.** Mère Agnès, sister of Angélique, knew the Psalms by heart at the age of nine (see *Mém. pour servir à l'hist. de P.-R.* vol. II, p. 338).

p. 218, l. 21. **the Adoration**—*i.e.* of the Blessed Sacrament. Port-Royal had a special devotion to the Blessed Sacrament. The full title of the community was *Monastère de Port-Royal du Saint-Sacrement*.

p. 218, l. 27. **Imitation.** The *Imitatio Christi* ascribed to Thomas à Kempis.

p. 219, l. 15. **talking to them**—*i.e.* in private. See *supra* pp. 230–233.

p. 223, l. 5. **speak less to them than to God on their behalf.** An echo of Saint-Cyran. See *supra* p. 115, l. 26.

p. 224, l. 21. **like little doves.** A feature of the convent buildings at Port-Royal des Champs was the *colombier* or dove-cot—a round tower, which is the only part of the original structure still standing. Jacqueline Pascal must often have watched the doves and noticed their solicitude for their young, so that this simile comes naturally to her mind.

p. 231, l. 19. **we must pray more than speak**—*plus prier que parler*; another echo of Saint-Cyran. His phrase was *plus prier que crier* (Lancelot, *Mém. de S.-C.* p. 336—see *supra* p. 115, l. 25).

p. 232, l. 2. **the violent who take heaven by force.** The reference is to Matthew xi, 12.

p. 233, l. 28. **to kiss the feet of their comrades.** See *supra* note on p. 210, l. 16. In a contemporary engraving of the refectory at Port-

Royal des Champs a nun is shown doing penance by kissing the feet of one of her fellows.

p. 235, l. 3. **the Imitation.** See *supra* note on p. 218, l. 27.

p. 235, l. 3. **the Sinner's Guide.** *Dux Peccatorum* or *Guia de Pecadores*, by Luis de Grenada (1504–1588), Archbishop of Braga and author of many devotional works.

p. 235, l. 3. **the Philothée**—*i.e.* the lover of God. A devotional handbook composed for the use of young ladies. It was the work of S. Francis of Sales (1567–1622) and had an enormous vogue in the seventeenth century.

p. 235, l. 3. **S. John Climacus.** See *supra* note on p. 75, l. 21.

p. 235, l. 4. **the Tradition of the Church.** See *supra* note on p. 213, l. 35.

p. 235, l. 4. **the letters of M. de Saint-Cyran.** See Introd. p. 37.

p. 235, l. 5. **the Familiar Theology.** See *supra* note on p. 139, l. 28.

p. 235, l. 5. **the Christian Maxims**—such as are found bound up with modern Roman Catholic devotional handbooks as, for example, the *Garden of the Soul* or *Key of Heaven* or the French *Paroissien*.

p. 235, l. 6. **the letter of a Carthusian Father.** I have been unable to identify this book. A certain Carthusian Dom Étienne wrote a letter to M. Singlin in praise of Port-Royal. It is dated July 10th, 1655, and is given in an appendix to Sainte-Beuve's *Port-Royal* (vol. VI, pp. 308–310). The letter may possibly have been written originally in Latin; but this seems doubtful; and I fear therefore that the reference here is to some other document which I cannot trace.

p. 235, l. 7. **the Meditations of S. Theresa.** See *supra* note on p. 109, l. 7.

p. 235, l. 12. **S. Jerome's letters.** See *supra* note on p. 78, l. 26.

p. 235, l. 12. **Christian Almsgiving.** *L'Aumône chrétienne* (2 vols., 1651). A work by Antoine le Maître.

p. 235, l. 14. **Lives of the Desert Fathers.** The Port-Royalists often alluded to Port-Royal des Champs as a "desert" (cf. *supra* note on p. 97, l. 9); and the solitaries were fond of regarding themselves as a kind of revival of the original Desert Fathers who had lived in the wilderness of Sinai or Syria.

p. 237, l. 29. **good Christians and good doctors**—as for example Victor Pallu, physician to the community from 1643 to 1650, who attended Saint-Cyran in his last illness and of whom Fontaine says, "It was almost agreeable to fall ill in order to have the pleasure of enjoying his conversation"; or Jean Hamon, physician from 1650 to 1657, mystic, ascetic, and scholar, who afterwards proved himself the consoler of the community during the years of persecution.

INDEX

For EU product safety concerns, contact us at Calle de José Abascal, 56–1°,
28003 Madrid, Spain or eugpsr@cambridge.org.

www.ingramcontent.com/pod-product-compliance
Ingram Content Group UK Ltd.
Pitfield, Milton Keynes, MK11 3LW, UK
UKHW020320140625
459647UK00018B/1944